BRITISH RADIO DRAMA, 1945–63

BRITISH RADIO DRAMA, 1945-63

Hugh Chignell

BLOOMSBURY ACADEMIC
NEW YORK • LONDON • OXFORD • NEW DELHI • SYDNEY

BLOOMSBURY ACADEMIC
Bloomsbury Publishing Inc
1385 Broadway, New York, NY 10018, USA
50 Bedford Square, London, WC1B 3DP, UK
29 Earlsfort Terrace, Dublin 2, Ireland

BLOOMSBURY, BLOOMSBURY ACADEMIC and the Diana logo are trademarks of Bloomsbury Publishing Plc

First published in the United States of America 2019
Paperback edition published 2021

Copyright © Hugh Chignell, 2019

For legal purposes the Acknowledgements on p. viii constitute an extension of this copyright page.

Cover design: Louise Dugdale
Cover image © Nnena Irina/Shutterstock

All rights reserved. No part of this publication may be reproduced or transmitted in any form or by any means, electronic or mechanical, including photocopying, recording, or any information storage or retrieval system, without prior permission in writing from the publishers.

Bloomsbury Publishing Inc does not have any control over, or responsibility for, any third-party websites referred to or in this book. All internet addresses given in this book were correct at the time of going to press. The author and publisher regret any inconvenience caused if addresses have changed or sites have ceased to exist, but can accept no responsibility for any such changes.

Library of Congress Cataloging-in-Publication Data
Names: Chignell, Hugh, author.
Title: British radio drama, 1945-1963 / Hugh Chignell.
Description: New York: Bloomsbury Academic, [2019] | Includes bibliographical references and index.
Identifiers: LCCN 2019008331 (print) | LCCN 2019012135 (ebook) | ISBN 9781501329708 (ePub) | ISBN 9781501329715 (ePDF) | ISBN 9781501329692 (hardback: alk. paper)
Subjects: LCSH: Radio plays, English–History and criticism. | Radio programs–Great Britain–History. | BBC Radio 3–History. | Radio and literature.
Classification: LCC PR739.R33 (ebook) | LCC PR739.R33 C45 2019 (print) | DDC 809.2/22–dc23 LC record available at https://lccn.loc.gov/2019008331

ISBN: HB: 978-1-5013-2969-2
PB: 978-1-5013-7722-8
ePDF: 978-1-5013-2971-5
eBook: 978-1-5013-2970-8

Typeset by Deanta Global Publishing Services, Chennai, India

To find out more about our authors and books visit www.bloomsbury.com and sign up for our newsletters.

For Sue

CONTENTS

Acknowledgements	viii
A note on terminology	x
INTRODUCTION	1
Chapter 1 POST-WAR BRITAIN	11
Chapter 2 THE POST-WAR BBC RADIO DRAMA DEPARTMENT	23
Chapter 3 RADIO DRAMA, 1945–53	37
Chapter 4 TECHNOLOGIES OF PRODUCTION AND CONSUMPTION	57
Chapter 5 RADIO DRAMA AND THE ABSURD	65
Chapter 6 GILES COOPER	87
Chapter 7 FEATURES DEPARTMENT DRAMATISTS	109
Chapter 8 REALIST RADIO DRAMA	127
Chapter 9 THE 1960s	149
CONCLUSION	159
List of programmes	167
Bibliography	174
Index	179

ACKNOWLEDGEMENTS

Bournemouth University has made it possible for me to spend much of the last three years thinking about, researching and writing this book, and I am very grateful to the institution for that support which included four months' research leave and funding to attend conferences. The Centre for Media History at Bournemouth has been a major source of inspiration and support, and particular thanks go to my former colleague Sean Street who led me down the radio path and to my current colleagues, Kate Murphy, Kristin Skoog, Kate Terkanian, Tony Stoller, Ieuan Franklin and many others.

I have learned a great deal about radio history from the work of three distinguished scholars and friends, and I thank them all for their inspiration and support: David Hendy, Michele Hilmes and Todd Avery.

I have also learnt a great deal about radio drama from conversations with Nina Garthwaite at In the Dark, the brilliant Danish scholar, Heidi Svømmekjær and Leslie McMurtry.

The Entangled Media Histories network, based at the universities of Lund, Bournemouth and Hamburg, has also been crucial for my development as a media historian even though this book is only partially influenced by the entangled approach. My thanks in particular to Marie Cronqvist, Patrik Lundell, Hans-Ulrich Wagner, Christoph Hilgert and Johan Jarlbrink for their friendship and inspiration.

I used the BBC Written Archives Centre mainly for the chapter on Samuel Beckett, and I am very grateful to all the WAC staff who advised and helped me; I know I should have spent longer there. I also consulted the Giles Cooper papers at the Columbia Rare Book and Manuscript Library, and I am very grateful for the support and advice of their staff.

Without the support and advice of the staff at the British Library, this book would not have been written. I am extremely grateful to Paul Wilson, curator of radio, for his enthusiasm and support and his ability to help me find and get access to obscure old radio programmes. The staff of the British Library sound archive's listening and viewing service have also been wonderfully helpful and surprisingly uncomplaining.

I am particularly grateful to members of the Cooper family, and in particular Guy and Giles (junior), for their support and for giving me access to the short biographical note of Giles Cooper's life probably written by his son Ric.

Michael and Melissa Bakewell provided a wonderful opportunity to revisit the early part of his illustrious career, and I benefitted greatly from both of their memories. It was also wonderful to meet John Tydeman whose exceptional recall of events and individuals contributed greatly to my understanding of historic radio drama.

I am very grateful to the wonderfully enthusiastic editorial staff at Bloomsbury Academic and, in particular, Mary Al-Sayed, Katie Gallof and Erin Duffy.

Finally my love and thanks to my partner and co-worker, Sue.

All extracts from British Broadcasting Corporation documents are published with the permission of the BBC Written Archives Centre.

A NOTE ON TERMINOLOGY

I refer in this book to the Drama Department and the Features Department of the BBC. Elsewhere I refer to Drama and Features and the capital D and F indicate that this is a reference to a department. I also refer to drama and features, with lower case d and f, and these are references to a genre of radio output.

INTRODUCTION

Any history of British radio in the twentieth century must acknowledge the importance of radio drama and especially in the period after the end of the Second World War up to the early 1960s. This is particularly interesting in terms of radio drama output partly because a number of celebrated writers wrote specifically for radio, including Samuel Beckett and Harold Pinter, and also because of the artistic freedom granted by the BBC's cultural network,[1] the Third Programme, launched in September 1946. There is a case for calling this period of time, from 1945 to 1963, the 'golden age' of radio drama; admittedly this is a slightly speculative shorthand but it captures a truth about the period when radio was still a dominant cultural medium and before television drama began to attract the best writers and producers.

As this book will show, there are a variety of radio dramas, including plays written for the stage, novels adapted for radio and, far less common, plays written specifically for radio. Adaptations from novels often took the form of serials, whereas stage adaptations tended to be single broadcasts, often running for well over an hour or in two parts over two hours. Dramas written specifically for radio, a phenomenon which became the norm in the 1960s, were relatively rare but as these emerged in the early 1950s they revealed some of the most interesting writing for radio which, as will be explained in later chapters, often directly addressed the idea of 'sound drama' or what Neil Verma has called 'the theatre of the mind'.[2] This book will mainly be about dramas written specifically for radio because they were so often the most interesting and innovative although I have also included some very important and apparently successful stage adaptations and also the occasional adaptation from a novel. My emphasis on plays written for radio reflects Mary James's 'hypothesis that the original play written for radio had the potential to be a specialized form of poetic drama, "poetic drama of the air".'[3]

What is missing, among the many things missing in this inevitably selective book, is the genre of popular drama and especially popular drama series including *Frontline Family*, *The Archers* and *Mrs Dale's Diary*, which are all in their own way highly significant and deserving of critical analysis and their own written histories as Heidi Svømmekjær has demonstrated in her account of the very early Danish 'soap opera' *The Hansen Family*.[4] My justification for excluding popular forms of radio drama is not derived from the quality or significance of the different types but is more to do with an interest in the extremely innovative and experimental work of some writers and producers at a time when the BBC gave all the appearance of being very conservative and cautious. This is perhaps not a very compelling argument, and it will no doubt leave some readers feeling I have omitted examples of interesting and important work, including not only the serial but almost all of the drama output of the Light Programme and most of the Home Service as well. However, in the chapters which follow, the extraordinary artistic creativity of a small group of writers, producers and script editors will show itself to be worthy of close attention.

Having narrowed the scope of this book to a certain type of drama, either written for radio or adapted from the stage or novel, I should add that some of this output was produced by the BBC's Drama Department, but some of it was made in Features Department. The division of Drama from Features at the end of the war (as will be discussed in Chapter 2) resulted in the production of dramas in both departments, but, confusingly, some of the programmes made in Features Department were called 'features'. So, to take one example, the 1946 production of Louis MacNeice's *The Dark Tower*[5] although clearly a drama was in fact referred to as a 'feature' because it was made by Features Department. The radio feature is a combination of factually based content with creative, often musical or poetic, elements. This places features somewhere between drama and documentary, and the genre remains an important part of contemporary creative radio and audio, but Features Department also made radio dramas with no factual content, like *The Dark Tower*, and so they are included here.

The period of time covered by this book, from the end of the Second World War to 1963, requires some justification. The late 1940s and early 1950s witnessed the production of some extraordinary and ambitious dramas mainly by Features Department (including *The Dark Tower* as well as *In Parenthesis*[6] and *The Ascent of F6*[7]) and so the period after 1945 is important even though very few recordings still exist from that time. The 1950s themselves could easily be called a 'golden age' of radio drama as Beckett, Pinter and, the prolific, Giles Cooper among others were writing for the medium. The early 1960s was also a productive time but 1963 serves as a useful cut-off date as the long-serving head of Radio Drama, Val Gielgud, retired in that year and handed his baton over to a very different man indeed, Martin Esslin. What followed was, arguably, the decline of radio drama as television drama became increasingly confident and successful, a view expressed most forcefully by the radio critic David Wade who stated that 'by 1966 radio was deep in the depression induced by the runaway success of television, at which time it was even forecast that sound broadcasting was finished'.[8]

The choice of dramas discussed here is also heavily influenced by the very limited availability of recordings of historic British radio dramas. This is not the place to address the complex and frustrating situation regarding the inaccessibility of old radio programmes. I leave that to Ian Wittington who includes a forthright statement of the situation at the end of his analysis of literary radio studies: 'A great deal [of radio material] remains unreleased, accessible only through in-person listening at the British Library in London.'[9] He adds that 'significant foundational work must be done to bring these documents to a wider audience, whether through the publication of scripts, the release of audio recordings, or through newer, digital models of archival presentation that combine audio and textual information'.[10] There is a twofold problem for the radio historian here because not only are existing recordings rare or difficult to access but the selection process for retaining them in the BBC Sound Archive was skewed towards well-known writers. As a result, even radio dramas that were well thought of at the time were either not archived or subsequently destroyed. A notable example of this is the important radio dramatist Rhys Adrian, whose early work is largely missing. In one of the most important books about radio drama, Donald McWhinnie's influential *The Art of Radio*,[11] there are detailed accounts of production and aesthetics issues in relation to a number of radio dramas, including Giles Cooper's *Without the Grail*, Rhys Adrian's *The Passionate Thinker* and James Forsyth's *The Pier*, but I was unable to access any recordings of these dramas despite their prominence.

The consequence of this scarcity of recordings is that the history of the genre is skewed. The fairly comprehensive literature on Beckett's radio output is surely partly to do with the fact that all of his radio work is available in an admittedly rare CD box set. One solution may be to read the scripts, many of which are available in the BBC's Written Archives Centre. The problem with that approach is that it fundamentally denies the sonic quality of sound drama and removes from hearing the performance of actors, the use of music and sound effects. I have not included dramas which I have not been able to hear (with a few exceptions)[12] and that has significantly limited the range of programmes that could be examined here[13] although I believe and hope that what could be heard still represents a fascinating and useful record of the genre.[14]

Media historians seem to be presented with a particularly diverse range of sources, including written and audiovisual material, as well as burgeoning digital resources for interpreting and identifying historic programming. As a result this study of post-war radio is based not only on listening to old programmes but also on a variety of published sources, document archives in the United Kingdom and the United States, interviews, access to BBC oral histories and recently developed databases. As new resources become available, the media historian can find themselves standing on rapidly shifting terrain and this can directly influence the research journey. A good example of this is the relatively recent online resource *The Listener Historical Archive*[15] which gives the researcher access to the entire published output of what was in effect, from 1929 to 1991, the BBC's 'house magazine'. This is an extremely important resource for anyone interested in the history of radio drama as the weekly publication included sometimes very perceptive reviews of broadcast dramas. I had been used to consulting the bound back copies of *The Listener*, a very slow and cumbersome process, so when I gained online access to the archive

I changed my methodology and used these programme reviews far more systematically as the following chapters will reveal. This book makes extensive use of *The Listener* as a source of information about radio dramas but especially as an indicator of critical responses at the time in the articles titled 'The Critic on the Hearth'.

Perhaps the most important online development for media historians has been the BBC Genome,[16] a database which currently contains basic programme information on all programmes listed in the *Radio Times* from 1923 to 2009. There can be little doubt that the Genome has not only made some research activities significantly easier and quicker but also changed the stories told about the past. The ability to see at a glance, to take just one example, all of the dramas written for radio by Giles Cooper, has not only greatly speeded up the research process but also revealed far more clearly the diversity of his writing for the three radio networks and for television and how that distribution varied over time (as discussed in Chapter 6). Similarly, those individuals working for the BBC who have been neglected now have their contribution revealed in considerable detail. So the exceptionally multi-talented Features producer Nesta Pain was, before the launch of the Genome, a largely ignored and seriously underestimated woman but is now revealed as a prolific writer and producer of features and dramas on both radio and television.[17]

Interviews with former radio producers have been used sparingly, partly because the period covered ended over fifty years ago, but despite the challenges of trying to recall what might have happened in a different era, both Michael Bakewell and John Tydeman provided invaluable information and observations about the past. A new resource now becoming accessible to researchers is the archive of BBC oral histories which were conducted with selected members of BBC staff when they left the organization; in some cases, the interviews lasted several hours.[18] Despite the institutional flavour of these recordings, the tendency for interviewees to put a gloss on their careers and the occasional lack of sensitivity and understanding of the interviewers, they can provide extremely valuable insights. In the case of historic radio drama, the interviews with the influential 1950s' script editor Barbara Bray and with the head of Radio Drama, Val Gielgud, contain some of the emotional dimension of their work which would otherwise be missing. So, Barbara Bray's deep affection for Samuel Beckett and Val Gielgud's contempt for popular forms of drama are far more vivid in the interviews than on the printed page.

The first port of call for historians of the BBC has traditionally been the Written Archives Centre where the memoranda, meeting minutes and other institutional papers can be found. An over-reliance on this one source, however, can result in an institutional history as is probably the case in Asa Briggs's five-volume history of British broadcasting.[19] David Hendy's magisterial history of Radio Four[20] also draws heavily on BBC paper archives, but that is successfully leavened by the use of interviews and detailed discussion of individual programmes. I know from experience that searching the BBC archives can reveal hidden treasures which shine the most incandescent light on the past; my earlier work on BBC current affairs programmes drew heavily on the minutes of the Radio Weekly Programme Review Board, a truly remarkable record of attitudes to programming in the 1970s. But for various reasons the record of discussion within the post-war Radio Drama department is incomplete and superficial. The exception to this is the wonderfully detailed record of the BBC's dealings with, and discussion about, Samuel Beckett as will be shown in Chapter 5 where much of the analysis of Beckett's radio career is based on BBC archives. Much can be discovered about the largely forgotten radio dramatist Giles Cooper, who is the subject of Chapter 6, from listening to the available recordings of his plays and in addition for this study I consulted his private papers at the University of Columbia which include a comprehensive collection of scripts, some of which were not performed, as well as very revealing notebooks (or 'workbooks') which include early writing influenced by his experience of the Second World War.

As this book is about distinct literary and aesthetic artefacts, dramas written and performed at a particular moment in time and broadcast using varieties of transmission and reception technology, the programmes themselves, existing today as digitized recordings, are the foundation upon which this book is built. Theoretically, if sometimes not actually, the analysis here is derived from listening to historic radio: that has usually been the starting point for the research, and hopefully it has created a sense that this is a study which puts the programmes first. However, the act of listening to radio dramas made over half a century ago is problematic. It is an activity radically different from the experience of the listener to, say, Michael Bakewell's 1959 production of Ionesco's *Rhinoceros* at home one evening tuned into the Third Programme on VHF frequency using a non-portable valve radio set. The researcher's experience is mediated by having to hear this drama at the British Library in St Pancras, London, using headphones in a listening booth booked weeks previously following a request to the library's listening service to get a copy of the programme from the BBC Sound Archive. The researcher's engagement with the drama is of course slightly perverse, an experience in which the strangeness of the material is emphasized; the drama is heard separated from its context, from the voices and culture and concerns of the time. Post-war radio dramas sound strikingly unfamiliar and 'other'; we struggle to connect emotionally with them and instead resort to an analysis which, though worthwhile, is fundamentally different from the response of the intended listener. Attempts to de-individualize listening by forming public-listening events or 'gatherings' have been successful, most notably in the UK as pioneered by the collective, In the Dark.[21] This approach brings together a diversity of listeners to an appointment to listen perhaps in the way envisaged by Bull and Back: 'The kind of listening we envision is not straightforward, not self-evident – it is not easy listening. Rather, we have to work toward what might be called agile listening and this involves attuning our ears to listen again to the multiple layers of meaning potentially embedded in the same sound.'[22]

A final component of the research described here concerns the materiality of the media. This is an often neglected aspect of traditional radio studies but one which is gaining traction as researchers take a serious interest in the material means of production and consumption. The physical limits of the radio studio and the often poor quality of sound transmission directly influenced the listening experience as did the immobility of the valve radio set, the precursor to the portable transistor radio. This concern with the materiality of the media, for example, the type of paper used for newspapers,[23] the deficiencies of Long Wave and Short Wave radio transmission, and the cost of commercially available tape recording machines, are all examples of the way the physical attributes of the media influence what is made and how it is consumed. I have attempted, briefly, in Chapter 4 to address the materiality of radio broadcasting and listening because these factors clearly influenced the experience of hearing radio drama and as a result the nature of the drama that was made. In addition, the introduction of sound recording in the 1950s to allow rebroadcasts and the ability to edit dramas before transmission was clearly an important and influential development, and this is discussed later. We are fortunate that some very early, including pre-war, dramas were recorded in the era before magnetic tape and this has made it possible to hear a small but very significant sample of immediate post-war drama. Domestic tape recorders only became affordable in the late 1950s but the consequence of that was the beginning of off-air recording including the recording of dramas, and I will speculate about this in Chapter 4.

I have already explained that this is not a book about popular radio drama, despite the significance of that genre. There are additional parts of the radio drama story that I have not addressed and that should be clarified here. Inevitably I do make aesthetic judgements about individual radio dramas, and my focus on particular broadcasts is influenced by those judgements, but I have tried not to allow this to be a subjective analysis where my likes and dislikes take centre stage. Where possible I have searched for more objective criteria than my own personal opinion and in particular whether a drama seems to be innovative or influential. The consequence of this is that I do not subscribe to the idea of a radio 'canon', although I do think it is a rather interesting and stimulating challenge to wonder what might be 'in' and what is not. Clearly, for example, Louis MacNeice's 1946 radio feature (and drama) *The Dark Tower* would be part of any radio canon, but why? Not, I think, because as Frances Gray claims that it is MacNeice's 'best play' nor that he 'succeeds brilliantly'[24] nor that this is a 'masterpiece' but rather because this was such an influential radio drama which made a generation of future writers realize the potential of the genre. In addition, the lost dramas of Rhys Adrian which cannot be discussed in any depth here cannot be part of any radio drama canon simply because they no longer exist in audio form.

Also missing from this account is any systematic discussion of radio actors, and I have rarely recorded the names of actors in the list of programmes discussed at the end of this book. Actors were of course important to both writers and producers, and Nesta Pain's association with Michael Hordern and the influence of the Irish actor Patrick Magee on Samuel Beckett are both important examples but largely for reasons of space I have not explored this theme in any depth. Similarly I have considered the experience of listeners and especially in relation to the technology of radio receivers, but I have chosen not to examine the radio audience in terms of size or by looking at the BBC Listener reports. Given that many of the dramas were broadcast on the Third Programme they would have been heard by audiences so small that they were scarcely measurable and any attempts at quantitative analysis would be unproductive.

Some explanation is needed here, at the end of this introduction, to explain why radio drama is important and to suggest that there is something of special significance about the 'golden age' which might provide ideas about the future direction of the genre. I would like to claim that a close reading of radio dramas in what might be called the 'long 1950s' provides new ideas and examples for radio production today, more of that in the conclusion. For an understanding of the specificity of radio drama it is helpful to turn to the literature on radio drama, including that written in the 1950s and much more recent contributions. Neil Verma proposes an 'aesthetic history' of radio, one where the programmes themselves take centre stage and I am happy to follow him in that ambition. Moreover he points out that around the middle of the twentieth century, radio drama in America was not only a 'theatre of the mind' but also 'that as American broadcasters built a theatre *in* the mind, radio drama necessarily became a theatre *about* the mind, in an era in which that concept was a site of extraordinary contest'.[25] This appreciation of radio drama as having a unique capacity to understand and reveal psychological states was one identified fifty years earlier by arguably the most important radio drama producer of the post-war era Donald McWhinnie who wrote the following: 'Perhaps the most potent quality of the spoken word in close focus – not projected artificially to several hundred people – is its power to communicate secret states of mind, the inner world and private vision of the speaker.'[26] He describes the way actors whisper into the listener's mind and 'invades the listener's own solitude, recreates the illusion inside his own head'.[27] Thinking about the dramas that are discussed in this book, although some do contain action and plot, they are mainly concerned with states of mind; that is particularly true of Giles Cooper about whom McWhinnie wrote the following: 'Using every shorthand device of imaginative radio, Cooper paints vividly, with a blend of farce and bitter irony, a man's life, his aspirations, hopes, frustrations, failures.'[28] Ian Whittington also identifies an 'aesthetic turn' in radio studies citing the innovative work of Shawn Van Cour who called for renewed attention to the formal aspects of radio broadcasting, which would include 'analysis of narrative structure and broadcast genres, methods of spatial and temporal representation, styles of vocal performance, and experiential qualities of radio listening'.[29]

What follows is, therefore, a book which is influenced by the aesthetic turn and also by the proposition that mid-century radio drama revealed the inner world of its listeners. Another influential idea which has produced some of the most persuasive and insightful writing on radio is the importance of the relationship between the literary (and theatrical) world and radio, sometimes called 'literary radio studies' and often led by scholars of modernity. One of the most adept at drawing together the literary world with the complexities of the BBC is Todd Avery in his influential *Radio Modernism*.[30] For Avery, and for another modernist, Debra Rae Cohen, the 'intermedial' connection between radio and literature is fundamental to an understanding of mid-twentieth-century radio.[31] European scholars have stressed the importance of looking at the way different media intersect and encouraged a move away from 'monomedial' approaches. Marie Cronqvist and Christoph Hilgert's articulation of 'entangled media histories'[32] includes an emphasis on multimedial approaches to media history and the attempt is made here to understand the connection between literature, theatre and radio.

What follows is some necessary context about post-war Britain, a cultural history which provides just enough information to make sense of the creative world inhabited by writers and producers of radio drama. Then, a brief account of the post-war BBC and in particular some of the individual producers and script editors whose vision and commitment to radio drama made it possible for writers to use the medium of radio to tell the story of how post-war and cold war Britain was experienced.

Notes

1 The term 'network' is used by the BBC to refer to its different radio stations which at the time were the Home Service, the Light Programme and the Third Programme. The nature of these networks and in particular the very influential launch of the Third Programme in 1946 is explained in Chapter 2.
2 Neil Verma, *Theatre of the Mind, Imagination, Aesthetics and American Radio Drama* (Chicago: The University of Chicago Press, 2012).
3 Mary James, 'British radio drama: A critical analysis of its development as a distinctive aesthetic form' (PhD diss., University of Hertfordshire, 1994).
4 Heidi Svømmekjær, '*The Hansen Family* and strategies of relevance in the Danish Broadcasting Corporation 1925-50' (PhD diss., Rosskilde University, 2014).
5 *The Dark Tower*, 21 January 1946. BBC Home Service. All radio drama broadcasts mentioned in the text are included in a list of programmes with broadcast details in the appendix.
6 *In Parenthesis*, 19 November 1946. BBC Third Programme.
7 *The Ascent of F6*, 22 August 1950. BBC Third Programme.

8   David Wade, 'Popular radio drama', in *Radio Drama*, ed. Peter Lewis (London: Longmann, 1981), 95.
9   Ian Whittington, 'Radio studies and twentieth-century literature: Ethics, aesthetics, and remediation', *Literature Compass* 11, no. 9 (2014): 634–8.
10 Ibid.
11 Donald McWhinnie, *The Art of Radio* (London: Faber and Faber, 1959).
12 For example, I read the script of Cooper's *Without the Grail* and some other Cooper scripts and also Rhys Adrian's *A Nice Clean Sheet of Paper*.
13 The importance of hearing dramas is discussed in Elke Huwiler, 'Storytelling by sound: A theoretical frame for radio drama and for radio drama analysis', *The Radio Journal – International Studies in Broadcast and Audio Media*, 3, no. 1 (2005): 45–59.
14 Radio historians vary considerably in their use of recordings for research. I have listened to slightly less than fifty dramas for this book, whereas Verma in *Theatre of the Mind* states that he 'selected approximately six thousand broadcasts to study' (p. 231) adding that 'recordings were obtained commercially from the Old Time Radio Catalog'. This contrasts with Svømmekjær's study of *The Hansen Family* which is almost entirely based on reading scripts although she did manage to listen to a part of just one episode.
15 www.gale.com/uk/c/the-listener-historical-archive
16 https://genome.ch.bbc.co.uk/
17 Kate Terkanian and Hugh Chignell, 'Nesta Pain, the entangled producer', *Media History*, 2019 (forthcoming).
18 The AHRC-funded BBC Connected Histories' project's primary aim is to digitize and bring into the public realm the BBC's collection of over 600 recorded oral history interviews with key members of its staff.
19 Asa Briggs, *The History of Broadcasting in the United Kingdom*, 5 volumes (Oxford: Oxford University Press, 1995).
20 David Hendy, *Life on Air: A History of Radio Four* (Oxford: Oxford University Press, 2007).
21 In the Dark was established by the producer and cultural activist Nina Garthwaite. She has referred to 'gathered' listening as opposed to 'collective' listening which allows the experience to retain its essential individuality while benefitting from the gathered wisdom of the group. Some of the analysis in this book is derived from ideas expressed at listening events held at the British Library.
22 Michael Bull and Les Back (eds), *The Auditory Culture Reader* (Oxford: Berg, 2003), 3.
23 My interest in the materiality of the media is largely the result of being part of the Entangled Media Histories (EMHIS) network led by Patrik Lundell and more recently, Marie Cronqvist at the University of Lund. One of the network members, Johan Jarlbrink, has shown how the transition from rag-based to pulp-based paper in the eighteenth century changed the nature of newspaper conservation and use. Johan Jarlbrink, *Informations- och avfallshantering i papperstidningens tidevarv* [trans: Information and waste management in the age of the newspaper] (Lund: Mediehistoriskt arkiv, 2018).
24 Frances Gray, 'The nature of radio drama', in *Radio Drama*, ed. Lewis, 53–4.
25 Verma, *Theatre of the Mind*, 3.
26 McWhinnie, *The Art of Radio*, 57.

27 Ibid., 36.
28 Ibid., 163.
29 Whittington, 'Radio studies and twentieth-century literature', 14.
30 Todd Avery, *Radio Modernism: Literature, Ethics, and the BBC, 1922-1938* (London: Ashgate, 2006).
31 Debra Rae Cohen, Michael Coyle and Jane Lewty (eds), *Broadcasting Modernism* (Gainesville: University Press Florida, 2009).
32 Marie Cronqvist and Christoph Hilgert, 'Entangled media histories. The value of transnational and transmedial approaches in media historiography', *Media History*, 23, no. 1 (2017): 130–41.

Chapter 1

POST-WAR BRITAIN

Wrapped in the comfortable cloak of nostalgia, we can admire the heroics of the brave British men and women who survived the horrors of the Second World War. In the recent film *Dunkirk* (2017) the plucky English sailors and fishermen nobly rescued the stranded soldiers on the French beaches in their 'pleasure boats' and how thrilling it was to hear Winston Churchill's inspiring words exhorting the nation to fight the Germans on the beaches if necessary. Nothing quite encapsulates the famous 'Dunkirk spirit' better than J. B. Priestley's iconic radio broadcast of 1940, days after the evacuation from French beaches: 'Our great grand-children, when they learn how we began this War by snatching glory out of defeat, and then swept on to victory, may also learn how the little holiday steamers made an excursion to hell and came back glorious.'[1] There is something glamorous about the soldiers and nurses in uniform and their victory over a much-despised enemy; no wonder so many British films have looked back in wonder at that glorious moment in our history and embellished it.

Not so much is said, however, of the decade that followed. Somehow, between the joyous celebrations in Trafalgar Square on VE Day, May 1945 and the recording of the first Beatles album, 'Please, Please Me' in February 1963, Britain looks like it was a pretty drab place. Doris Lessing described London when she arrived immediately after the war from the sunshine and colour of South Africa as 'unpainted, stained, cracked, dull … war-damaged' and characterized by 'ruins, cellars, dark fogs'.[2] She noted that there were no cafés or good restaurants, and clothes were dismal and ugly. Everyone was indoors by ten and the streets emptied, 'the war still lingered, not only in the bombed out places but in people's minds and behavior'.[3] Similarly, Cyril Connolly described London as a sad, dirty city, 'its crowds mooing round the stained green wicker of the cafeterias in their shabby raincoats, under a sky permanently dull and lowering, like a metal dish-cover'.[4] As David Pattie argues so persuasively, an account of the post-war period has to start in the Second World War and the Blitz, with bombed-out British cities creating a legacy of material deprivation and hardship including rationing, a militarized culture with young men doing national service and film, comedy, radio all packed with war and military references.[5]

There are many useful histories of the post-war period,[6] and they share a view of a society whose culture was influenced mainly by a post-war militarism, Cold War anxieties, austerity and a hierarchical conservatism based on rigid class and gender divisions. Austerity was most graphically expressed by food rationing: in 1947 the average adult was allowed thirteen ounces of meat, two pints of milk and one egg a week.[7] Housing remained inadequate with many people living in cold, dark and dirty terraced houses; a survey in 1950 showed that almost half of all homes had no bathroom and outdoor and shared toilets were common.[8] Social class and elitism based on a public school and Oxbridge education produced a hierarchical and divided society. David Kynaston describes a society 'riddled by petty snobbery and gradations of class'[9] citing the case of a golf club where members opposed new entrants because 'they were engaged in trade' and Old Etonian[10] National Trust committee members against letting the general public into Montacute House 'because they smelt'.[11] The historian Correlli Barnett had first-hand experience of British industry in the early 1950s: 'At the summit of the industrial system stood an elite predominantly blessed with the accent of the officer's mess: men bowler-hatted or hamburged, wearing suits of military cut either bespoke or at least bought from such approved outfitters as Aquascutum or Simpsons of Piccadilly'[12] who lived in the suburbs, played golf and bridge and belonged to men's clubs.

The mid-1950s saw the end of austerity and the beginnings of a far more affluent society, one in which consumerism was a defining characteristic. Rationing ended in 1954 and at the same time there was a relaxation of hire-purchase regulations allowing people to buy the attractive consumer goods advertised on commercial television which was launched the following year. Televisions, fridges, record players and vacuum cleaners were affordable to a working population whose wages doubled between 1955 and 1959 and about whom the Conservative prime minister Harold MacMillan famously said, 'You've never had it so good.'[13] But the legacy of war and the persistence of military involvement remained a feature of the post-war period. The 1947 National Service act introduced compulsory service in the armed forces for all eighteen-year-old men initially for eighteen months and then for two years after the outbreak of the Korean War in 1950. It must have seemed that no sooner was that military conflict over in 1953 than Britain was readying itself for war again following the nationalization of the Suez Canal by President Nasser of Egypt. The Conservative prime minister Anthony Eden epitomized membership of the British upper class, educated at Eton and at that most prestigious of Oxford colleges, Christ Church. He developed an irrational hatred of Nasser[14] and in an act of reckless colonial aggression directed the invasion of Egypt by British troops on 5 November 1956. Following international condemnation and fury from Washington, Britain was forced into a 'shabby and humiliating retreat'.[15] These events ran hand in hand with the wider conflict between America and its allies and the Soviet Union, the so-called Cold War, and Soviet troops rolled into Hungary at the same time as British and French troops entered Egypt.

Britain between 1945 and the early 1960s must have appeared to be a society where military matters, personnel and memories were pervasive and so was the ever-present threat posed by the Soviet Union. Irrespective of how real that threat was, it justified the development of the most poignant Cold War symbol, the atomic bomb. On 6 August 1945 the first atomic bomb was dropped on Hiroshima and then, three days later, on Nagasaki. Japan surrendered the following day. As tensions between the USSR and the West developed years later with the blockade of Berlin in 1948, Britain, under a Labour government, was developing its own nuclear weapons and these were first tested in 1952. To add to the febrile Cold War atmosphere in the early 1950s, Senator Joe McCarthy had launched his hysterical crusade against supposed communists, 'building conspiracy theory upon fantasy and suggesting America had "lost" China – and almost the whole cold war – because of Reds in high places'.[16] The following year two Soviet spies, Guy Burgess and Donald Maclean, defected having served in the British foreign office. I mention these post-war characteristics (the hierarchies, anxieties, militarism and deprivation) because they clearly had a powerful impact on radio drama writing and provided not only the background noise but also the core themes explored by dramatists. In addition, developments in cultural life itself, in the theatre and literature also had a powerful influence on radio drama.

The British theatre after the end of the war,[17] and in particular in the unrivalled capital of the stage, London, was dominated by commercial theatre companies of which the most important was H. M. Tennent managed by Hugh 'Binkie' Beaumont; at the end of the war, Tennent had twelve productions on in the West End.[18] Outside London there were over 100 'repertory' companies which managed to present a different play each week in what was a treadmill for actors (including Harold Pinter who worked in repertory throughout the 1950s). What was there on offer for theatregoers at this time? The answer is not entirely straightforward. The more negative assessment goes something like this: British post-war theatre was mainly concerned with giving middle-class audiences a peek at a glamorous world, often located in an English country house where the leading ladies wore the latest Dior gowns flown over from Paris and the plays themselves, with titles like *Mary Had a Little*, *The White Sheep of the Family* and *Waggonload of Monkeys* resolutely refusing to address social issues or question the status quo.[19] The celebrated theatre critic Kenneth Tynan, who wrote for *The Observer* from 1954 to 1963 (alongside the other famous theatre critic of the 1950s: Harold Hobson, who was the critic for the *Sunday Times*), invented the term 'Loamshire plays' to describe typical dramas on the London stage, 'its setting is a country house … the inhabitants belong to a social class derived partly from romantic novels' adding that 'Loamshire is a glibly codified fairy-tale world. … Loamshire's greatest triumph is the crippling of creative talent in English directors and designers. After all, how many ways are there of directing a tea party?'[20]

Another line of criticism of British theatre was how divorced it was from the reality of post-war Britain. The American writer Arthur Miller commented in 1956, 'I sense that the British stage is hermetically sealed against the way society moves.'[21] The same point was made by Harold Hobson in 1952 following a visit to Paris: 'I came back to a country whose newspapers are mainly filled with tidings of war, insurrection, industrial unrest, political controversy, and parliamentary misbehavior, and to a theatre which it seems to me, in the first shock of reacquaintance, that all echoes of these things is shut off as by sound-proof walls.'[22]

It would, however, be a mistake to characterize British theatre as exclusively glamorous, merely an evening out when a bourgeois audience got the opportunity to dress up, be amused by extravagant sets and costumes and light-hearted fare before standing for the National Anthem and then off for an after-theatre dinner. Given the relentless dreariness of post-war life it is not surprising that this was a popular activity but it was far from all that the theatre, or even H. M. Tennent, had to offer. At times Tennent did put on adventurous plays including the 1949 production of Tennessee Williams's *A Streetcar Named Desire* and also in 1949, and despite difficulties with the censor, Arthur Miller's *Death of a Salesman*.[23] But Kenneth Tynan saw the success of imports, mainly from America and France, as underlining the fact that 'there is nothing in the London theatre one dares discuss with an intelligent man for more than five minutes'.[24] The main imports from France included the plays of Jean Anouilh, which although not country house capers were romantic and fantastical dramas thoroughly divorced from British realities. More challenging for the theatregoer would have been the 1946 production of Sartre's *Huis Clos* directed by Peter Brook and starring Alec Guiness in which three dead characters are condemned to stay in a room for eternity. Another reason for not dismissing London theatre entirely was the work of one of Tennent's in-house playwrights, Terrence Rattigan, whose 1946 play *The Winslow Boy* dealt with a father's attempt to clear the name of his son, wrongfully dismissed from a military academy. *The Browning Version* (1948) was a 'brilliant psychological depiction of the academic and personal failure of a deeply disliked schoolmaster'.[25] *The Deep Blue Sea* was another of Rattigan's plays in which characters struggled against the pressures exerted on them by a changing world. Rattigan was a troubled figure, a celebrated and famous writer forced to hide his homosexuality at a time when its revelation would have spelt disaster;[26] his plays were an intelligent and perceptive addition to the London stage.

There were other signs that culture, despite its great limitations, was moving in the post-war years, and one of these was the establishment of the Arts Council in 1946 which encouraged the creation of theatres outside London. This use of state subsidy made possible some experimental and less commercial theatre. Although the Arts Council had very little cash to play with, a good deal of that was spent subsidizing the elite metropolitan cultural institutions (the Royal

Opera House, Sadler's Wells, the Old Vic theatre and orchestras) that played in London.²⁷ However, regional theatres like the Glasgow Citizen's Theatre and others in Cambridge, Coventry and Bristol did receive state support and in addition touring theatre companies, subsidized by the Arts Council, took theatre to 'theatreless' regions of the country. Other signs of cultural progress included the Festival of Britain in 1951 which had a modest artistic impact and focused on the development of the South Bank region of London and in particular the opening of the Royal Festival Hall. It followed the launch of two other highly successful arts festivals, the Edinburgh International Festival and the Aldeburgh Festival, led by the prominent British composer Benjamin Britten whose musical contribution to radio drama was particularly significant.

In the mid-1950s British theatre experienced what might be called a 'revolution' in the way it responded not only to a post-war, Cold War world but also to themes of class and to a lesser extent, gender. There are several components of this watershed and also different accounts of what happened, but for the purposes of this book it is enough to say that the establishment of the English Stage Company in 1954, moving to the Royal Court Theatre two years later, and the appointment of the twenty-five-year-old Peter Hall to direct plays at the Arts Theatre Club were significant developments in the dramatic 'revolution'. This was followed in August 1955 with the English premiere of Samuel Beckett's play, *Waiting for Godot*, directed by Hall at the Arts Theatre Club (to an audience of 300) and then in May of the following year, the opening of John Osborne's *Look Back in Anger* at the Royal Court.

Waiting for Godot could hardly have been more different from the 'Loamshire' dramas. The almost complete absence of a set or of narrative structure, the fact that the central characters were tramps, characters without motivation and the incomprehensibility of the play all conspired to make this the cause of shock and dismay.²⁸ Tynan saw *Godot*'s radical break from dramatic convention and wrote that it had 'no plot, no climax ... no beginning, no middle, no end. ... *Waiting for Godot* frankly jettisons everything by which we recognize theatre'.²⁹ For students of radio drama, *Godot*, although it was not broadcast on radio until 1960, is extremely important because of its influence on a generation of writers. In 1962, the then head of Radio Drama at the BBC, Martin Esslin, coined the term 'theatre of the absurd' to describe the work of Beckett, Eugene Ionesco and others,³⁰ and later commentators such as Dominic Shellard continued to write about 'absurdist drama' as a non-problematic term. Ionesco's *The Lesson*, directed by Peter Hall in 1955, is a good example of bafflingly illogical drama (a professor murders his student, the fortieth murder of the day), and other Ionesco plays were performed in London during the 1950s including *The Chairs* (also 1955) and, perhaps most significantly for radio drama, *Rhinoceros* which was to be adapted as a radio drama in 1959 by Michael Bakewell.

Two other important developments in British theatre should be mentioned here, at least in passing, to add to the general sense that the tectonic plates of

British and especially London drama were shifting rapidly and loudly in the mid-1950s. Bertolt Brecht's Berliner Ensemble presented a London season beginning in August (the month in which Brecht died) putting on *Mother Courage* and then in November, *The Good Woman of Setzuan*. To many more traditional theatregoers, the Marxist playwright Bertolt Brecht was boring, as the *Daily Telegraph* critic W. A. Darlington put it having seen *The Good Woman of Setzuan*: 'One of the dullest evenings I have had in the theatre ... three hours by the watch but they felt like six.'[31] It is probably true to say that Brecht was more influential in Britain in the 1960s than during the 1950s, and Michael Billington has described Brecht's influence on the theatre director Richard Eyre and the playwright David Hare in the 1960s as well as on approaches to Shakespeare at the same time.[32] Also in the early 1950s, Ewan MacColl and Joan Littlewood created the Theatre Workshop (a group derived from the pre-war Manchester-based Theatre of Action, a left-wing and anti-fascist theatre group) in 1945 and eventually based it at the Theatre Royal Stratford East in 1953. Productions included important versions of Shakespeare, a revival of Brecht's *The Good Soldier Schweik* in 1956 and Shelagh Delaney's well-known realist drama *A Taste of Honey* in 1958.

The play which is, perhaps not entirely correctly, seen as creating the 'firebreak' in the British theatre,[33] opening at the Royal Court Theatre on 8 May 1956, was John Osborne's *Look Back in Anger*. The play inspired the moniker 'Angry Young Men' to describe a generation of writers, referred to rather more pithily by the doyen of British theatre, Somerset Maugham, as 'scum'. In *Look Back in Anger*, the curtain rose to a rather shabby and cramped suburban room in which Alison Porter is ironing; it is little surprise that *Look Back in Anger* and the realist plays which followed it were referred to as 'kitchen sink' dramas. The central, angry character, Jimmy Porter, even broke convention by speaking in a regional accent and mouthing implicitly left-wing views: 'To many, in particular the young and the university-educated, this depiction of a re-invigorated, eloquent, liberal conscience at work was the revelation they had been waiting for.'[34] *Look Back in Anger* may not have been as revolutionary as *Godot* or as sophisticated as Brecht, but this was an immensely important symbolic moment for British theatre because it represented such a deliberate break with the past and such a declaration of a new social realism, which was to influence radio drama in the late 1950s and early 1960s. Jimmy Porter was a character who spoke from the heart, lacked emotional inhibition and was prone to passionate outbursts.[35] Above all, Porter was a voice for the new post-war generation, captured perfectly by the drama critic of the *Daily Express*, who wrote that play was 'intense, angry, feverish, indisciplined. It is even crazy. But it is young, young, young.'[36]

The major trends in British theatre in the 1950s included the country house dramas so beloved of the smart theatregoing bourgeoisie, the largely French-based challenge of absurdism and Brecht's epic theatre, but *Look Back in Anger* was perhaps the most explicit expression of a new realism, opening up to the stage the everyday world of kitchen sinks, working-class voices, poverty, boredom, pubs, railway stations, swearing and squalor; these took to the stage and almost at the same time were to appear in radio dramas and at the same time in television drama. Following the production of Shelagh Delaney's *A Taste of Honey* at Stratford East, Tynan encapsulated the thrill of realist drama: 'Miss Delaney brings real people on to her stage, joking and flaring and scuffling and eventually, out of the zest for life she gives them, surviving.'[37] Realism was to extend its influence over British drama with the arrival of Harold Pinter (see Chapter 8) and on television across a range of output including the comic anti-hero, Tony Hancock, 'permanently frustrated by the gulf between his own pretentious aspirations and the glum drudgery of reality'[38] and from 9 December 1960 (to the present) the realist 'soap opera' on Granada Television, *Coronation Street*.

It would of course be wrong to think that *Look Back in Anger* was an unchallenged triumph. Later in 1956, in fact almost immediately after the disaster of Suez, Noel Coward's reactionary play *Nude with Violin* opened starring John Gielgud. It was a cruel satire on the pretentiousness of modern art and characterized by a casual racism and sneering contempt for the lower social classes. It ran for a year, and Dominic Shellard warns us that 'the reception of the play by London theatregoers, therefore, provides a salutary reminder that it is erroneous to talk of a Royal Court revolution, dating from the premiere of *Look Back in Anger* in May 1956, that swept all before it'.[39]

Developments in the theatre had a particularly profound influence on radio drama, hardly surprising as most radio dramatists also wrote for the stage (and for television). Of the main writers considered here, Beckett increasingly wrote for the stage after writing six pieces for radio between 1957 and 1964, Pinter of course became primarily a writer for the stage (and then a writer of screenplays) after his three commissions for the BBC and even Giles Cooper, most radiogenic of writers, was mainly concerned with television from the early 1960s as he became the main writer for the television series *Maigret*. The interconnection of theatre and radio drama will be studied in later chapters, but there were also extremely important developments in literature, including novels and poetry.

Many of the most interesting developments in post-war literature can be seen as reactions against the dominance of a Bloomsbury-inspired,[40] modernist and London-centric elite. Figures like T. S. Eliot, E. M. Forster and Cyril Connolly (editor of the influential literary magazine *Horizon*) were powerful men of letters after the war. Perhaps nowhere reflected the sub-Bloomsbury elite more than the Third Programme which became an unofficial institutional centre of British cultural life headed by its first controller, George Barnes, whose Bloomsbury connection was through his mother, a member of the Strachey family and close friend of the very prolific broadcaster E. M. Forster.[41] As before the war, the BBC created an institutional home for a particular literary elite who were mainly male, middle aged and part of the same social circle. But this was not the only literary grouping and a 'New Wave' of writers emerged partly in reaction against what they saw as an experimentalist, elitist and old establishment: this group included Martin Amis and Philip Larkin and was referred to as 'The Movement'. Writers like Osborne, Doris Lessing, Colin Wilson and John Wain were also associated with the Movement and sometimes, with some justification, referred to as the 'Angry Young Men' [sic]. Many of the most important Movement writers contributed to the revealing *Declaration*[42] in which Lessing, Osborne, Wain and others provided summaries of their beliefs. The book starts with these words:

> A number of young and widely opposed writers have burst upon the scene and are striving to change many of the values which have held good in recent years. No critic has yet succeeded in assessing them or correlating them *objectively* one to another. This volume aims at helping the public to understand what is happening while it is actually happening – at uncovering a certain pattern taking shape in British thought and literature.[43]

Dominic Sandbrook describes the bond between Amis and Larkin, both born in 1922, as 'the most important relationship in post-war letters'.[44] Amis's *Lucky Jim* of 1954 and Larkin's collection of poems *The Less Deceived* (1955) contributed to their prominence and together with some Cambridge graduates influenced by F. R. Leavis denounced the 'Mandarins of Bloomsbury'.[45] Poets in the early 1950s reacted against the experimentalism and obscurity of Eliot and Ezra Pound and denounced the 'tags from foreign tongues, cribs from authors and learned references' of the modernists.[46] One of the characteristics of the BBC, then as now, was a capacity to do the unexpected, and this was certainly the case with the BBC radio poetry programme, *New Soundings*, presented by the established literary heavyweight, John Lehman in 1952. So successful was the programme that, of course, Lehman was fired and then, remarkably, replaced by the close associate of Amis and Larkin, John Wain who renamed the programme *First Reading*. He declared, belligerently, in his first broadcast, that he was going to use it 'as a means of putting over a certain point of view about contemporary letters'.[47] Wain's first item in this programme was a provocative reading from the unpublished *Lucky Jim*. This was the first broadside in a cultural spat which was to be played out in publications like *The New Statesman*. Hewison sees the BBC's role here as important: 'The arguments over *First Reading* were more useful in dramatizing a growing conflict between generations than in deciding any issues about poetry. They help to show the process by which the carnivorous young men of 1951 were growing into the angry young men of 1956.'[48]

For the purposes of this account of 'golden age' radio drama it is possible to pick out some influential themes in New Wave literature. Britain's decline, certainly as an imperial power, is powerfully captured in Osborne's second major play, *The Entertainer*, in which Lawrence Olivier played a washed-up music-hall comedian. In the play, the death of music hall is used to represent the end of empire with echoes of the very recent humiliation of the Suez crisis. An affirmation of youth is also a core theme, young new artists, kicking against the establishment at a time of the first coffee bars, students wearing duffel coats, listening to skiffle music or jazz, seeing Elvis Presley in his first big film *Heartbreak Hotel*.[49] Associated with the theme of youth is quite simply one of anger and especially towards a soft, complacent and comfortable older generation. This is well put in Osborne's chapter in *Declaration*:

> I can't go on laughing at the idiocies of the people who rule our lives. We have been laughing at their gay little madnesses, my dear, at their point-to-points,[50] at the postural slump of the well-off and mentally under-privileged, at their stooping shoulders and strained accents, at their waffling cant, for too long. They are no longer funny, because they are not merely dangerous, they are murderous.[51]

Osborne's anger was not only directed at a different class and different generation but also at women, as identified by Dominic Sandbrook who sees 'an extraordinarily aggressive treatment of women' in New Wave writing.[52] Jimmy Porter in *Look Back in Anger* is clearly misogynistic, and throughout New Wave novels and films women are the victims of 'lies, treachery and verbal abuse'.[53] Sandbrook argues that 'the explanation for all this lies in the identification of supposedly feminine values with modernity and mass culture. Women were closely identified with the new affluent society.'[54] Amis was a great fan of Ian Fleming's superhero James Bond about whom Sandbrook is particularly critical for his sadism and adolescent sexuality. 'Bond's women' were disposable consumer goods, and the Bond books can be seen as a reaction against the image and role of women (and homosexuals) which had changed since the end of the war. This was of course before the changes brought about from the 1960s by second-wave feminism and the American women's liberation movement, and it is hardly surprising that some post-war radio dramatists represented women in a negative light. Giles Cooper is a case in point, and many of his dramas depict women as domineering and threatening. In addition prostitutes were common in post-war radio dramas often humiliating and belittling men.

The conclusion of this brief survey of post-war British society and culture examines the way radio drama itself was represented by a leading cultural publication *The New Statesman* (before 1958 titled *The New Statesman and Nation*), a weekly publication famed for its extensive cultural and literary reviews. Although increasingly thought of as a political journal expressing the views of the left, during the late 1950s and early 1960s, it had extensive coverage of cultural developments over several pages each week. It is instructive therefore to look at how *The New Statesman* responded critically to the 'golden age' of radio drama: instructive but also rather depressing. Just to take the most active period of innovative BBC radio drama production, 1957–62, there were no reviews of radio drama at all. In fact the 'Arts and Entertainment' section is extremely instructive as a measure of the way the arts were viewed at that time (books and poetry were in a separate section of the magazine). There is a distinctly hierarchical quality with painting and architecture always appearing first and often at some length, followed by theatre reviews and opera and classical music and then sometimes jazz, film and maybe broadcasting. The main reviewer of broadcasting from 1957 to 1961 was Tom Driberg who made occasional references to radio but mainly wrote about television. His reviews were fascinating as an expression of what must have been a commonly held view that television had 'won' and was superior in almost every way to radio. In 1958, Driberg discussed the demise of radio: 'In the next few years radio will surely do less and less of the sort of programmes that TV can do as well or better' including here 'most plays'.[55] This opinion that radio drama was simply inferior to the television version was implicit throughout his reviews. Driberg was replaced by some rather more balanced voices, notably Louis MacNeice who, although he apparently was only tasked with reviewing television programmes, wrote these wonderfully dismissive words about watching the great English potter Bernard Leach at work on television: 'The close-up of his hands on that wet and whirling wheel is one of the few things I have lately seen on television, always excepting sports, that have made me feel grateful for the medium.'[56] Similarly, Clancy Sigal, who had a three-month assignment as a television reviewer starting in late 1961, was generally very critical because 'TV emphasizes the worst aspects of our society. … It will never achieve a balance of good and bad.'[57]

It is significant that during radio drama's 'golden age' when the form was at its height and the most important and indeed famous radio dramatists were producing their best work, a journal which prided itself on its coverage of all forms of culture, from sculpture to jazz, should completely ignore radio output. What do we learn from this? Although with the benefit of hindsight we can see considerable creative activity in BBC Radio Drama with some writers, especially Beckett, Pinter and Cooper, becoming important cultural figures, the reality at the time is that their work for radio was largely ignored outside the world of the BBC and its publication, *The Listener*. No wonder, perhaps, that they all left radio to work in other media. One also wonders what determination it must have taken for those who remained in radio to persist.

In this brief survey of post-war British society and culture I have attempted to indicate some of the context for the analysis of radio dramas which will follow. The dominant themes of a post-war and Cold War Britain included austerity, class and cultural divides and the end of empire which both the theatre and literature in their different ways hoped to address. The absurdism and realism of some post-war radio dramas or adaptations of stage plays on radio can be seen as attempts to respond to that world but were sometimes limited by the prejudices of the time as the chapters which will follow will reveal.

Notes

1. J. B. Priestley, *Postscripts* (London: William Heinemann, 1940), 4.
2. Doris Lessing, *Walking in the Shade, Volume Two of My Autobiography, 1949-1962* (London: Flamingo, 1998), 4.
3. Ibid., 5.
4. Quoted in Robert Hewison, *In Anger, Culture in the Cold War 1945-1960* (London: Methuen, 1988), 16.
5. David Pattie, *Modern British Playwriting in the 1950s* (London: Methuen Drama, 2012), 4.
6. For the purposes of this book I have found Hewison's *In Anger* particularly helpful and have also learnt a lot from David Kynaston's *Austerity Britain, 1945-51* (London: Bloomsbury, 2007); Dominic Sandbrook's *Never Had It So Good: A History of Britain from Suez to the Beatles* (London: Abacus, 2006).
7. Sandbrook, *Never Had It So Good*, 48.
8. Ibid., 105.
9. Kynaston, *Austerity Britain*, 174.
10. Former students of Britain's most prestigious public school, Eton College.
11. Kynaston, *Austerity Britain*, 174–5.
12. Quoted in ibid., 446.
13. Quoted in Sandbrook, *Never Had It So Good*, xii.
14. Kenneth O. Morgan, *The People's Peace; British History 1945-1990* (Oxford: Oxford University Press, 1990), 147–53.
15. Ibid., 153.
16. Peter Hennessy, *Never Again, Britain 1945-1951* (London: Vintage, 1993), 409.
17. My comments on the theatre here are based on Pattie, *Modern British Playwriting*.
18. The 'West End' is London's theatre quarter.
19. Dominic Shellard (ed.), *Twentieth Century British Theatre: Industry, Art and Empire* (Cambridge: Cambridge University Press, 2008); Michael Billington, *State of the Nation: British Theatre since 1945* (London: Faber and Faber, 2007).
20. Kenneth Tynan, *The Observer*, 31 October 1954 quoted in Dominic Shellard (ed.), *Kenneth Tynan: Theatre Writings* (London: Nick Hern Books, 2007).
21. Pattie, *Modern British Playwriting*, 36.
22. Ibid., 44.
23. The Lord Chamberlain's office controlled what could be performed in British theatres and actively deterred nudity, swearing, references to homosexuality and blasphemy. The Lord Chamberlain's powers were revoked in 1968, and they did not extend to the output of the BBC; see Pattie, *Modern British Playwriting*, 38–9.
24. Quoted in Hewison, *In Anger*, 84.
25. Dominic Shellard, *British Theatre since the War* (New Haven and London: Yale University Press, 1999), 30. It is interesting to note that the subject of the schoolmaster as total failure is central to Giles Cooper's most famous radio drama *Unman Wittering and Zigo* (1958).
26. Pattie, *Modern British Playwriting*, 125.
27. Claire Cochrane, *Twentieth Century British Theatre, Industry, Art and Empire* (Cambridge: Cambridge University Press, 2011), 147.

28 Billington, *State of the Nation*, 78.
29 Kenneth Tynan, *The Observer*, 7 August 1955, in Shellard (ed.), *Kenneth Tynan*, 69.
30 Martin Esslin, *The Theatre of the Absurd* (London: Penguin, 1962/1980).
31 Quoted in Shellard, *British Theatre since the War*, 76.
32 Ibid., 80.
33 Pattie, *Modern British Playwriting*, 1.
34 Shellard, *British Theatre*, 52–3.
35 Ibid., 53.
36 John Barber, *Daily Express*, 9 May 1956, quoted in Shellard, *British Theatre*, 54.
37 Kenneth Tynan, *The Observer*, 1 June 1958, quoted in Shellard (ed.), *Kenneth Tynan*, 187.
38 Sandbrook, *Never Had It So Good*, 399.
39 Dominic Shellard (ed.), *The Golden Generation: New Light On Post-war British Theatre* (London: British Library, 2008), 78.
40 The term 'Bloomsbury' is used to describe the modernist circle of writers and artists some of whom lived on or near Bloomsbury Square in London; this included Virginia Woolf, Lytton Strachey, T. S. Eliot and E. M. Forster. The complex and very important relationship between Bloomsbury and the BBC is discussed in Todd Avery's *Radio Modernism*.
41 Hewison, *In Anger*, 39.
42 Tom Maschler (ed.), *Declaration* (London: MacGibbon and Kee, 1957).
43 Ibid., 7.
44 Sandbrook, *Never Had It So Good*, 148.
45 Hewison, *In Anger*, 100.
46 Ibid., 109.
47 Ibid., 111.
48 Ibid., 113.
49 Sandbrook, *Never Had It So Good*, 29.
50 A type of horse race much loved by the fox-hunting rural elite.
51 John Osborne in Maschler (ed.), *Declaration*, 67.
52 Sandbrook, *Never Had It So Good*, 214.
53 Ibid., 214.
54 Ibid., 215.
55 Tom Driberg, *New Statesman*, 2 August 1958.
56 Louis MacNeice, *New Statesman*, 4 August 1961.
57 Clancy Sigal, *New Statesman*, 9 February 1962.

Chapter 2

THE POST-WAR BBC RADIO DRAMA DEPARTMENT

For a variety of reasons, the BBC had, to use a term which would have been very familiar at the time, a 'good war'. Despite government efforts to control if not censor the organization through the vast bureaucracy of the Ministry of Information, installed grandly at Senate House, the BBC managed to produce a highly successful and largely honest news operation which peaked magnificently after D Day with the famous daily 'War Reports'.[1] In addition, the BBC grew in popularity by beginning to think seriously about the needs of listeners, both men and women. Magazine programmes were developed for those on the home front while the music-based Forces Network tried to keep up the morale of the troops. In December 1939, soon after the outbreak of war, the head of Features and Drama,[2] Val Gielgud (more on him later in this chapter), developed a drama policy for wartime: 'It seems to me that few things can be more important during a war than the preservation of the civilized values for which that war is being fought.'[3] A particularly important development during the war years was the attempt to replace theatres (many of which were closed during the war) with a 'national theatre of the air' created by regular broadcasts of classic stage plays. For a while, the Features and Drama Department moved to Evesham and then to Manchester where drama and features producers worked closely together, both motivated by the war effort. During the war years this intermingling of producers appears to have been largely positive and, according to Ian Rodger, drama producers learnt the benefit of collaboration between writers, actors, musicians and producers which was pioneered in Features.[4] At the same time, it became necessary to create a Radio Drama Repertory Company which resulted in radio acting less derived from stagecraft and more sensitive to the needs of radio.

While Drama enacted the policy of a 'national theatre' with regular offerings of adaptations from Rudyard Kipling, Somerset Maugham, the Bible, the whole of *War and Peace*, Dorothy L. Sayers's twelve-part life of Christ (*The Man Born to be King*) and so on, Features produced probably some of the most important wartime drama and especially the work of the celebrated poet and classicist, Louis MacNeice.[5] Although lying outside the range of this book, MacNeice's wartime dramas were influential and important contributions by one of the very few radio drama writer/producers. *Christopher Columbus* (October 1942) was an epic drama starring Lawrence Olivier with music by William Walton; *Alexander Nevsky* (April 1942) was based on the film by Eisenstein while the moving tale of a close friend of MacNeice's who had died in the war, *He Had a Date*, was broadcast in June 1944. Wartime dramas began to be broadcast in two different 'slots', Saturday and Monday evenings. *Saturday Night Theatre*, which began in 1943, was mainstream (or 'middle-brow'), while radio drama on Monday evenings was more intellectually challenging. The establishment of distinct radio drama places in the broadcast schedule contributed to large audiences and the success of radio drama after the war.[6]

At the end of the war, various changes in the BBC directly impacted on Drama, the first of which was the separation from Features. In February 1945, Val Gielgud complained to the controller of Programmes, Lindsey Wellington, of an uneasy relationship with the senior features producer, Lawrence Gilliam, and suggested that Features be split in two with the literary and dramatic work being absorbed by Drama and everything else going off to News. Gielgud's typically high-handed request was only partly accepted by Wellington who simply separated the two departments but, to Gielgud's great and increasing annoyance, leaving the literary part of Features under Lawrence Gilliam.[7] As Chapter 3 will show, in the immediate post-war period up to 1953 the most important radio drama was made in Features, while Drama persisted with an unadventurous policy of adapting classic stage plays and canonical novels.

The director general of the BBC at the end of the war, William Haley, is famous among those with an interest in the history of the BBC for creating the cultural and challenging Third Programme alongside two other networks, The Light Programme (based on the earlier Forces Network) and the Home Service. Haley's motivation can be traced back to his hero and inspiration, the first manager and director general of the BBC, John Reith. Reith was himself influenced by the Victorian philosopher Matthew Arnold who saw the potential in the arts to civilize the masses.[8] This broadcasting policy, which still influences the output of the corporation today, is usually known as 'Public Service Broadcasting' based on the idea of using broadcasting to provide the listener and viewer with education, information and entertainment.[9] Reith's commitment to maintaining high standards and use of the BBC to broadcast the civilizing benefits of a certain type of established high culture is an important part of the story of post-war radio drama. Reith appointed Val Gielgud as the BBC's productions director on 1 January 1929,[10] and many of Gielgud's rather venomous opinions have a distinctly Reithian flavour. In addition, Haley was perhaps more Reithian than Reith, a fact which was expressed in his policy of a 'cultural pyramid' whereby he imagined listeners to the populist Light Programme being tempted to listen to something on the Home Service which would eventually lead them to the more demanding output of the Third.[11]

2. The Post-War BBC Radio Drama Department

The Third Programme was launched on 29 September 1946. Haley's view of the likely audience was 'one already aware of artistic experience and will include persons of taste and intelligence, and of education'.[12] It was envisaged that output would be approximately half classical music and half speech, the latter mainly drama, features (including documentary) and that BBC staple, 'talks'. The first week of the Third Programme featured an uncut production of Bernard Shaw's *Man and Superman*[13] (lasting three and a half hours) and an unabridged version of Sartre's *Huis Clos*[14] directed by the Drama Department producer Mary Hope Allen.[15] Over the following two decades, until the Third became Radio 3 in 1967, it represented a home for a particular type of radio drama: experimental, avant garde, difficult, innovative and the main subject of this book. The first controller, Third Programme, George Barnes (see Chapter 1), was a representative of the modernist, Bloomsbury-inspired cultural elite, and there can be little doubt that the Third Programme reflected the modernist world of literary London at least for the first few years of its existence. The controllers of the Third were drawn from an extremely small social group; Barnes and the later Third controller John Morris together with the young and influential radio drama producer Michael Bakewell were all alumni of King's College, Cambridge. To add to this social exclusivity, Features and Drama producers gravitated to the pubs close to Broadcasting House: The Stag's Head, The Horse and Groom and, above all, The George in Great Portland Street. This heavy drinking culture is described with a rather self-deluded frankness by the features producer Rayner Heppenstall whose alcohol-fuelled career is the subject of *Portrait of the Artist as a Professional Man*.[16] Somehow this small,[17] predominantly male, socially and educationally exclusive group, which although employed by the BBC spent as much time as possible outside it, managed to produce some Prix Italia dramas and features and work of the calibre of Dylan Thomas's *Under Milk Wood*.

It may be a rather sweeping generalization but the great strength of Features, at least up until the mid-1950s when it began to decline, was the quality and artistic creativity of some of its producers, and especially MacNeice and the most important of all features producers, Douglas Cleverdon[18] not to mention the pioneering Nesta Pain, D. G. Bridson, Francis Dillon, Henry Reed and W. R. Rodgers[19] among many others. The other great strength of Features was a willingness to experiment combined with great ambition. So the magnetic tape recorder was used in Features long before other parts of the BBC (with the exception of the News Department) and most spectacularly by Denis Mitchell in 1954 who interviewed 'ordinary' people in the iconic series *People Talking*. Nesta Pain's remarkable science programmes gave flies, spiders and other insects the features treatment and topical and historical features were equally innovative. As for ambition, *The Canterbury Tales*[20] was a seven-part adaptation of Chaucer's work by Nevil Coghill of which Thomas wrote, 'The series was a superb example of the ambitious large-scale literary project.'[21] Similarly Henry Reed's adaptation of Thomas Hardy's *The Dynasts*[22] in six ninety-minute episodes was a bold and prestigious production.

The talent and philosophy of Features in the decade after the end of the war produced some major radio dramas which are discussed in Chapter 3. The story of post-war features and drama is intriguing because, as Jeanette Thomas explains, during the 1950s Drama grew in ambition and stature as Features went into decline: 'As far as the art of radio is concerned, the first ten years after the war marked the ascendancy of Features. The next ten years marked the rise of Drama and relative decline of Features, ending with the death of Lawrence Gilliam and the disbandment of Features in 1964.'[23] There are many possible explanations for the demise of the Features department, including the emergence of the radio documentary as a way of providing information about the world, making use of portable tape recorders, especially when produced by Denis Mitchell and D. G. Bridson, and the fact that the cost of the large-scale 'musico-literary' programmes was increasingly prohibitive and appeared old fashioned in the rapidly changing culture of late 1950s and early 1960s. This is not the place to dwell on the demise of the once glorious BBC Features department, and it is encouraging to see that the radio feature remains an exciting and dynamic radio form, but it could be argued that the success of Drama in expressing something of the 1950s' zeitgeist, a Cold War, post-war sensibility in both absurdist and realist dramas simply outplayed the elitist, rarified output of Features. To use a contemporary expression, Drama 'got it', Features did not.

The story of the post-war Drama Department is partly about individuals,[24] from the culturally conservative and long-serving head of department Val Gielgud who was in effect in charge of radio drama from 1929 to 1964, an extraordinary thirty-five years, to the far younger producers under him, including from 1953 his assistant Donald McWhinnie, a name which will be repeated endlessly in the examples to follow and the first head of the Script Unit, Barbara Bray, the more established figures of Lance Sieveking and Raymond Raikes who had unique approaches to their craft and the very young recruits Michael Bakewell and John Tydeman, both Cambridge graduates with apparently ravenous appetites for new drama.

What we know about post-war radio drama producers is the product of rather uneven sources of information. Val Gielgud, for example, wrote a number of personal accounts of his career and beliefs about drama[25] and was also interviewed at length by the BBC when he retired, and his views are also well documented in the files at the BBC Written Archives Centre. Barbara Bray is also well represented in the archive and was the subject of a BBC oral history; she is also mentioned in biographies of Samuel Beckett with whom she had a close, long-term relationship. Both Michael Bakewell and John Tydeman were interviewed for this book, and in addition Tydeman was also the subject of an exit interview and has also published about radio drama.[26] There is a fairly comprehensive literature about Louis MacNeice including specifically his time at the BBC.[27] Donald McWhinnie, a central figure in the history of radio drama, wrote the extremely informative *Art of Radio*[28] but there is nothing about his life other than passing references in the archive. As for Douglas Cleverdon, although his work is widely reviewed and admired, there is no published account of his life or expression of his opinions.[29] With the benefit of hindsight no doubt, McWhinnie and Cleverdon are revealed as towering figures in twentieth-century radio drama, but they exist only as passing references in other peoples' obituaries[30] and reminiscences. It follows that this account of Drama producers is uneven and, like the radio archive itself, very incomplete.

Val Gielgud's appointment as Productions Director on 1 January 1929 made him the de facto head of drama, and he retained that position until 1963 when his assistant, Martin Esslin, took over and he retired. Like many other radio drama producers, Gielgud was able to say on his appointment that 'my experience of the practical problems of Radio Drama was nil'.[31] However, Gielgud was given some instructions to guide him: 'The general directive given me by Roger Eckersley[32] in 1929 included the stipulation that at least eight of Shakespeare's plays should appear in our programmes each year.'[33] Despite his lack of experience of theatre production, Gielgud was an extraordinarily prolific writer of novels, plays and radio dramas, and during the 1930s he became a regular producer of different types of radio drama including some of his own plays for radio (such as *Esiles*, 1932, and *Friday morning*, 1934). He also adapted stage plays including the work of Ibsen and Chekhov (whose stage plays arguably lend themselves to audio-only versions) as well as Somerset Maugham and Oscar Wilde (both particular Gielgud favourites) and in 1939 *The Finest Stories in the World*, inspired by stories from the Bible (Part 1, 'Ruth', Part 2, 'Elijah', etc.). During the war when, as already described, Drama was moved from London to Manchester and back again, Gielgud was producing almost weekly dramas, many of which were parts of serials written by popular authors including Norman Edwards, Clemence Dane and Mabel Constanduros. This light and entertaining output was motivated by the war effort and the need to produce uplifting and universally popular dramas. Gielgud's production of Dorothy L. Sayers's twelve-part *The Man Born to be King* (1941) is typical of his activity during the war; the long-running life of Christ began as a programme for children and was then broadcast on the Home Service. During the war, Drama also produced a serial drama about life in wartime Britain titled *Frontline Family*, written by Mabel Constanduros, a popular writer and comic actress.[34] An idea developed to make this into a daily fifteen-minute drama designed to reach American audiences as part of the propaganda effort prior to America's entry into the war. However, this would mean that the Drama Department was engaging in the production of the much-reviled radio soap: 'Val Gielgud … had for many years resisted any notion of serial production on the grounds of its inferiority as a cultural form as well as the way that the demands of series production would disrupt normal BBC practices.'[35] But by March 1941, *Frontline Family* was in production and was to run for seven years. Fairly soon the decision was made to bring in a more authentic 'radio soap' writer in the shape of 'Mrs Ronnie Colley', an American living in London with serial writing experience who produced sample scripts and an outline of the ongoing narrative more closely aligned to an American radio soap. The response from Gielgud is worth quoting at length:

> My own view of these Colley scripts is that they are perfectly frightful. The sentiments may be unexceptionable but they are also unbelievably dull. There is no characterization worth a damn and this is surely an essential thing in a programme of this kind, because without it there is no reason why people should take an interest in the characters concerned, considering how flimsy the plots are bound to be. The dialogue is not only undistinguished, it is incompetent.[36]

Despite Gielgud's reservations, *Frontline Family* continued till 1948 when it was replaced by *Mrs Dale's Diary* and then in 1950 the longest running of all British radio serials, *The Archers*. Gielgud's strategy for distancing himself from radio soaps was to set up a semi-independent serial drama unit inside the Drama Department and let them get on with it. He was, however, clear about his views on the subject in his BBC exit interview stating that he 'hated' and had only 'contempt' for programmes like *Mrs Dale's Diary* and also the popular thriller *Dick Barton*.[37] After the war, Gielgud was given the job of head of Television Drama from 1949 to 1951, but he did not enjoy the experience[38] and was pleased to return 'home' to Radio Drama. His return was quickly followed by a decisive moment in the history of British radio drama, the appointment of Donald McWhinnie as his assistant in 1953.

Gielgud's return to Radio Drama and the arrival of McWhinnie (soon followed by the equally important appointment of Barbara Bray as head of the Script Unit) seemed to have released Gielgud from the day-to-day running of the department and allowed him to do more producing. His preferred choice of dramas were serial adaptations from popular novels or the stage. In 1953–4 he 'directed' a twelve-part series of Sherlock Holmes tales starring his brother John Gielgud and Ralph Richardson. In 1955 he co-produced the twelve-part *The Golden Butterfly*,[39] a very traditional drawing room drama, and then between 1957 and 1960 he produced three long-running adaptations of novels by John Galsworthy, *Maid in Waiting*, *Over the River* and *Flowering Wilderness*. In the last few years of his BBC career, Val Gielgud produced some important adaptations for the Third Programme including Rattigan's *The Deep Blue Sea*,[40] Anouilh's *The Lark*[41] and a number of adaptations of ancient Greek tragedies by Aeschylus and Sophocles.[42]

Gielgud was a complex and contradictory figure. His oral history interview suggests someone deeply conservative and conventional but under Gielgud, Radio Drama flourished in the 1950s and early 1960s, even though he strongly disliked much of the new drama for which the BBC was becoming well known. His reactionary views are particularly well expressed in *Years in a Mirror* published shortly after his retirement. He was adamantly opposed to state funding for bodies like the Royal Shakespeare Company and the National Theatre: 'If the theatre, fortified by subsidies, is enabled to disregard audience reaction; if the pretentious, the self-consciously obscure, the dreary but sociologically significant, can rely on the backing of critics who forget that they exist to represent as well as to influence public taste, then the theatre will operate in a vacuum of its own creation.'[43] He was pleased that the mass audience for radio dramas at the end of the war (presumably for radio drama serials) had deserted radio for television: 'That vast body of moronic listeners whose innate and unalterably conservative tastes had always acted as a brake upon the adventurous, the novel, and the experimental in radio.'[44] In the 1950s, Gielgud seemed to relinquish leadership of drama to younger producers, including Barbara Bray and then Michael Bakewell and John Tydeman, although the departure of McWhinnie, Bray and Bakewell all in the early 1960s suggests disagreements with Gielgud and his successor, Martin Esslin.[45]

Donald McWhinnie, as already explained, has left little biographical trace and so any account of his contribution to post-war radio drama must depend on the record of his productions derived from *The Radio Times* and his book on 'the art of radio'.[46] McWhinnie's first production for BBC Drama was broadcast in 1949 on the Home Service; *Broken Battlements*[47] by Frederick Lidstone was a 'Saturday matinee'. After that, McWhinnie was busily producing dramas on all three networks before being the assistant producer with the eminent features producer, E. A. Harding in the Third Programme broadcast of Goethe's *Faust*[48] in an adaptation by Louis MacNeice. In 1950, McWhinnie produced a number of poetry programmes and then that particular favourite of BBC Radio Drama, an eight-part adaptation of a novel by John Galsworthy, *The Country House*.[49] McWhinnie's career thus far seems unremarkable for a jobbing radio producer, but in the late summer of 1950 he truly arrived on the radio dramatic scene. *The Ascent of F6* by W. H. Auden and Christopher Isherwood (discussed in more detail in Chapter 3) was published in 1936 and performed on the London stage the following year. It was a verse drama with music written for it by Benjamin Britten. McWhinnie was then given the high-profile task of producing a radio version for the Third Programme[50] starring the eminent stage actor Marius Goring.

Three years later, McWhinnie was promoted to the position of Assistant Head of Drama (Sound) and was to play a vital role in the promotion of new writing for radio up to 1960. He was the main producer of radio dramas written for the BBC by Beckett, Giles Cooper and Harold Pinter and as such was the principal architect of radio drama's 'golden age'. Despite the lack of biographical information on McWhinnie, we are fortunate that he wrote *The Art of Radio* which includes detailed accounts of the production of his most famous successes, including Beckett's *All That Fall* and Cooper's *Under the Loofah Tree*.[51] Not only did he have the ability to identify and then support, against considerable opposition, the work of particular writers but he also had a unique understanding of sound drama. Apart from detailed descriptions of the process of radio drama production, his analysis of the role of sound, whether realistic or unrealistic, is extraordinarily perceptive and ahead of his time. A particularly important example of this is his account of the use of sound in Beckett's *All That Fall*,[52] including what he calls 'stylized' sound effects.[53] For McWhinnie, radio drama is at its best an exploration of the inner world, an intimate representation facilitated by the original use of sound. He was, unsurprisingly, one of the main advocates for the development of the Radiophonic Workshop which was partly the consequence of his 'painstaking and brilliant'[54] use of sound effects in *All That Fall*.

McWhinnie's career as a radio drama producer came to an end in October 1960 and is connected to the beginning of Harold Pinter's rise to fame. The failure of Pinter's *The Birthday Party* at the Lyric, Hammersmith on 19 May 1958 (discussed in more detail in Chapter 8) did not stop Pinter from writing to McWhinnie about his plans for a radio drama. Pinter was then commissioned to write three radio dramas for the BBC, and McWhinnie produced the first two of these (*A Slight Ache*[55] and *A Night Out*[56]). Pinter clearly established a good relationship with McWhinnie and asked him to direct *The Caretaker* at The Arts Theatre Club in 1960 which was a great success. McWhinnie then moved into television direction and left behind his glorious but, today, largely forgotten radio career.

Barbara Bray was asked in her BBC oral history interview how it was that given she had no experience of the theatre she got the job of Head of the Script Unit in 1953; she replied that the fact that she was 'young, beautiful and brilliant'[57] with a first-class degree from Cambridge was probably the reason. Interestingly she claims in the same interview that McWhinnie himself did not have a theatrical background so she was certainly not alone in that. Bray was one of the most influential young figures in Drama and, alongside McWhinnie and then Bakewell, helped in the process of commissioning Samuel Beckett and Harold Pinter to write for the BBC. She also translated important French dramas including those by Marguerite Duras (a personal friend), Arthur Adamov, Sartre and Anouilh. Her friendship with Beckett played a very important part in his critically important BBC career and became a central part of her life; she moved to Paris to be near him in 1961, and she was his 'personal and intellectual partner for more than 30 years'.[58] Bray saw her role as extending beyond the BBC to more general support for British theatre, actors and writers. She attempted to see almost all London stage plays and looked out for struggling writers in order to offer them support and encouragement.[59] The impact this had on British drama was described by John Tydeman, a future head of Radio Drama and contemporary of Bray, who claimed the Script Unit under Bray was 'public service radio at its best', adding that it was 'a service for the dramatic life of the country'.[60] One struggling writer who benefitted from the support and encouragement of BBC staff was Harold Pinter, and Barbara Bray produced the third of his early radio plays, *The Dwarfs*.[61]

2. The Post-War BBC Radio Drama Department

Michael Bakewell was born in 1931 in Birmingham and attended Bishop Vesey's Grammar School till the age of eighteen. On leaving school he did National Service and then in 1951 went to study English Literature at King's College, Cambridge. His tutor there was the eminent British scholar and theatre director George 'Dadie' Rylands. Rylands's excellent Bloomsbury credentials included the fact that Lytton Strachey wrote the introduction to his dissertation for the position of fellow at King's, and Virginia Woolf describes having lunch in Rylands's rooms at Cambridge in *A Room of One's Own*. Rylands was actively involved in the creation of the Cambridge Arts Theatre and fostered the vibrant theatrical life of the university which contributed to a generation of actors and directors including Michael Bakewell and John Tydeman.

Immediately after graduating, Michael Bakewell applied to work at the BBC and Val Gielgud gave him a job as a drama producer: 'I went directly into doing things and I started directing plays almost immediately.'[62] Bakewell was twenty-four years old, had no professional theatre experience at all and yet was given one of the most prominent positions in British drama; his first production was with Donald McWhinnie, Schiller's *The Death of Wallenstein*,[63] and he quickly proceeded to produce plays by Giles Cooper, André Gide, Eugene Ionesco, Arthur Adomov and other major writers. As McWhinnie departed, Michael Bakewell became the most important of the drama producers specializing in the avant garde, and he produced three particularly important and successful adaptations from the stage: Ionesco's *Rhinoceros*,[64] Pinter's *The Caretaker*[65] and Beckett's *Endgame*.[66] Bakewell was also the main producer of plays by Rhys Adrian whose work he championed (he produced three plays by Adrian in 1963 alone). In 1962 he produced the first radio drama by the celebrated writer Caryl Churchill,[67] who was then associated mainly with John Tydeman.

Michael Bakewell, passed over for the position of Val Gielgud's deputy on McWhinnie's departure in 1960, did not find Gielgud's replacement, Martin Esslin, to his liking ('a terrible bore'[68]) and soon embarked on a career in television. He made an important and distinctive contribution to the 'golden age' of radio drama, but the question of why he was appointed in the first place is important and needs an answer. Bakewell was, according to his own version of events, a precocious undergraduate, he was told by Rylands after two years of his degree, 'there is no point in you going on doing English any longer, I can't teach you any more, go off and do something else'.[69] This combination of youth, academic brilliance but almost no theatrical experience is identical to that other Drama fire-brand, Barbara Bray and their surprising appointments by Gielgud suggests that he valued raw intelligence over anything else. As it turned out he was right, both Bray and Bakewell made very important and successful contributions to radio drama despite their almost complete lack of relevant experience, a theme which I will return to in the conclusion.

John Tydeman arrived in the Drama department in 1960 and so missed the culture wars associated with Gielgud and his precocious young producers. Born in 1936 he was educated at Trinity College, Cambridge, where he made full use of the opportunities to direct and act in plays. He directed fourteen plays while an undergraduate and benefitted from having some very talented actors to work with, including Derek Jacobi and Ian McKellen. Some of the Cambridge student productions went to London and to the BBC for broadcast.[70] It follows from this semi-professional experience that unlike some of his contemporaries in BBC Drama, Tydeman was already an experienced theatre director, admittedly at an amateur level. He joined the BBC Trainee scheme and was then appointed to the role of producer for the Drama Department and up to 1964 produced a modest variety of afternoon plays for the Home Service and in 1962 a number of editions of *The Dales*.[71] His first production for the Third Programme was Genet's *The Maids*,[72] and it is striking that despite his experience he was not offered the same amount of work as a drama producer, especially for the Third Programme, as the young Michael Bakewell or Donald McWhinnie; this may have reflected a more cautious approach by Martin Esslin to using unproven talent.

John Tydeman's undergraduate experience as a prolific theatre director schooled him in the work of Shakespeare and Marlowe, and he was a great enthusiast for adapting Shakespeare for radio, describing *Macbeth* as 'the perfect radio play' adding that 'the soliloquys are pure radio'.[73] This and other views about the suitability of playwrights for adaptation are useful for an understanding of why some stage plays and not others were adapted for radio. Tydeman took the view that Chekhov's plays did not adapt well whereas Ibsen and Shaw both did. One factor in Tydeman's judgements was the availability of actors; the abundance of Shakespearian actors encouraged performances of the bard on radio, and surprisingly, despite Tydeman's reservations about Chekhov, the ability to get actors like Ian McKellen and Paul Schofield to perform Chekhov for radio overruled concerns about his adaptability for sound.[74]

Raymond Raikes was an important and very active radio drama producer of the post-war period but in many ways profoundly different from the cohort of young producers around Donald McWhinnie. He is not a central part of the story told here because he rarely produced dramas written for radio and his adaptations were mainly of the classics. However, his career is a useful reminder of how extremely versatile some drama producers were. Born in 1910, he studied Classics at Oxford and was actively involved as a director and actor in the Oxford University Dramatic Society. He became a professional actor in the 1930s and after the start of the war was a presenter on the Forces Programme. After the war in 1946 he introduced the Home Service programme, *Top of the Bill*, as a sort of early radio disc jockey. Raikes was one of the drama producers tasked with producing radio drama serials including *The Robinson Family* (1947) and *Dick Barton* (1947) on a daily basis in March and April and then in May 1947, *The Daring Dexters* (a thriller serial about circus life) which he produced on a daily basis for three months in the summer of 1947. Given Raikes's labelling as a drama serial producer it is remarkable that he also produced *Scenes from the Frogs*[75] by Aristophones in the original

2. The Post-War BBC Radio Drama Department

Greek acted by Cambridge University students. Towards the end of 1947 Raikes ceased producing the popular serials and became more of a Home Service drama producer and in 1948 he produced Dickens's *Great Expectations*[76] in a thirteen-part adaptation by Mabel Constanduros. The turning point in Raikes's career was his production of Edward Sackville-West's *The Rescue*[77] (discussed in Chapter 3). This was one of Gielgud's favourite radio dramas and indeed Gielgud had produced it himself only three years earlier so the choice of Raikes to produce this third production was surely a huge vote of confidence in him by the head of Drama and not dissimilar to giving McWhinnie *The Ascent of F6* in 1950. During the 1950s, Raikes was established as one of the most important drama producers specializing in adaptations of canonical plays, including from ancient Greece but also Ibsen, Chekhov and the Restoration dramatists, Webster and Jonson. At the beginning of the 1960s Raikes was a key figure in the Home Service's *The National Theatre of the Air*, an odd selection of Restoration drama, Somerset Maugham, Shakespeare and the Mystery plays in a lightly concealed final statement from Gielgud, the man associated with the original concept of the national theatre of the air. This was perhaps a final swansong for both Gielgud and Raikes, a deeply conservative affirmation of everything that was not Pinter, Beckett, Osborne and the modern English stage. Despite the fulsome words of admiration in Tydeman's obituary for Raikes,[78] he was rather less guarded in an interview describing him as a 'dreadful old fogey' and a 'supreme amateur'.[79]

This account of the post-war Drama Department has focused mainly on the individuals who produced dramas against the backdrop of a post-war BBC emerging confidently into the 1950s. The combination of a tabula rasa Third Programme schedule and a collection of highly intelligent and culturally adventurous young producers, only partly restrained by older more conservative managers, was the seedbed of radio drama's 'golden age'. McWhinnie, Bray and Bakewell, despite a remarkable lack of theatrical experience, were trusted by Gielgud and the controllers of the Third to produce a form of public service broadcasting which both supported English actors and dramatists as well as introducing radio listeners to the latest and most important developments in drama.

Notes

1 This analysis is based on the definitive account of the wartime BBC, Sian Nicholas, *The Echo of War: Home Front Propaganda and the Wartime BBC, 1939-45* (Manchester: Manchester University Press, 1996) and also my own survey of BBC factual output, Hugh Chignell, *Public Issue Radio: Talks, News and Current Affairs in the Twentieth Century* (Basingstoke: Palgrave, 2011).
2 Until immediately after the war, Features and Drama were one department under Gielgud.

3   Quoted in Ian Rodger, *Radio Drama* (London: Macmillan, 1982), 54.
4   Ibid., 57.
5   MacNeice's BBC career is the subject of Barbara Coulton, *Louis MacNeice in the BBC* (London: Faber and Faber, 1980).
6   At least this was the view of Val Gielgud in his BBC interview, http://www.bbc.co.uk/historyofthebbc/bbc-memories/val-gielgud.
7   Jeanette Thomas, 'A history of the BBC Features Department, 1924-1964' (D.Phil diss., University of Oxford, 1993), 177–9.
8   Avery, *Radio Modernism*, 23–8.
9   For a contemporary account of Public Service Broadcasting see David Hendy, *Public Service Broadcasting* (Basingstoke: Palgrave Macmillan, 2013).
10 Val Gielgud, *British Radio Drama, 1922-1956, A Survey* (London: George Harrap, 1957), 34. The book has a photograph of Reith at the beginning and is dedicated to him.
11 This movement upwards is particularly well explained by Tony Stoller in his history of classical music on the BBC, *Classical Music Radio in the United Kingdom, 1945-1995* (Basingstoke: Palgrave Macmillan, 2018), 45.
12 Quoted in Kate Whitehead, *The Third Programme, A Literary History* (Oxford: Clarendon Press, 1989), 16.
13 *Man and Superman*, 1 October 1946 (in 4 acts). BBC Third Programme.
14 *Huis Clos*, 4 October 1946. BBC Third Programme.
15 Kate Murphy, *Behind the Wireless, A History of Early Women at the BBC* (Basingstoke: Palgrave Macmillan, 2016), 132–5.
16 Rayner Heppenstall, *Portrait of the Artist as a Professional Man* (London: Peter Owen, 1949).
17 There were approximately fifteen features producers and a similar number of drama producers.
18 Jeanette Thomas points out in her study of the Features Department that of forty-three Prix Italia entries by the BBC in the post-war period, a remarkable seventeen were produced by Cleverdon, and he was also responsible for the two undisputed masterpieces of the post-war years, *Under Milk Wood* and *In Parenthesis*. Thomas, 'A history of the BBC Features Department'.
19 W. R. Rodgers, a Presbyterian minister from Northern Ireland and poet, was recruited to Features, along with Sam Hanna Bell, by Louis MacNeice on a trip to Northern Ireland in search of talent. Both made extremely important contributions to features production in London and Belfast.
20 *The Canterbury Tales*, 21 October 1946 (in seven parts). BBC Third Programme.
21 Thomas, 'A history of the BBC Features Department', 223.
22 *The Dynasts*, 3 June 1951 (in six parts). BBC Third Programme.
23 Ibid., 383.
24 The observation that histories of the BBC need to acknowledge the decisive interventions of individuals on the corporation, its culture and output is not new and best expressed in David Hendy, 'Biography and the emotions as a missing "narrative" in media history', *Media History*, 18, no. 3-4 (2016): 361–78.
25 Including Val Gielgud, *British Radio Drama* and *Years in a Mirror* (London: The Bodley Head, 1965).
26 For example, John Tydeman, 'The producer and radio drama: A personal view', in *Radio Drama*, ed. Lewis.

27 Coulton, *Louis MacNeice in the BBC*; Amanda Wrigley and S. J. Harrison (eds), *Louis MacNeice: The Classical Radio Plays* (Oxford: Oxford University Press, 2013).
28 McWhinnie, *The Art of Radio*.
29 Like Giles Cooper, Douglas Cleverdon did leave a substantial collection of personal papers now held in the Lilly Library, Indiana University Bloomington, Indiana.
30 For example, there is some useful information about Douglas Cleverdon in the obituary of his wife, Nest Cleverdon, *The Independent*, 5 January 2004.
31 Gielgud, *British Radio Drama, 1922-1956, A Survey*, 34.
32 Roger Eckersley was the director of Entertainment (the other 'output' director was the director of Talks, Hilda Matheson).
33 Gielgud, *Years in a Mirror*, 180.
34 Michele Hilmes, *Network Nations, A Transnational History of British and American Broadcasting* (New York and London: Routledge, 2012), 148.
35 Ibid., 149.
36 Val Gielgud quoted in Hilmes, *Network Nations*, 150.
37 BBC oral history interview with Val Gielgud, http://www.bbc.co.uk/historyofthebbc/bbc-memories/val-gielgud.
38 Gielgud described this as follows: 'It was late in 1949 before the experiment was tried of seconding the Head of Sound Drama to Alexandra palace and adding Television Drama to his other activities. The experiment lasted some eighteen months. No one is in a better position than the present writer to assert that it was not a success.' Val Gielgud, *British Radio Drama*, 142.
39 *The Golden Butterfly*, 22 February 1955 (in ten parts). BBC Home Service.
40 *The Deep Blue Sea*, 2 August 1958. BBC Home Service.
41 *The Lark*, 29 December 1961. BBC Third Programme.
42 See Amanda Wrigley, *Greece on Air: Engagements with Ancient Greece on BBC Radio, 1920s–1960s* (Oxford: Oxford University Press, 2014).
43 Gielgud, *Years in a Mirror*, 167.
44 Ibid., 171.
45 This view of an argumentative and unhappy Drama Department in the early 1960s is supported by Barbara Bray in her BBC exit interview in which she regretted the failure to appoint McWhinnie as Gielgud's successor. In the interview with Michael Bakewell conducted for this book (21 June 2017) he stated that Bray was driven out of Drama by Gielgud following McWhinnie's departure and that he, Bakewell, was passed over for the head of Drama position because he was too junior and so Martin Esslin was Gielgud's replacement.
46 McWhinnie, *The Art of Radio*.
47 *Broken Battlements*, 5 February 1949. BBC Home Service.
48 *Faust*, 1 November 1949 (in four parts). BBC Third Programme.
49 *The Country House*, 2 April 1950 (in eight parts). BBC Home Service.
50 *The Ascent of F6*, 22 August 1950. BBC Third Programme.
51 *Under the Loofah Tree*, 3 August 1958. BBC Third Programme.
52 *All That Fall*, 13 January 1957. BBC Third Programme.
53 McWhinnie, *The Art of Radio*, 134–51.
54 Paul Ferris in *The Observer* quoted in Louis Niebur, *Special Sound: The Creation and Legacy of the BBC Radiophonic Workshop* (Oxford: Oxford University Press, 2010), 24.

55 *A Slight Ache*, 29 July 1959. BBC Third Programme.
56 *A Night Out*, 1 March 1960. BBC Third Programme.
57 BBC Oral History interviews. Barbara Bray.
58 Barbara Bray, obituary. *The Guardian*, 4 March 2010.
59 BBC Oral history interviews. Barbara Bray.
60 John Tydeman, extract from his BBC oral history interview, http://www.bbc.co.uk/historyofthebbc/radioreinvented/radiodrama?lang=gd
61 *The Dwarfs*, 2 December 1960. BBC Third Programme.
62 Interview with Michael Bakewell, 21 June 2017.
63 *The Death of Wallenstein*, 16 January 1955. BBC Third Programme.
64 *Rhinoceros*, 20 August 1959. BBC Third Programme.
65 *The Caretaker*, 20 March 1962. BBC Third Programme.
66 *Endgame*, 22 May 1962. BBC Third Programme.
67 *The Ants*, 27 November 1962. BBC Third Programme.
68 Interview with Michael Bakewell.
69 Ibid.
70 For example, Marlowe's *Edward II*, 31 March 1959.
71 Formerly *Mrs Dale's Diary*, the name changed in February 1962.
72 *The Maids*, 4 June 1963. BBC Third Programme.
73 John Tydeman interview, 23 November 2017.
74 Tydeman produced Chekhov's *The Three Sisters* for the Home Service, 24 May 1965 (so outside the time frame for this book). He described Schofield as 'the supreme radio actor with such an interesting vocal quality and he achieved such depth of thinking and feeling'. (John Tydeman, interview, 23 November 2017).
75 *Scenes from the Frogs*, 20 February 1947. BBC Third Programme.
76 *Great Expectations*, 19 September 1948 (in thirteen parts). BBC Home Service.
77 *The Rescue*, 13 September 1951. BBC Third Programme.
78 John Tydeman, 'Raymond Raikes', *The Independent*, 7 October 1998.
79 John Tydeman, interview, 23 November 2017.

Chapter 3

RADIO DRAMA, 1945–53

The years between the end of the war and the broadcast of Dylan Thomas's celebrated *Under Milk Wood* in January 1954 were marked by a combination of established or canonical output of drama from the Drama Department, almost all adapted from the stage and some individually remarkable dramas made by both the Drama and the Features Departments. This chapter will focus on relatively few radio dramas and will attempt to provide some new insight as well as place those examples in the wider context.

The two main organizational changes for radio drama at the end of the war were the separation of the Drama and Features departments into separate units under Val Gielgud and Laurence Gilliam, and then in September 1946 the launch of the Third Programme which would create major new opportunities for the broadcast of dramas. As already explained, under Val Gielgud, the Drama Department pursued a policy of a 'national theatre of the air' whereby the BBC would give listeners the opportunity to hear the classical dramatic repertoire. The *Saturday Night Theatre* was more populist in intention and attracted huge audiences, often over twelve million,[1] to hear mainly popular drama by British writers and adaptations of classic novels (Austen Hardy, Dickens, among others). As Kate Whitehead explains, the launch of the Third Programme allowed an extension of the national theatre of the air to include classical Greek drama, Elizabethan and Jacobean plays and European dramatists including Anouilh, Sartre and Betti as well as the perennial favourites: Ibsen, Strindberg and Chekhov.[2]

In any one year, the listener could expect to hear a number of Shakespeare's plays across the networks (Home Service, Light Programme and Third Programme); so in 1954, to take just one year, the BBC broadcast *Romeo and Juliet*, *King Lear*, *Henry IV Part 1*, *Antony and Cleopatra*, *The Taming of the Shrew* and *All's Well That Ends Well*. Taking just one of Shakespeare's tragedies we can see how it was broadcast repeatedly in different productions; *Hamlet* was broadcast in 1946 as part of 'World Theatre' in December 1948 starring John Gielgud,[3] then repeated in December and June 1949, in July 1951 a 'revival' with John Gielgud and a repeat in April 1950 followed by a new production with Michael Redgrave in October 1960 repeated in January and April 1961. In the immediate post-war years up to 1954, it is striking how many broadcasts there were of the greats of European theatre. The plays of Henrik Ibsen, for example, were repeatedly broadcast; in the three years following the end of the war there were productions of *The Wild Duck*, *John Gabriel Borkman*, *Peer Gynt*, *A Doll's House*, *Rosmersholm* and *The Master Builder*. In the same period of time five of Chekhov's plays were adapted for radio and seven of the plays of Bernard Shaw.

Set against this backdrop of canonical adaptations fulfilling the requirements of the 'national theatre' were a few outstanding and iconic productions of work created specifically for radio. Louis MacNeice was one of the most important of all radio producers: classicist, poet, playwright and producer of radio dramas and features.[4] In addition, MacNeice made a very important contribution to the BBC's war effort by writing and producing the very imaginative propaganda features series *The Stones Cry Out* aimed at an American audience prior to American involvement in the war. Just before the end of the war, MacNeice returned to the place of his birth, Northern Ireland, and in May and June 1945, two months before the bombing of Hiroshima and Nagasaki, he was writing his epic radio drama *The Dark Tower*, which was broadcast before the creation of the Third Programme on the Home Service at the end of January 1946. While he was in Northern Ireland, in a fairly typical act of generosity, he recruited two new features producers to the BBC, Sam Hanna Bell (who remained in Belfast) and W. R. Rodgers, both of whom were to make an outstanding contribution to features production.[5] MacNeice's career in radio drama is considered in more detail in Chapter 7, but this is the place to consider *The Dark Tower*, one of a small number of radio dramas for which the title 'masterpiece' is appropriate,[6] indeed for some it is the greatest of all BBC radio dramas. Although technically this was a Drama Department production made immediately following the division of Drama and Features, in reality it had all of the qualities of a Features production, and MacNeice sent synopses and scripts to the Head of Features, Laurence Gilliam rather than Gielgud.[7] He also recruited Benjamin Britten to compose the music which proved to have a decisive impact on the quality and success of the drama.

Like many of the dramas discussed here, *The Dark Tower* is a 'verse drama' or 'poetic drama' although like Auden and Isherwood's *The Ascent of F6*, the dialogue sounds quite realistic. This was a tradition particularly associated with T. S. Eliot, and it gave a seriousness and lyrical quality to the dialogue. The drama was broadcast at 9.30 pm on a Monday and lasted one hour fifteen minutes. It begins with the announcer informing listeners that this is a 'parable' play suggested by Robert Browning's poem, 'Childe Roland to the Dark Tower Came'.[8] We are also told that the theme of the drama is the quest, an adventure undertaken in this case by Roland who we meet at the very beginning of the play having trumpet lessons. We soon learn that Roland is destined to follow his brothers and his father on a quest to slay the dragon who he will find in the dark tower. Roland's mother explains that this is a dangerous adventure which has claimed the lives of his brothers:

Roland: And did they all die the same way?
Mother: They did, Roland.⁹

Meanwhile, Roland's brother, Gavin, has learnt how to play the trumpet and, with some reluctance, is ready to set off for his probable death. Britten's dramatic orchestral music is used to provide a transition to the school room where Roland is being instructed by the tutor who had taught his six brothers. The tutor's role is to explain to Roland why he must seek the dragon because if it is allowed to live people 'would lead a degraded life, for the Dragon would be supreme'. Roland, who is sceptical about the existence of the dragon, goes to see Blind Peter who describes life when the dragon was at large, when he had succumbed to temptation and become an informer, sending members of his own family to their deaths. Blind Peter has faith in Roland and believes he will challenge evil:

Blind Peter: You're like your father – one of the dedicated
Whose life is a quest, whose death is a victory.
Yes! God bless you! *You've* made up your mind!

What follows is Roland's journey in which we meet character types including Sylvie, his love, Soak (the drunk), Neaera, a 'lady of pleasure' who seduces him, a steward and a ticket collector on a boat, a 'tout', a priest and the voices of a clock, a raven and a parrot. Throughout his journey, Roland is beset by doubt and at one point chooses to marry Sylvie and abandon his quest. In this part of the drama any pretence at realism is abandoned, and as the announcer stated at the beginning of the play, 'the manner of presentation is that of a dream – but a dream that is full of meaning'. To add to the dreamlike and fantastic quality of the play, music is used and we hear the voices of different characters including birds and the clock. This is a climactic moment in which Roland seems at last to assert himself:

Clock Voice: Tick Tock etc.
Soak: Left right, etc.
Steward: Golden days, etc.
Neaera: Kiss me, etc.
Sylvie: You and I, etc.
(*The five voices swell in the foreground, driving as it were at the camera, till Roland can bear it no longer.*)
Roland (*screaming*): NO!

At this point Roland cries out, 'Mother where are you?' and then realizes that the ring she has given to him, which shines a blood red colour to signify her desire for him to go on the quest, has no colour left. In this final section of the drama, Roland is caught between his mother's desire to have her son back and his own inner struggle to be independent:

> Roland: Everyone I have met
>   Has played his music on me. Own free will!
>   Three words not one of which I understand!
>   All right, Mother dear, I'm coming.

Finally, Roland approaches the dark tower and sees those who have gone before him to fulfil the quest. They encourage him to fight the dragon but first to blow the trumpet as he has been taught and so call the dragon to him:

> Roland: Yes, dear friends, I will blow it the way you taught me.
>   I Roland, the black sheep, the unbeliever –
>   Who never did anything of his own free will –
>   Will do this now to bequeath free will to others.

He raises the trumpet to his lips, the 'challenge call' rings out and the play ends.

MacNeice wrote an introduction to the published version of *The Dark Tower* which contains some useful clues about his intentions and the drama's meaning. By calling it a 'parable' play he makes it clear that the writing is allegorical, so we are free, for example, to interpret the dragon as fascism or the trumpet's call as propaganda. He states that 'my own impression is that pure "realism" is in our time almost played out'[10] and so we are presented by a fantasy, a parable which we are free to interpret. In his discussion of *The Dark Tower*, Donald McWhinnie praises the artistic qualities of the work including the use of 'compression', the very rapid changes of scene, 'the compressed telescoping of situation and emotion makes for clean, crisp listening'.[11] This is particularly evident at the beginning of the drama; the first scene in which Roland is taught to play the trumpet segues directly into him asking: 'Mother! What's tradition?' After she has answered, the two of them hear Gavin practising the trumpet, and there is no pause between Roland stating that he has got it right at last to Gavin saying, 'Mother! I know the challenge. When can I leave?' McWhinnie's identifies in *The Dark Tower* a quality which we will return to repeatedly; this is not in any sense an adventure story but a sonic exploration of the emotional, the inner word: 'The writer is not simply telling a story or resolving conflicting actions; at the same time he is generating atmosphere, music, colour, perpetually stimulating the inner vision, guiding the listener (as a composer does) through an infinitely variable world of sound.'[12]

That *The Dark Tower* is perceived as a radio drama classic is not surprising; it was the work of two of the last century's most distinctive and creative voices, Benjamin Britten and Louis MacNeice. It was written and produced towards the very end of the Second World War, and it is tempting to interpret the dragon and the dark tower as representations of fascism. But its themes are also more personal and psychological. The dreamlike quality of some of the production suggests a Freudian reading of an inner world, the world of consciousness in which Roland seems constantly at odds with his mother, his love and the 'lady of pleasure'.[13] The play also addresses philosophical questions, the nature of free will and personal responsibility in a refreshingly direct and comprehensible manner. At the same time, as McWhinnie states, McNeice's storytelling technique is dazzling. The rapid transition of scenes, the powerful narrative as we follow Roland onto the boat, across the ferry to the dark tower and the light-hearted moments of realism which drag the listener back to a post-war reality are brilliant examples of radio drama scripting and production. The combination of psychological and philosophical elements with such assured production was a statement for all those who listened that radio drama had great artistic potential. As a result, *The Dark Tower* was one of a few exceptional immediate post-war radio dramas that motivated the next generation of writers and producers.

Another Features Department drama which would surely have influenced the future of production was also the work of several remarkable talents. *In Parenthesis* by the artist and poet David Jones was produced by Douglas Cleverdon and featured music by the established composer Elizabeth Poston.[14] *In Parenthesis* was published in 1937 and is an account of Jones's experiences in the First World War between 1915 and 1916 in the Royal Welch Fusiliers engaged in the battles of the Somme and Ypres. The book almost defies description as it has the length of a novel but is a combination of verse, highly realistic dialogue and long excursions into Welsh legend and the myths and legends of ancient Welsh soldiery. In his introduction to the book, T. S. Eliot describes it as a work of genius and places Jones in a group of four writers: Eliot himself, Ezra Pound and James Joyce.[15] Douglas Cleverdon wanted to adapt the work for radio following the award of the prestigious Hawthornden Prize for poetry in 1938, but the first broadcast, scheduled for November 1942, was cancelled due to the book's harrowing subject matter.[16] Eventually, *In Parenthesis* was broadcast in the third week of the Third Programme's existence, on 19 November 1946.[17] Evidence of its success can be seen in the number of repeats of the programme: on 20 November, 13 December and 26 December 1946 and then on 4 January 1947 and twice in 1948.

The drama begins with Elizabeth Poston's orchestral music and a strikingly haunting song from the Song of Solomon: 'This is my beloved and this is my friend'.[18] After this biblical introduction (followed throughout by references to the Bible) we hear the voice of the sergeant shouting at his men and asking, 'Where's Ball?' and so introducing us to Private Ball who represents David Jones in the play. Cleverdon's production of *In Parenthesis* combined a realistic representation of soldiers waiting to embark for France with the voices of three narrators, the 'Narrative' of Action, Thought and Memory and, in addition, some powerfully emotive music.

We follow the soldiers as they arrive in France where it is freezing cold and wet. The speech of the soldiers is fractured and colloquial and full of 'bleedings' and 'buggers' and 'cushies' whereas the narration is poetic and literary, 'Guides met them at an appointed place; pilots who knew the charting of this gaining wilderness; the road continued its undeviating eastward thrust. They passed where was a ruin, they hear muted voices: the dark seemed gaining on the hidden moon.'[19] Added to these contrasting styles of speech are quotations from literature, including the sixth-century Welsh epic poem *Y Gododdlin*:

On Tuesday they put on their dark blue raiment;
On Wednesday they prepared their enameled shields.[20]

In the printed version of *In Parenthesis*, David Jones explains the importance of *Y Gododdlin* and why it was used in his play: 'The whole poem has special interest for all of us of this Island because it is a monument of that time of obscurity when north Britain was still largely in Celtic possession and the memory of Rome yet potent; when the fate of the Island was as yet undecided.'[21]

As the drama proceeds the soldiers get closer to the front and after slightly over quarter of an hour we hear the first explosion. The men are moving at night and we share their intense foreboding: 'They stood miserably. They stretched encumbered limbs to take their rifles, listless, bemused, to slowly scrape away the thicker more caked, with deadness in their eyes and hands as each to each they spoke.'[22]

A soldier is heard singing a hymn and in the distance is the sound of machine gun fire. It is morning and the soldiers are standing miserably, uncomfortable and afraid. At this point there is one of the most dramatic and powerful moments in the play when Private Dai Evans (acted in different versions of the play by Richard Burton and Dylan Thomas) speaks the 'boast of dai'. According to Jones's footnotes this is based on the 'boast of Taliessin' from the 1200s; he was a bard of the Welsh court, and as part of courtly tradition he spoke to portray himself and his like as divinely inspired, wise, erudite and in the case of Dai, present at all important battles and historical events. This is how Dai begins:

My fathers were the Black Prince of Wales
They served in these fields,
It is in the histories that you can read it, Corporal – boys
Gower, they were
I was with Abel when his brother found him,
Under the green tree.[23]

The 'boast' ends with Dai's claim that he was at the crucifixion.

> The Dandy Tenth are my regiment;
> who diced
> Crown and Mud-hook
> Under the tree, of Calvary
> I watched them work the terrible embroidery, the crown of thorns that
>   He put on.
> I saw cock-robin gain
>   His rosy breast
> I heard him cry
> I saw him die.[24]

In Parenthesis continues after Dai's boast with mounting tension and the sounds of further suffering: explosions, screams and the call for stretcher bearers. Then it is night, the sky is like porcelain, Private Ball reads his book, they drink tea and 'you could hear foreign men cough and stamp with foreign feet'. Amid the general horror which the drama describes is a touching moment of quiet and intimacy for Private Ball and his friends,

> John Ball heard the noise of the carpenters where he squatted to clean his rifle. ... He'd take a walk. He'd go and find his friend with the Lewis guns. And perhaps Olivier would be there. No orders were out yet, and tea would not yet be up.
> These three loved each other, but the routine of their lives made chances of fore-gathering rare. These two with linked arms walked together in a sequestered place above the company lines and found a grassy slope to sit down on.[25]

The final part of the drama features the assault on Mametz Wood, part of the Battle of the Somme. More men are killed, Private Jones is injured, more explosions are heard and more screams. Three more dead soldiers 'distinguished only in their variant mutilation'. Then Dai is killed and screams for his mother. The wood is like a crypt and Private Jones crawls away to wait for the stretcher bearers. The drama ends with music and singing.

In his review of a recent biography of David Jones, Chris Power provides a convincing overview of *In Parenthesis*: 'It blends infantryman demotic with a Shakespearean register, Christianity, Welsh legend, chivalric romance, a Joycean collapsing of past into present. ... Dense with allusion, the text is sometimes a maze, but for all its darkness and difficulty it is also an extraordinarily beautiful, unforgettable reading experience.'[26] Cleverdon's production of Jones's great poem has all of these qualities and the sonic representation of the soldiers' 'demotic', the rich Welsh voice of Dylan Thomas and the collapsing of time is also, as Power rightly says, 'extraordinarily beautiful'. In his review of *In Parenthesis* in *The Listener*, Philip Hope-Wallace praised the translation of the poem into sound but wondered if anyone who had not read the book would have understood it.[27] This is surely a legitimate criticism, the 'maze' like difficulty of the text, alleviated in the printed form by the extensive use of footnotes, resulted in a profoundly moving and beautiful radio drama but one which required the listener to have extensive prior knowledge (of the war, Welsh legend and the Bible) or a copy of the book in front of them.

Another epic radio drama of the immediate post-war years was Edward Sackville-West's *The Rescue* which was first broadcast in 1943 with music by Benjamin Britten. Strictly speaking it lies outside the scope of this book and has been discussed in some detail elsewhere,[28] but the fact there were two new productions of the play, one in 1948 and one in 1951, make it a significant contribution to post-war radio drama. In 1942, Sackville-West had written to Val Gielgud suggesting 'a dramatic composition on the Return of Odysseus, designed to bring out the parallel between the position in Ithaca then and that in Greece generally now'.[29] The proposal was accepted and Benjamin Britten was invited to compose the music. There is an explicitly propagandist message in the return of Odysseus to rescue his people from the 'usurpers' who have driven them into poverty and who fight among themselves for the hand of Odysseus's wife, Penelope. In the Preamble to the published version of *The Rescue*, Sackville-West is clear what Penelope's suitors represent: 'Her suitors … I have chosen to display in a semi-comedic light, for two reasons: Because Homer himself does so, and because gangsters, Fascists, and other childish persons are, when looked at by themselves, essentially figures of farce.'[30]

Odysseus returns and slaughters the suitors and so the drama has a positive and uplifting outcome. *The Rescue* was broadcast again after the war, this time in a production by Val Gielgud himself; the drama is in two parts and the Gielgud production was broadcast on the Third Programme on 3 March 1948 with a thirty-five minute interval and repeated on 4 March. It is striking that only three years later there was a new production of the play with Raymond Raikes as the producer[31] and repeated on 14 September 1951. Gielgud's enthusiasm for *The Rescue*, allowing three productions between 1943 and 1951, was reflected in the critical reviews of the play. J. C. Trewin, who took over from Hope-Wallace as *The Listener*'s 'Critic on the Hearth', praised 'the clear definition of the characters' in a drama which was 'quick, exciting and subtly judged'.[32] This was a somewhat orthodox, and in places melodramatic, production of a Greek classic featuring a script by Sackville-West (a very established BBC critic) with music by Benjamin Britten. Trewin was right that the combination of very clearly drawn characters and rapidly paced action, together with Britten's well-judged composition, produced a radio drama which would have kept its audience listening.

Gielgud's enthusiasm for *The Rescue* was probably surpassed by his admiration for and strongly held belief that Ibsen's plays worked well on radio. He made his position very clear on his appointment in 1928: 'From the date of my first appointment to the drama Department I announced that I intended to include the plays of Chekhov, of Ibsen and of Strindberg in programmes as part of our regular repertory of classical productions.'[33] As mentioned above, six different Ibsen plays were broadcast between 1945 and 1948, but it was surely no surprise that when he retired and was allowed to produce any play he wished that he chose Ibsen's *Brand*, 'another of those plays which in my opinion broadcasts infinitely more satisfactorily than it can ever be staged'.[34] *Brand* was broadcast in December 1949[35] in an adaptation from the stage starring Ralph Richardson and Sybil Thorndike and produced, unsurprisingly, by Val Gielgud. The play is a 'dramatic poem' written in verse and, like *Peer Gynt*, not originally written for the stage but for publication. As a radio drama it probably suffers from its intense seriousness, so although the intellectual and spiritual themes are conducive to the invisible medium of radio and the verse makes the drama lyrical and arresting, the lack of light and shade did not make for a dramatic success. In an unusually critical review, Philip Hope-Wallace wrote, 'Of all Ibsen's self-appointed supermen Pastor Brand is the most repellent.'[36] He found Brand's relentlessly negative proclamations too much: 'But even if we dare to drain Brand's cup of bitterness with him, may we not feel that the cup is too large?' adding that this contrasts negatively with *Peer Gynt*'s 'humour and variety'.[37] In addition, Hope-Wallace was unimpressed by the leading actors: 'I thought Mr Richardson and Miss Leighton[38] seemed to believe in the play as little as I did ... a total lack of sincerity rang loud and clear throughout the performance which in the principal roles sounded to me stagey and mannered beyond bearing.'[39]

Radio drama in the late 1940s could be heard not only on the Third Programme but also on the Home Service which broadcast less challenging but at times significant and original productions, the more popular and accessible of which were then transferred to the Light Programme. One of these was *Silence in Heaven*[40] written and produced by Lance Sieveking, among the most original and important pre-war radio drama producers. When Val Gielgud was appointed to lead BBC radio drama in 1928, Lance Sieveking and two other writers, Tyrone Guthrie and L. du Garde Peach, experimented with the new genre of sound drama. Sieveking's highly experimental *The Kaleidoscope*[41] was an original, modernist experiment in radio and made full use of the new Dramatic Control Panel, an ingenious piece of studio technology which allowed the producer of live drama to mix together sounds from different studios, including actors, a narrator, sound effects and music. Between 1932 and 1940, Sieveking produced over 200 radio plays and during the war took responsibility for the West Region.[42] From 1945 to 1956 he was a producer but also a script editor. In his account of Sieveking's BBC career, David Hendy identifies a contradiction in Sieveking as, on the one hand, 'a reputation for incomprehensibility has clung to the man',[43] while, on the other hand, he occupied solid mid-level positions in the BBC as regional manager and then 'producer-cum-editor'.[44] There is something therefore rather intriguing in Sieveking's contribution to radio drama: on the one hand the modernist obscurantist who embraced technical innovation like a First World War fighter pilot skimming over the skies[45] and on the other hand the radio drama functionary who helped Val Gielgud produce large quantities of popular drama in a career spanning almost forty years at the BBC. Perhaps it says something about the development of BBC radio drama over that period of time that Sieveking could begin with his high modernist acoustic experiments, 'which melded together performances taking place simultaneously in different rooms so that listeners heard a collage of dramatic scenes and poems mixed with classical music or jazz, all interspersed with sound-effects'[46] and from that become, in the early 1960s, the adapter and producer of classic, middle-brow writing including long multi-part adaptations of two Jules Verne novels.[47]

Lance Sieveking's *Silence in Heaven* is a good representation of the later and considerably safer expression of his talent. Based on his 1936 novel it tells the story of the unpleasantly authoritarian Stanley, his downtrodden wife, Fanny and their troublesome children. Stanley owns a factory and employs a young doctor, Francis, with whom Stanley's daughter becomes pregnant. Stanley is an erratic and vindictive character and held in contempt by other characters. On visiting his solicitor with a business partner he suffers a lapse of memory and meets the father of the now sacked Francis and in his state of amnesia is confronted with his own bad behaviour. The father mistakes Stanley for Mr Goss, the solicitor:

> Mr Goss, have you ever met a devil incarnate? A really bad man?
> He's ruined the lives of everyone he comes into contact with.[48]

In a complicated plot twist Stanley dictates a letter to himself confessing his own appalling behaviour before regaining his memory. The play ends with the death of the son following an operation, the daughter reluctantly agrees to marry Francis and the play ends where it started with the self-deluded Stanley shouting to his wife, 'Fanny! Fanny!' and her sad reply, 'All right Stanley, I'm coming.'

Silence in Heaven was reviewed by Philip Hope-Wallace, and it is hard not to agree with his fairly dismissive assessment: 'It abounded in radiogenic detail, pounding feet, and the sound of time's chariot hurrying by, but the characterization was blatant, flat and repetitive, so that little human interest attached to the fable.'[49] Hope-Wallace was right that the characters were rather crudely drawn stereotypes: the grumpy, authoritarian father, the rather camp son who acted and then died and the wimpish and ultimately defeated wife. The 'pounding feet' in his review refers somewhat cruelly to the relentless pace of the action feeling at times like a not very subtle attempt to hold the listener's attention.

The creative collaboration between the celebrated English poet W. H. Auden and the American writer Christopher Isherwood produced three verse stage plays at the end of the 1930s including, most successfully, *The Ascent of F6* in 1937.[50] The play was a major contribution to the English stage, unsurprisingly so given Auden's celebrity and place as one of the most important English poets of the last century, together with Isherwood's skill as a writer (famous for his stories about Berlin in the 1930s), augmented by music composed by Benjamin Britten. F6 is an unconquered mountain in the Himalayas; an experienced and celebrated climber; Michael Ransom leads an expedition of fellow Britons up the slopes in competition with a group of climbers from another country. En route, all Ransom's climbers perish; Ransom dies when he reaches the peak. The drama contains a number of different elements including ruling-class characters driven by British, imperialist ambitions (the group includes Ransom's brother, James) and a working-class couple, Mr and Mrs A, who provide a sparkingly funny left-wing commentary on the hopeless mountain adventure. The play reflected Auden's socialist politics and through the mouths of Mr and Mrs A provides a critique of capitalism and the oppressive nature of social class differences before the war. The various failings of different men in the play constitute a fascinating dissection of masculine frailties and inadequacies culminating in Ransom's death. In addition, in an interestingly modernist touch, radio itself is a feature of the stage play, used by the ruling elite to disseminate their propaganda message and heard by Mr and Mrs A.

The first broadcast of *The Ascent of F6* was as a television programme in September 1938.[51] There was an abbreviated (one-hour) version on radio in December 1938 and then, after the war, it was broadcast on 22 August 1950 from 9.30 pm to 11.15 pm on the Third Programme in a production by Donald McWhinnie. It is worth pausing here to consider Gielgud's decision to offer the production of the play to the newly arrived, McWhinnie. As mentioned previously, McWhinnie's first production for the BBC was in February 1949, so he was selected to produce *The Ascent of F6* less than eighteen months later. It was a feature of Gielgud's leadership of Radio Drama that gave production jobs of great responsibility and prominence to some of his very young, but clearly very talented, producers and editors, and McWhinnie's production of *The Ascent of F6* is an important example of this. One of the most important stage plays of the 1930s with music composed by Benjamin Britten and starring the famous actor Marius Goring was produced by someone who had less than two years' experience of radio drama production and almost no experience of drama production for the Third Programme.

The play begins with a long musical introduction on the piano of approximately four minutes. Ransom, the hero and mountaineer, is heard delivering a monologue reflecting on the themes of virtue and knowledge. In complete contrast, emphasized by the transition from prose to verse, we meet Mr and Mrs A who bemoan their fate as workers complaining about politicians:

> Mrs A: Smiling at all the photographers, smoking,
> Walking in top hats down by the lake,
> Treating the people as if they were pigeons,
> Giving the crumbs and keeping the cake.
> When will they notice us? When will they
> flatter us? When will they help us? When
> There's a war!
> Then they will ask for our children and kill
> them; sympathize deeply and ask for some
> more.[52]

Much of the drama concerns the heroic Ransom who is initially opposed to climbing the mountain, only to be persuaded by his mother while denying that she loved his brother, the reactionary Sir James Ransom, more. Once the decision is made it is announced on the radio in a pastiche of an early radio talk; the announcer describes Sudoland where F6 is to be found: 'The natives are delightful people, of wonderful physique and very humorous and artistic.'[53] The expedition is turned into an heroic propaganda adventure and Mr and Mrs A follow the adventure in the media:

> Mr A: Cut out the photos and pin them to the wall,
> Cut out the map and follow the details of it all,
> Follow the progress of this mountain mission,
> Day by day let it inspire our lowly condition.[54]

The mountaineering party led by Ransom consists of an eclectic group of men, all flawed in different ways. Of these the most interesting is Gunn, a coward and a thief but the one chosen to accompany Ransom to the peak of F6. Shawcross is consumed with jealousy and self-loathing, 'F6 has broken me, I am rotten weakling' he says before throwing himself off the precipice. Another mountaineer, Lamp is a collector of flowers and his obsession takes him to a dangerous ledge where an avalanche carries him away. The different versions of his death are provided by Lord Stagmantle who eulogizes him claiming 'this is as he would have wished', and then Mr A who draws on his experience in the trenches of the First World War claims this:

> Mr A: If you had seen a dead man, you would not
> Think it so beautiful to lie and rot;
> I've watched men writhing on the dug-out floor
> Cursing the land for which they went to war;
> The joker cut off halfway through his story,
> The coward blown involuntary to glory.[55]

The radio drama ends in a dreamlike trial of Ransom in which his fellow climbers are called to give evidence. The verdict is that Ransom must die for England and in the final minutes Mrs Ransom sings of her son's heroism:

> Mrs Ransom: Reindeer are coming to drive you away
> Over the snow on an ebony sleight
> Over the mountain and over the sea
> You shall go happy and handsome and free.[56]

The Ascent of F6 succeeds on a number of different levels. McWhinnie's light touch edit of the original play[57] produced a fast moving and compelling narrative, subtly supported by Britten's music. The drama is emotionally varied with moments of real pathos and tragedy combined with the satirical exchanges in verse of Mr and Mrs A. In addition, the play addresses themes of nationalism, propaganda, social inequality and the presence of the radio in peoples' lives. As a critique of the way governments, then as today, use media events (often sport related) it is highly effective. Another way of reading the play, and perhaps not entirely unrelated to Auden and Isherwood's homosexuality, is as a commentary on masculinity, on the different types of men who fail in their different ways: Ransom, the self-destructive hero; his brother James, the uncaring reactionary; Gunn, the treacherous coward; Lamp, the obsessive botanist; Shawcross, the jilted lover; Mr A, the downtrodden clerk and so on. This interpretation is encouraged by experiencing a British stage classic as a radio drama and not a visual experience. The sonic version pushes the listener to reflect on the nature of the male characters in particular and also to focus on the verse dialogue of Mr and Mrs A. This need to orient the listener to words and ideas is particularly important at the end of the radio drama: in the stage version there is a highly visual ending in which James Ransom is the dragon on the mountain 'in full ceremonial dress' and other characters are in a chess game as full-size chess pieces, but the radio version uses verse and singing to capture finally Mrs Ransom's rather deluded love for her son.

In October 1933, the BBC broadcast a poem by the eighteen-year-old Welsh poet Dylan Thomas.[58] Later, in 1937, Thomas was offered fifteen shillings to broadcast his poem 'Especially When the October Wind'.[59] He continued to contribute to BBC radio on an occasional basis and by the end of the war was an established reader of poetry, both his own and other poets'. In August 1945, Thomas gave a radio talk, 'Quite Early One Morning',[60] which formed the basis for his 1954 production, *Under Milk Wood*.[61] The eminent features producer Douglas Cleverdon played a vital role in the development of this iconic drama, and after the war he encouraged Thomas to write a dramatic and poetic adaptation of his 1945 talk.[62] In 1953, by which time Thomas was a regular visitor to America as a reader of his poetry, he finished the first complete draft of *Under Milk Wood* which he then read in public before it received two performances with actors at the Kaufman Auditorium in New York on 15 May and 29 May 1953.⁶³ A final version for broadcast was sent to the BBC at the end of October 1954, two weeks before Thomas's death.

Under Milk Wood was a Features Department production by Douglas Cleverdon for the Third Programme and broadcast in the Monday evening drama slot from 7.25 pm to 8.55 pm.⁶⁴ In many ways it was the quintessential 'radio feature' as Cleverdon was the quintessential features producer. The drama combines poetry (the drama is mainly written in verse) and a simple narrated story, without a plot in the dramatic sense of the word, in a fanciful description of one day in the life of Llareggub, a Welsh seaside town. The drama starts (in the 1954 and most subsequent versions) with the voice of Richard Burton:

> FIRST VOICE (*Very softly*)
> To begin at the beginning: it is spring, moonless night in the small town, starless and bible-black, the cobblestreets silent and the hunched, courters'- and-rabbits' wood limping down to the sloeblack, slow, black, crowblack, fishingboat-bobbing sea.⁶⁵

What is striking about this opening, in arguably one of the most famous and recognizable radio programmes of the last century, is Dylan Thomas's linguistic invention. Throughout the drama and especially in the words of the two narrators, First Voice and Second voice, we hear 'transferred epithets, invented and compound adjectives, personification, unusual metaphorical identifications, departures from normal word order'.⁶⁶ It is also apparent that this is drama written for the ear, the result of a career spent working in radio was a script designed to stimulate the imagination, to oblige the listener to visualize the 'bible-black' town and briefly savour that image. This radiogenic quality of the work is identified by Kate Whitehead: 'Not only is the language carefully selected for its aural effect but the almost symphonic arrangement of voices and sounds, overlapping and contrasting with each other marks out the piece as arguably the most successful piece of creative writing to have emerged from the medium of radio.'⁶⁷

After the long opening monologue, the drama unfolds and we are introduced to the sleeping and dreaming characters who populate Llarregub: Captain Cat, the blind former sea captain, Miss Price and her lover, Jack Black, Evans the Death (the undertaker), Mister Waldo, Mrs Ogmore-Pritchard and her two dead husbands who she sleeps with, Organ Morgan and many others. These characters are all described in Thomas's powerfully evocative words, here in a description of Mister Waldo:

> FIRST VOICE
> His fat pink hands, palms up, over the edge of the patchwork quilt, his black boots neat and tidy in the washing-basin, his bowler on a nail above his bed, a milk stout and slice of cold bread pudding under the pillow.⁶⁸

The drama is both funny and sad in its description of the romantic and sexual frustrations and disappointments of the dreaming and then waking characters of the town. It also has a highly descriptive, even documentary quality which provides a sharply observed account of everyday life in a small Welsh seaside town:

SECOND VOICE

Titbits and topsyturvies, bobs and buttontops, bags and bones, ash and rind and dandruff and nailparings, saliva and snowflakes and moulted feathers of dreams.[69]

It is the morning and everyone is getting out of bed. Mr Pugh takes tea to Mrs Pugh (who he plans to poison), Dai Bread hurries to the bakery, the pub opens and Sinbad pulls a pint. Willy Nilly the postman takes news and messages to people; there are no secrets in Llareggub. Then the morning is over and First Voice describes the sounds of the town: 'Bread is baking, pigs are grunting, chop goes the butcher, milk-churns bell, tills ring, sheep cough, dogs shout, saws sing. Oh, the Spring whinny and morning moo from the clog dancing farms, the gulls' gab and rabble on the boat-bobbing river and sea ....'[70]

The day passes, men talk about women in the pub, and the children play a cruel kissing game resulting in one boy being bullied. We move from afternoon to evening, the pigs snore their 'deep after-swill sleep'. Mr Ogmore and Mr Pritchard reluctantly enter their widow's house. Cherry Owen drinks seventeen pints of 'flat, warm, thin Welsh bitter beer' in the pub. Captain Cat says good night to the drowned sailors of his dreams. Finally, 'the thin night darkens. A breeze from the creased water sighs the streets close under milk waking Wood' and so the drama ends.

The critical response to *Under Milk Wood* is typified by Peter Lewis's 1981 assessment: '*Under Milk Wood* is easily the most celebrated full-length play for radio, or "play for voices" as Dylan Thomas designated it, that the BBC has produced in more than fifty years of broadcasting, and it is for many people the outstanding example of the genre, an unsurpassed and virtually unsurpassable achievement.'[71] As a radio drama it is unique in its dissemination and longevity. Following its first broadcast in January 1954 (it won the Prix Italia for that year) it was then repeated on 27 January, 18 and 20 February, 20 April, 28 September (Home Service) and again in 1955 and 1956. Just two weeks after the first broadcast, Douglas Cleverdon produced a stage reading of the play and then in 1956 the first acted stage performance which was a triumph at the Edinburgh Festival and ran for seven months in the West End. This performance was then televised in May 1957. Since the 1950s there have been new radio productions and a film, and *Under Milk Wood* is studied in book form as a classic of twentieth-century British literature. No other radio drama has had this level of success in the published script, audio and audiovisual form.

Before reflecting on the radio dramas mentioned above and trying to draw some conclusions about immediate post-war radio drama, this is a useful place to consider the critical reaction to BBC drama output and especially by *The Listener* critic, Philip Hope-Wallace. Each week, the semi-official BBC publication published reviews of radio and television programmes under the title 'The Critic on the Hearth'. There were different critics for different types of output, and one of these wrote under the heading 'Broadcast Drama'. From 15 February 1945 to 12 July 1951 the critic was Philip Hope-Wallace.[72] What is particularly interesting and valuable about Hope-Wallace's reviews is that they provide an idea of the experience of listening to radio drama on a weekly basis as well as some very interesting reflections on the nature of immediate post-war radio drama. So, for example, he claimed in early 1946 that adaptations from the stage will always be inferior to the stage version whereas some adaptations of novels work very well.[73] No doubt this would have upset Val Gielgud who prioritized adaptations of classic stage plays in his policy of a national theatre of the air. Hope-Wallce returned to this theme two months later and criticized Gielgud specifically stating, 'The true art of radio drama is more and more neglected in favour of reviving all and any stage success irrespective of whether it makes good radio or not.'[74] He referred to a radio production of Chekhov's *The Seagull* which he described as 'at very best a pale ghost of the play as it should be'.[75] This is an important observation from one of Gielgud's most influential critics and with hindsight explains the move, partly inspired by the success of *Under Milk Wood*, towards radio drama written specifically for radio.

The restart of the BBC's television service in June 1946 clearly posed a threat to radio drama, and Hope-Wallace urged producers to 'take stock of its true nature' in the hope that television would not cause the death of 'drama for the ear alone'.[76] Hope-Wallace was not dogmatic about stage adaptation, however, and believed that the work of a few playwrights transferred to radio very well. George Bernard Shaw was, for example, 'the radio dramatist *par excellence*'[77] and, in words which Gielgud himself would have approved of, he claimed that 'with Ibsen we sometimes positively seem to see the play *more* clearly when we don't see it at all!'[78] Hope-Wallace returned to this theme many times during the 1940s arguing that one of the reasons stage plays so often failed on radio was because we cannot see the way other characters react to what is said, a particular problem in the work of Chekhov.[79] By doing this he was implicitly attacking Gielgud's policy of the national theatre of the air and also contributing to the gradual movement towards drama written specifically for radio.

This has been a highly selective account of immediate post-war radio drama. Given the ambition of this book to be based on listening to radio dramas and the very few recordings from the pre-1953 era, that should not be a surprise. There are only seven dramas discussed in any detail here, but of those five could be described as triumphs of radio drama production in their different ways. Do we learn anything about the development of the genre at this time from this highly selective group of plays? The answer to that question I think is yes.

The Dark Tower, In Parenthesis, The Rescue and *The Ascent of F6* can all be described as epic dramas. There is a sense in all of them that a great task must be achieved or quest fulfilled, and in all of these dramas one or more men have heroic qualities. In all of these dramas the nature of heroism is also questioned; Roland in *The Dark Tower* like Ransom in *The Ascent of F6* and John Ball in *In Parenthesis* are heroic figures who doubt themselves and even Odysseus in *The Rescue* is questioned by his son and wife despite his return and the slaughter of the suitors. The epic quality of these four plays is greatly enhanced by the use of music and the use of verse rather than a more realist form of speech; this is particularly evident in *In Parenthesis* where Elizabeth Poston's use of orchestral instruments and solo and group singing combined with epic verse, most notably in the extraordinary 'boast of Dai', produce a drama of truly epic quality. These themes of the uncertain hero and the quest to be achieved reflect the militaristic culture which resonated for several years after the end of the war. Demobilized soldiers and active servicemen and young men on national service were to be seen on the streets while the cruel reality of war, as a lived experience by so many, would have made unproblematic representations of heroism impossible. This epic, masculine and soldierly quality of radio drama seemed to die with Richard Burton's softly spoken words, 'to begin at the beginning'.[80] The year 1953 was a watershed year for radio drama; in June, Queen Elizabeth's coronation took place, and as the broadcasting historian Andrew Crisell rightly claims, this was the moment when, huddled round their neighbours' television sets, the British public made the move from radio to television.[81] Just as the coronation was a watershed in broadcasting history, so *Under Milk Wood* was the landmark radio drama of the immediate post-war era. Before it, there were occasional epic triumphs, suffused with a military sensibility and benefitting from verse scripts written by some of the foremost poets of the time, accompanied by music composed by the best British composers. *Under Milk Wood* signalled the end of all that, and although it was unrepeatable and unrepeated, its triumph suggested new possibilities and new ambition for the genre in the era of television. Radio drama could survive, but it would require original writing and dramas specifically written for radio. Like Dylan Thomas's masterpiece, radio drama would also need to create new worlds in the imagination of the listener which exploited the essence of the invisible medium.

Notes

1 Whitehead, *The Third Programme*, 136.
2 Ibid., 138.
3 Most radio productions of Hamlet were in three parts over three nights; see http://genome.ch.bbc.co.uk
4 Coulton, *Louis MacNeice in the BBC*. Two other MacNeice dramas from this period will be considered in Chapter 7 which attempts an overview of MacNeice's

radio career: *The Death of Gunnar* (7 April 1947) and *Trimalchio's Feast* (22 December 1948).
5   Probably the fullest critical account of the work of these two producers is provided by Portia Ellis-Woods, 'BBC Northern Ireland Drama and Features Programming 1924-1956: Development, identity, and cultural history' (PhD diss., Queen's University Belfast, 2018). See also Hugh Chignell, 'Sam Hanna Bell and the ideology of place', in *Regional Aesthetics: Mapping UK Media Cultures*, ed. Ieuan Franklin et al. (Basingstoke: Palgrave Macmillan, 2015), 185–95.
6   See, for example, Rodger, *Radio Drama*, 71.
7   Coulton, *Louis MacNeice in the BBC*, 77.
8   *The Dark Tower*, 21 January 1946. BBC Home Service.
9   Louis MacNeice, *The Dark Tower* (London: Faber and Faber, 1947). All the quotations from the play are taken from this source.
10 Ibid., 21.
11 McWhinnie, *The Art of Radio*, 165.
12 Ibid., 168.
13 This was to be one of Giles Cooper's abiding themes, a man-made impotent by the women in his life, but Roland faces the end heroically unlike all of Cooper's men.
14 *In Parenthesis*, 19 November 1946. BBC Third Programme.
15 David Jones, *In Parenthesis* (London: Faber and Faber, 1937), vii–viii.
16 Whitehead, *The Third Programme*, 120.
17 The *Radio Times* listings for *In Parenthesis* show that the 1946 version was ninety minutes long, but the 1955 version was two hours.
18 Song of Sol. 5:15.
19 David Jones, *In Parenthesis*, 29.
20 Ibid., 11.
21 Ibid., 191.
22 Ibid., 63.
23 Ibid., 79. The Boast of Dai in the radio version is much shorter than that in the published poem and is adapted in places so, for example, the explanatory 'crown of thorns' was provided for the radio audience but is not in the published original.
24 Ibid., 83.
25 Ibid., 138–9.
26 Chris Power, 'David Jones by Thomas Dilworth review', *The Guardian*, 29 March 2017.
27 Philip Hope-Wallace, 'Critic on the hearth', *The Listener*, 28 November 1946.
28 Amanda Wrigley, 'A Wartime Radio *Odyssey*: Edward Sackville-West and Benjamin Britten's *The Rescue* (1943)', *The Radio Journal – International Studies in Broadcast and Audio Media* 8, no. 2 (2010): 81–103.
29 Sackville-West quoted in Wrigley, 'A Wartime Radio *Odyssey*', 85.
30 Edward Sackville-West, *The Rescue: A Melodrama for Broadcasting Based on Homer's Odyssey* (London: Secker and Warburg, 1945), 12.
31 *The Rescue*, 13 September 1951. BBC Third Programme.
32 J. C. Trewin, 'The critic on the hearth', *The Listener*, 20 September 1951.
33 Gielgud, *Years in a Mirror*, 62.
34 Ibid., 185. Gielgud's commitment to Ibsen and belief in the radiogenic nature of his plays is interesting. Ibsen's stage directions are famously detailed; for example, the description of the set at the beginning of *Hedda Gabler* is 320 words long

which indicates that he had a very specific idea of how the play should look. Perhaps the naturalistic and realist quality of his writing and the abiding nature of the themes he addressed made his work adapt well.

35 *Brand*, 11 December 1949. BBC Third Programme.
36 Philip Hope-Wallace, 'The critic on the hearth', *The Listener*, 15 December 1949.
37 Ibid.
38 Brand, Ralph Richardson; Brand's mother, Sybil Thorndike; Agnes, Margaret Leighton.
39 Ibid.
40 *Silence in Heaven*, 14 March 1949. BBC Home Service. Repeated 1 May 1950. BBC Light Programme.
41 *The Kaleidoscope*, 4 September 1928.
42 David Hendy, 'Biography and the emotions as a missing "narrative" in media history; a case study of Lance Sieveking and the early BBC', *Media History* 18, no. 3/4 (2012): 365.
43 Ibid., 366.
44 Ibid., 370.
45 Ibid., 365.
46 Hendy, *Public Service Broadcasting*, 52.
47 *Around the World in Eighty Days* (from 22 March 1960). BBC Home Service; *Twenty Thousand Leagues under the Sea* (from 11 July 1961). BBC Home Service.
48 *Silence in Heaven*, 14 March 1949. BBC Home Service.
49 Philip Hope-Wallace, 'The critic on the hearth', *The Listener*, 17 March 1949.
50 W. H. Auden and Christopher Isherwood, *The Ascent of F6* (London: Faber and Faber, 1937). The play was first produced on 26 February 1937 at the Mercury Theatre, London, with music by Benjamin Britten.
51 The television broadcast does not appear in the BBC Genome although it is mentioned in the *Radio Times* as having been televised in September 1938, with photographs of the set (*Radio Times*, 5 December 1938).
52 *The Ascent of F6*, 22 August 1950. BBC Third Programme. All the quotations from the play are taken from the published version, Auden and Isherwood, *The Ascent of F6*.
53 Ibid.
54 Ibid.
55 Ibid.
56 Ibid.
57 McWhinnie did, however, succeed in removing from the play an early version of one of arguably Auden's most famous poems, 'Stop all the clocks, cut off the telephone, prevent the dog from barking with a juicy bone'.
58 'The Romantic Isle', 28 June 1933.
59 Ralph Maud (ed.), *Dylan Thomas, The Broadcasts* (London: J. M. Dent, 1991), 283. In fact the poem was not broadcast.
60 'Quite early one morning' 31 August 1945. Welsh Home Service.
61 Daniel Jones, 'Preface', in Dylan Thomas, *Under Milk Wood* (London: Dent, 1975), viii.
62 Whitehead, *The Third Programme*, 79.
63 Jones, 'Preface', x.
64 *Under Milk Wood*, 25 January 1954. BBC Third Programme.

65 Ibid.
66 Peter Lewis, 'The radio road to Llareggub', in *British Radio Drama*, ed. John Drakakis (Cambridge: Cambridge University Press, 1981), 79.
67 Whitehead, *The Third Programme*, 121.
68 *Under Milk Wood*, 25 January 1954. BBC Third Programme.
69 Ibid.
70 Ibid.
71 Lewis, 'The radio road to Llareggub', 72.
72 The radio drama critics of *The Listener* in the post-war period were Philip Hope-Wallace (1945–51), J. C. Trewin (1951–6), Roy Walker (1957–8), Ian Rodger and Frederick Laws (1958–62), Martin Shuttleworth (1962–3).
73 Philip Hope-Wallace, 'The critic on the hearth', *The Listener*, 31 January 1946.
74 Philip Hope-Wallace, 'The critic on the hearth', *The Listener* 28 March 1946.
75 Ibid.
76 Philip Hope-Wallace, 'The critic on the hearth', *The Listener*, 6 June 1946.
77 Philip Hope-Wallace, 'The critic on the hearth', *The Listener*, 1 August 1946.
78 Ibid.
79 There are interesting similarities and differences between Hope-Wallace and John Tydeman (see Chapter 2), as both stated that the audience's attention should not always be with the speaker but on the character spoken to.
80 *Under Milk Wood*, 25 January 1954. BBC Third Programme.
81 Andrew Crisell, *An Introductory History of British Broadcasting* (2nd edn) (London: Routledge, 2002), 81–2.

Chapter 4

TECHNOLOGIES OF PRODUCTION AND CONSUMPTION

As the story of radio drama takes us further into the 1950s, the impact of various technological changes on the listening experience becomes more significant. This short and quite speculative chapter identifies some of the issues around technological advances and the production and consumption of radio drama. To understand these it is necessary to consider the nature of the listening experience and the process of production. Accounts of the development of British radio drama have been remarkably silent in this area. The essential reading provided by Ian Rodger,[1] John Drakakis[2] and Peter Lewis,[3] for example, all fail to acknowledge the listening experience and the technical dimension of transmission and reception of radio programmes. In recent years, however, the materiality of the media, including radio sets, tape recorders, transmission masts and so on, has become an increasingly important part of media history.[4] Radio drama was to a greater or lesser extent influenced by technological change, in transmission, production and reception, and this influence was both direct, affecting the nature of the listening experience, and indirectly, altering the radio broadcasting environment in which radio drama sat.

When radio became a popular mass medium in the early 1920s, the main type of radio receiver was the crystal radio set. Often made at home from a kit, the device was difficult to use and required headphones in the absence of speakers. As Susan Douglas describes, the listener had to painstakingly move a thin wire (the 'cat's whisker') around a crystal in an activity as frustrating as it was thrilling.[5] Those who listened were mainly male, and as a result the early phase of radio, and especially in the United States, had a masculine quality.[6] But there was a significant market for radio sets which incorporated bulky valves (or 'tubes') and were designed to integrate into the home as a piece of furniture. Increasingly, radio receivers took the form of wooden cabinets and were connected to the mains electricity supply, and later in the 1920s and early 1930s the radio came to occupy a 'central place in the household as a source of entertainment and news'.[7] During the pre-war period there was only one radio service, the BBC's national station (although that had local variations at different times of the day)[8] and so the experience of listening to the radio was a very limited and collective affair. The family would listen together to a radio service designed to appeal to the population as a whole and so inevitably ignore minority tastes.

Before and after the war the fiercely competitive radio set market encouraged the development of smaller sets and those manufactured not in wood but in the early form of plastic, bakelite. After the Second World War, war bakelite was replaced by plastic, and tabletop sets became more common. In 1947 the development of the transistor radio was announced with the potential, given their use of small dry batteries, to replace the bulkier and less mobile valve sets. At the moment that television in the United Kingdom was becoming the dominant broadcasting medium, the new transistor gave radio a new impetus.[9] Early transistor radios were expensive but the launch of Japanese radios introduced new competition into the market and the price of radios began to fall. The launch of small, increasingly cheap, portable transistor radios is intimately connected in the literature with the rise of popular culture. Susan Douglas, for example, draws on her own teenage years in the 1950s to describe the way teenagers adopted the transistor radio and listened to the new radio DJs playing rock 'n' roll. The result was a segregation of listeners: 'Gone were the days when families would cluster round their Philco listening to Jack Benny. Now, just like in the early 1920s, listening was more often a personal affairs, done in the privacy of the kitchen, the bedroom, the car, even the bathroom.'[10] It is hard to know what impact this had on listening to radio drama in the 1950s and early 1960s, but there can be little doubt that given the specialist nature of Third Programme drama in particular, the availability of more than one radio set in the house would have made it possible for the dedicated cultural listener to take themselves off to the kitchen or shed and experience challenging content alone. It would be a mistake to exaggerate this impact but the new segregation of the audience at the time when television was in its pomp (aided by the launch of ITV in 1955) would surely have facilitated listening to the niche programming of radio drama.

Radio transmission was also undergoing change in the post-war period. Amplitude modulation (AM) was the standard process by which sound signals were transmitted on radio waves.[11] However, AM signals were susceptible to interference and especially at night, a potential problem for anyone trying to listen to a radio drama. Frequency modulation (FM), also referred to as VHF, had a number of advantages including better sound quality and less interference. In America, FM was originally developed in the 1930s but really took off after the end of the war when it was adopted by non-profit and educational radio stations. In Britain, VHF experiments began in 1945, but it was another ten years before the BBC began VHF transmission. On 2 May 1955, the postmaster general (representing the government) and the chairman of the BBC launched the VHF service from a new transmitter at Wrotham in Kent serving the south east of England. The BBC director general, Sir Ian Jacob, gave a talk on the Home Service welcoming VHF transmission and from that moment there were regular broadcasts of gramophone records on the Light Programme. The first advertisement for a VHF radio set appeared in *The Listener* on 15 September 1955; the Ferguson 401 RG sold for a very expensive ninety-five guineas[12] and offered 'interference free reception of highest quality'.[13] The *Radio Times* provides an important record of the introduction and take-up of VHF radio in the advertising it carried for radio sets. In 1955 there were advertisements in every edition of the magazine for radio sets, some with VHF, some valve radio sets and some portable radios. Alongside these were the television sets advertised as receiving both BBC and ITV signals.

Following the launch of VHF radio, the BBC then began 'simulcasting' programmes (transmitting both AM and FM) on all its networks.[14] One person who was delighted about the development of VHF was Val Gielgud. He described it as 'a technical advance of the greatest possible importance'[15] while adding that unlike developments in television he thought VHF received very little publicity. For the Head of Radio Drama, VHF solved more than one problem: 'Enthusiasts for the Radio Play had continually complained that with indifferent, or varying, reception subject to every kind of "interference," the subtleties, and accordingly the basic possibilities, of the broadcasting of pays were too frequently wasted.'[16] He claimed, perhaps a little optimistically, that VHF made the problem of interference practically non-existent and even that this had a considerable effect on the morale of radio producers. It is hard to find evidence to support Gielgud's optimism, but at least for a small minority of radio drama enthusiasts there would have been the possibility of evening listening to radio dramas using a VHF receiver and a greatly enhanced aural experience. The director of Sound Broadcasting, Lindsay Wellington, was also an enthusiastic supporter of VHF. Writing in 1956 he claimed that VHF would solve the problem of poor quality reception resulting from interference to the AM signal from foreign stations or other electrical installations.[17] However, many of the early VHF radio sets advertised in the *Radio Times* cost over ten guineas which would be several hundred pounds today. The VHF radio set was clearly a luxury item and not available to the mass of the population.

Early radio was an essentially live medium. Given the elementary and often very cumbersome recording technology not only was almost all broadcasting live but very few attempts at recording broadcasts were made. Sean Street provides the most complete account of recording technology used at the BBC before the advent of magnetic tape recording.[18] The Blattnerphone/Marconi-Stille system used steel tape: a spool weighed twenty-one pounds and the tape travelled at five feet per second, sections of tape had to be welded together. The device was both cumbersome and probably lethal, but the incentive for the BBC to record programmes was the need to feed the Empire Service to the British colonies from 1932. On Friday, 13 January, *Pieces of Tape* was a successful compilation of recorded extracts,[19] and thousands of hours of recordings were made using the steel tape system. Direct disc recording, developed by the inventor Cecil Watts, involved cutting directly on to a disc, similar to a gramophone record. Disc recording existed alongside steel tape, but it had the great advantage of being much more portable. Because of their portability, direct disc recorders were used extensively during the Second World War by BBC correspondents and especially to provide audio for the daily evening news programme following the allied invasion of France on 'D Day', *War Report*.[20]

Sound recording on magnetic tape, which was to have such a huge impact on both the production and consumption of radio, was originally developed in Nazi Germany to record Hitler's speeches for rebroadcast. After the war the BBC took a while to see the potential of tape recording; in 1951 all sound recording was on disc or one of the other pre-war technologies, but in 1952 six EMI Midget recorders arrived at Broadcasting house, and by 1955 magnetic tape recording had become the dominant recording technology.[21] Lindsay Wellington wrote that in just two or three years the Midget tape recorder 'has brought about a minor revolution in some areas of sound broadcasting'.[22] The benefit of recording, and especially the far more practical tape recording, for radio drama production is obvious. Dramas could be pre-recorded for broadcast and then available for further broadcasts as needed. Producers could interrupt recordings if mistakes were made, and the whole process was less stressful than going out live. Recording also made it possible to ensure dramas did not exceed their designated time slot. Michael Bakewell welcomed recording and almost all of his dramas were pre-recorded.[23] However, it is one of the quirks of broadcasting philosophy in the BBC that many of the older producers were opposed to broadcasting recorded as opposed to live speech. In the case of that staple of BBC output up to the 1950s, the radio talk, BBC managers like John Green (a Reith appointee) opposed pre-recording talks arguing that there was a moral imperative on the talker to address the listener live.[24] Green imposed a policy of restricting recorded talks as much as possible, and despite the obvious inconvenience there was little opposition from within the BBC reflecting the widespread scepticism about the use of recording in radio broadcasting. In his account of radio drama from 1922 to 1956, Val Gielgud asks if there was any difference between a live drama production and one recorded and then 'canned'.[25] Gielgud's answer is an interesting one; he felt that the occasion of the live broadcast (presumably like the live theatrical performance) created the 'fine edge' of acting and that 'an awareness of the audience *at the moment of playing* does heighten the emotional response of the actor'.[26] In addition he suggested that live performances make actors concentrate on the play as a whole, building in emotional intensity and creating a 'living organic unity'.[27]

If the tape recorder introduced a more convenient and practical approach to radio drama production in the 1950s, but perhaps lessening the tension and sense of occasion of a live broadcast, it also had the potential to change the experience of the listener. As was the case with the introduction of VHF and transistor radio sets it is possible to learn something about consumer behaviour from the advertisements in the main broadcasting publications.

In the late 1950s there were increasing numbers of advertisements for tape recorders and for different makes of tape in publications like *The Listener* and the *Radio Times* which were presumably designed to encourage recording off-air. In the 1960 BBC Handbook, an advertisement for a Walter tape recorder (priced at fifty-seven guineas) stated that it had 'sockets for recording from microphone, radio set ....'[28]

As Chapter 3 has described, some radio dramas were repeated, and it was Third Programme policy to repeat plays at least once and often the following week. However, despite the occasional repeat, it would still have been likely that the radio drama enthusiast would have missed many programmes. It is hard to assess whether the commercially available tape recorder was bought and used by listeners of radio drama, but the potential was clearly there to record off-air and to listen again and even to lend the recording to other radio drama enthusiasts.[29] For the first time, as music fans had been doing with record collections, radio drama listeners could become collectors and the experience of listening to an often demanding play might be repeated for fuller appreciation. Although there is insufficient evidence to prove this with any certainty, the sale of domestic tape recorders can be seen as the beginning of 'time shifting', of listening to programmes but not at the time at which they were broadcast. With time shifting and repeated listening, collection and lending, *some* radio drama listeners in the 1950s experienced a fundamentally different listening experience.

The use of tape recording did have an effect on radio production, but in the post-war period the most significant technological development for radio drama was the launch of the Radiophonic Workshop in April 1958: a unit within the BBC designed to use electronic means to develop new sounds to enrich radio and then television broadcasts. Donald McWhinnie argues that in the 1950s, audiences were beginning to tire of the use of standard 'realistic' sound effects: 'A certain stylization is always necessary in deploying real sounds in an artistic context. It is often more rewarding to use real sound unrealistically – that is to say, distorted, with some of its original characteristics removed.'[30] It is worth quoting McWhinnie at length on the subject as he was one of the main proponents of radiophonic effects:

> The principle is simple: take a sound – any sound – record it, and then change its nature by a multiplicity of operations. Record it at different speeds, play it backwards, add it to itself over and over again, subject it to the influence of frequency filters, acoustic variations, combine one segment of magnetic tape with another, unrelated segment; by these means, among others, we can create sounds which have never been heard before and which have a unique and indefinable quality of their own.[31]

There were a number of factors influencing the development of the Radiophonic Workshop including the early experimental use of sound in the comedy series

The Goon Show (1951–60) and the increasingly strange or absurd nature of radio drama which seemed to require other-worldly sounds. However, before the workshop began working, Beckett's *All That Fall* (discussed in Chapter 5) was praised for the creative use of sound and the stylized sound effects in McWhinnie's production. Philip Hope-Wallace, no longer at *The Listener* but still reviewing radio, was particularly impressed by the sound of *All That Fall*: 'A miraculous web of sound effects … like a dull bad dream recounted to you by some forcible bore in a Dublin pub.'[32] Another influence was the avant-garde approach to music composition 'Musique Concrete' which devised new techniques of sound production heard by BBC producers on their many visits to Paris. Following the launch of the Radiophonic Workshop, Donald McWhinnie used the new facility to provide sound for one of Giles Cooper's unsettling and fantastic dramas, *Under the Loofah Tree*.[33]

There is no doubt that over the period covered by this book the technology of radio production, transmission and reception changed in important ways and that as a result the experience of listening to radio drama also changed. For a limited number of listeners with VHF radio sets the sound quality would undoubtedly have been better from the mid-1950s. In addition, the arrival of television (both BBC and ITV) as well as transistor radios would have created a more segregated domestic media environment in which those who wanted to hear Third Programme radio dramas might have found their own space. It would, however, be a mistake to see all technological developments as inevitably producing better radio drama. A revisionist interpretation might be that Val Gielgud was to an extent right in thinking that live radio drama had advantages in terms of actors' performance and for the listener a sense of occasion. The Radiophonic Workshop was an interesting addition to the resources of the radio drama producer, but it is striking that praise was heaped on drama special effects (e.g. in *All That Fall* and Giles Cooper's *The Disagreeable Oyster*) *before* the arrival of radiophonics and that some of the radio drama associated with it was, with the considerable benefit of hindsight, self-conscious and pretentious. Michael Bakewell remembers his original enthusiasm fading: 'I was totally into that. In the end it killed itself – in the end I had reservations about it, it became a thing in itself, in the end it didn't lead anywhere.'[34]

Notes

1 Rodger, *Radio Drama*.
2 Drakakis, *British Radio Drama*.
3 Lewis (ed.), *Radio Drama*.
4 A particularly good example of this new emphasis on the materiality of the media is to be found in Jarlbrink, *Informations- och avfallshantering i papperstidningens tidevarv*.
5 Susan Douglas, *Listening In; Radio and the American Imagination* (Minneapolis: University of Minnesota Press, 1999), 55.

6   The definitive account of early radio and gender is to be found in Michele Hilmes, *Radio Voices, American Broadcasting, 1922-1952* (Minneapolis: University of Minnesota Press, 1997).
7   Stephen Lax, *Media and Communication Technologies* (Basingstoke: Palgrave Macmillan, 2009), 47.
8   Sean Street, however, has described the competition before the war between the BBC and radio stations based in continental Europe; Sean Street, *Crossing the Ether; British Public Service Radio and Commercial Competition 1922-1945* (Eastleigh: John Libbey, 2006).
9   Lax, *Media and Communication Technologies*, 48.
10 Douglas, *Listening In*, 225.
11 Lax, *Media and Communication Technologies*, 49.
12 Approximately £2,000 at the time of writing in 2018.
13 *The Listener*, 15 September 1955.
14 *Radio Times*, 2 May 1955.
15 Gielgud, *British Radio Drama*, 186.
16 Ibid.
17 Lindsay Wellington, 'Impact of VHF', *The Times*, 22 August 1956.
18 Street, *Crossing the Ether*.
19 Ibid., 119.
20 In addition to steel tape and disc recording, sound was also recorded on 35 mm film, the Philips-Miller System described in Street, *Crossing the Ether*, 127.
21 Chignell, *Public Issue Radio*, 66.
22 Wellington, 'Impact of VHF'.
23 Michael Bakewell, interview, 21 June 2017.
24 Chignell, *Public Issue Radio*, 69.
25 Gielgud, *British Radio Drama*, 115.
26 Ibid.
27 Ibid., 116.
28 BBC Handbook 1960.
29 Tape recorders were certainly expensive items in the 1950s. The Grundig Stenorette, a dictating machine but perfectly able to record off-air, was sold for fifty-two guineas in 1958 or rather more than £1,000 in 2018.
30 McWhinnie, *The Art of Radio*, 82.
31 Ibid., 86.
32 Quoted in Niebur, *Special Sound*, 24.
33 *Under the Loofah Tree*, 3 August 1958. BBC Third Programme.
34 Interview with Michael Bakewell, 21 June 2017.

Chapter 5

RADIO DRAMA AND THE ABSURD

In Eugene Ionesco's *Rhinoceros* all the residents of a French provincial town turn into rhinoceroses, in Samuel Beckett's *Endgame* the main character's parents are seen in trash bins on either side of the stage and in Arthur Adomov's *Le Ping Pong* two men meet in a café and play pinball until the machine eventually takes over their lives.[1] It is perhaps unsurprising that a theatrical movement, based in Paris and including writers like Becket and Ionesco, should be called the 'theatre of the absurd'. Martin Esslin, who became head of Radio Drama after Val Gielgud's retirement in 1963, wrote an influential book about the theatre which discussed the work of Beckett, Adomov and Ionesco in particular in terms of absurdism.[2] Esslin also included Harold Pinter as someone following in the footsteps of the pioneers of the absurd and N. F. Simpson, both of whom contributed to radio drama. He did not include Giles Cooper, the prolific radio dramatist and the subject of Chapter 6, who also had strong absurdist tendencies.

Absurdism is associated mainly with three émigrés: Beckett, Adomov and Ionesco, all living in Paris after the end of the Second World War. The Russian, Arthur Adomov's first play was *The Grand and Small Manoeuvre* (1950) while, the Romanian, Eugene Ionesco's first stage production was *The Bald Soprano* (1952). Both plays preceded Beckett's first stage play, *Waiting for Godot*, in 1953. All of these plays were characterized by minimal scenery and action, the depersonalization of characters and, on occasions, elements from the circus or music hall.[3] Ionesco provided this definition: 'Absurd is that which is devoid of purpose. ... Cut off from his religious, metaphysical, and transcendental roots, man is lost; all his actions become senseless, absurd, useless.'[4]

For the purposes of the history of radio drama it is useful to identify some of the key characteristics of absurdism. Starting with Ionesco's own definition, the meaningless of existence is often expressed by the absurdity or incomprehensibility of the drama; in Ionesco's *The Lesson* (1951), for example, an aged professor gives a lesson to a young girl during which he grows in stature while she is diminished and he eventually stabs her. In Ionesco's *The Chairs*, the stage is gradually filled with chairs and an orator enters whose speech is incoherent; he writes on a blackboard, a jumble of meaningless letters. Repeatedly in absurdist drama the audience is left searching for meaning and perhaps a realization that there is none. Associated with the loss of meaning, the inability to understand the world, is the failure of language itself to communicate. This was a particularly important theme for Beckett, in his effort to communicate the absurdity and meaninglessness of life Beckett modifies and reinvents language, using unexpected words and expressions, juxtaposing the familiar and the unfamiliar.[5] At the same there is a sense of language in decay. Martin Esslin describes 'the radical devaluation of language' in Beckett.[6] Elsewhere, we read of Beckett's need to 'tame [language] to express what he wanted'[7] and the need to 'bore one hole after another in it'.[8] A consequence of this attack on language was the shortening of his work; his earlier novels were substantial, *Waiting for Godot* is a full length play, but his later plays had fewer and fewer acts, and *Breath* (1969) is only a few minutes long.

Absurdist dramas also dwell on human anxiety, anguish and pain. They feature the expression of suffering and the experience of anguish so alien no doubt to the theatregoing public who were more used to drawing room capers. Human suffering is a powerful theme in Beckett's *Endgame* where the servant, Clov, states, 'I say to myself – sometimes, Clov, you must learn to suffer better than that if you want them to weary of punishing you – one day. I say to myself – sometimes, Clov, you must be there better than that if you want them to let you go – one day.'[9] Beckett lived through the extreme violence and cruelty of the Second World War in occupied France and he visited Nazi Germany several times. He was able to observe first-hand the ruthlessness of those in power and the sadistic cruelty of the Nazi regime.

Of all the absurdist writers, Beckett had the most decisive impact on British radio drama. He was born in Dublin in 1906 and after university moved from Dublin to Paris in 1928 as a *lecteur* at the Ecole Normale Superieure and spent time with another Irish literary great James Joyce. Beckett's writing career began with work written in English (he was later to be famous for writing in French). His first novel, *Murphy* (1938), was followed by *Watt* (eventually published in 1953) and what Anthony Cronin calls 'the great trilogy of novels, *Molly, Malone Dies* and *The Unnamable*.'[10] The trilogy, all initially written in French, marked a decisive development in Beckett's writing and were characterized by the abandonment of any conventional plot, the difficulties of language as a mean of communication and the lack of character development. Cronin suggests that in this creative period, at the end of the 1940s, Beckett was finding his own voice and writing something (to use a hugely non-Beckettian word) 'true'.[11] The result was the creation of a 'Beckett man', an anti-hero in the same tradition as Joyce's Bloom: 'He lays no claim to any virtue that can be named, except to a rather dubious humility and a too eagerly embraced resignation. His principal emotion when confronted with humanity at large is fear.'[12]

While Beckett's novels were still incomplete and all unpublished, Beckett completed his most famous and popular work, *Waiting for Godot*, between

October 1948 and January 1949. The play succeeds in combining humour with the worst aspects of human existence. The humour is strongly reminiscent of a certain style of Irish music-hall comedy in which two funny men exchange banter – comparisons have been made with Laurel and Hardy, and when the play eventually reached America it was very much seen as a comedy in that vein. After the play was finished, *Molly* and *Malone Dies* were published, and as a result, Beckett became better known in France. Extracts from the unperformed *Godot* were broadcast on French radio (RTF) on 17 February 1952, almost a year before the first performance.[13] Then, three years after *Godot* had been completed, at last a small theatre, 'Theatre de Babylone' became available for the beginning of 1953. Beckett was then working with the director Roger Blin, and on 5 January 1953 *Waiting for Godot* opened for the first time.[14] There were good reviews and in particular from the famous playwright Jean Anouilh, who wrote, '*Godot* is a masterpiece that will cause despair for men in general and for playwrights in particular.'[15]

Waiting for Godot features two tramps, Estragon and Vladimir, waiting on a lonely road by a tree for a man called Godot. After a while a local landowner Pozzo and his servant, Lucky, arrive: the unfortunate Lucky is made fun of and then these two leave. Before the end of the first act a boy arrives to say that Mr Godot will not be coming today but will come tomorrow. The second act is similar to the first: the two tramps are joined by Pozzo (who is now blind) and Lucky, they eventually leave, and the boy arrives to repeat his message that Godot is not coming but can be expected tomorrow and the play ends.

Although not written for radio, Beckett's best-known play provides an introduction to his thinking and writing which is important for radio scholars. Reaction to *Godot* from within Drama department shines the brightest possible light on BBC attitudes not only to the theatre but also to the nature of radio drama and public service broadcasting. The reaction to *Godot* in Drama Department created very clearly demarcated battle lines between the cautious and reactionary managers of BBC radio and the younger producers and script editors. This was the watershed moment for BBC Radio Drama. The first response to *Godot* was provided by the BBC's 'Paris representative' Cecilia Reeves and the established features producer Rayner Heppenstall. It is worth quoting her thoughts in full:

> From: Miss C. Reeves, Paris Representative
> Subject: En Attendant Godot by Samuel Beckett
> To: A.H.D. (Sound)[16] copy to Rayner Heppenstall
> 17 March 1953
>
> Rayner Heppenstall was going to talk to you about Samuel Beckett's play 'En attendant Godot' which we went to see together and which we thought might be suitable material for the Third. I am attaching the text of this. Perhaps you would let me know if you are interested in doing anything about it.

The first part of it is extraordinarily effective on the stage but it ceased to be convincing after we had a drink at the interval so that it would probably be easier to hold the attention with a radio version.[17]

The potential for adapting *Godot* for radio was identified very early, even though it was not broadcast for another seven years. The response in the BBC itself was varied. One producer, E. J. King Bull, saw the play as 'pretty funny' with a 'recurring gag' and suggested various comedians for casting in a memo to Val Gielgud.[18] Gielgud's response was perhaps not surprising:

I am left with the impression of something that is basic 'phoney', and I was incidentally interested to see the notice in the *Times* last week on a production of the play in Germany which strongly confirmed this impression. I shall advise C.T.P. [Controller, Third Programme, John Morris] that in my view we should do well to drop the subject.[19]

Gielgud made his views even clearer ten years later when he told his successor, Martin Esslin, 'I hate Brecht, I hate Beckett, I hate Pinter. But I know what my duty is. That's why I've appointed you to deal with these people.'[20]

So despite the excitement around Beckett's play, Gielgud rejected it on the grounds of its 'phoneyness', and in the Drama Department of 1953 few were prepared to disagree. However, interest in *Godot* continued to grow not only in Paris but also in London. At that time, the English stage was censored by the Lord Chamberlain but 'theatre clubs' were exempt, and it was in the small Arts Theatre Club that the precocious young British director, Peter Hall, put on Ionesco's *The Lesson* in March 1955 and then *Waiting for Godot* on 3 August. The response of the audience was hostile: laughter in the wrong places, inappropriate cheering and by the second half most of the audience had left.[21] It was perhaps unsurprising that an audience used to lavish sets, clever plots, leading ladies in haute couture gowns and an evening of undemanding entertainment would have struggled with Beckett for as Kenneth Tynan explained, 'It has no plot, no climax, no *denouement*; no beginning, no middle and no end. ... *Waiting for Godot* frankly jettisons everything by which we recognise theatre.'[22] He went on to praise the play, noting the 'double-talk of vaudeville' referencing Keaton and Chaplin. For Tynan, *Godot* 'forced me to re-examine the rules which have governed the drama', adding, 'it is validly new: and hence I declare myself, as the Spanish would say, *godotista*'.[23] The other main critic of British theatre, Harold Hobson, agreed with Tynan. For Hobson the tramps Vladimir and Estragon 'are like humanity, which dawdles and drivels its life, postponing action, eschewing enjoyment, waiting for some far-off, divine event, the millennium, the Day of Judgement'.[24] Hobson urged his readers to go and see *Waiting for Godot*, and at best they might discover something 'that will surely lodge in the corner of your mind for as long as you live'.[25]

5. Radio Drama and the Absurd

The approval of Britain's two most celebrated theatre critics no doubt contributed to uncertainty in Drama Department. Despite Gielgud's rejection of *Waiting for Godot* there were a growing number of voices at the BBC arguing that somehow Beckett's work had to be aired on radio. The script editor Helena Wood was one of these who argued that *Godot* should be broadcast:

> For radio it is not without dangers. The setting and the appearance of the tramps are essential, and will have somehow to be conveyed on the air. ... There is so much significance, vitality and poetry in the dialogue and subtle music in the phrasing that it is obviously radio material.[26]

Another supporter of broadcasting *Godot* was Raymond Raikes (discussed in Chapter 2) who shared many of Gielgud's more conservative views about drama. Gielgud decided to get Raikes's opinion about the London production of *Waiting for Godot* after it had moved to the Criterion Theatre. Raikes was enthusiastic but his opinion was the result not so much of any deep appreciation of Beckett's work rather a concern about the reputation of the BBC: 'May I suggest that we record and broadcast this production as soon as possible lest it be said that the BBC has once again "missed the boat".'[27] Over the following months the pressure on Gielgud to do something about broadcasting Beckett's work, for reasons of reputation if nothing else, clearly built and involved the director of Sound Broadcasting, Lindsey Wellington, who called a meeting of drama producers on 3 November 1955 to discuss the subject of 'experimentalism in drama programmes'. It is clear from the archived memoranda that the Drama Department was heavily criticized by Wellington and in particular for the lack of experimentation in drama output. Barbara Bray wrote to Gielgud following the meeting and expressed the views of the younger producers and editors:

> Good, unconventional *ideas* are sometimes stifled for lack of a more encouraging atmosphere. ... If the Programme Planners would agree to break with the old routines, so that the public might be more prepared to listen with an open mind, we could increase the proportion of unconventional material in our output.[28] (Emphasis in the original)

This was Gielgud's own written response to Wellington (note the implicit suggestions that the fault lay with junior staff):

> Following upon the recent meeting when, with every justification, you passed certain generally critical observations regarding the work of this department, and expressed your wish for the injection of a considerable new dose of 'experimentalism' into our output as a whole, I took the occasion of a departmental meeting to lay the criticism and the suggestions squarely before my producers.[29]

Gielgud's apparent capitulation to external criticism of his department reflects his complex character: at times resolutely opposed to the avant garde as well as prepared to allow others to take the lead against his own personal preferences.

John Morris, controller, Third Programme, following Gielgud's lead joined the pro-Beckett movement within the BBC. In July 1956, Morris visited Beckett to discuss the idea of him writing something for the Third Programme and then sent a memorandum to Gielgud: 'As arranged, I saw Samuel Beckett in Paris this morning. He is extremely keen to write an original work for the Third Programme and has indeed already done the first few pages of his script.'[30] Suddenly, the progressive forces in the Drama Department were mobilized and Donald McWhinnie was chosen as the producer of a new radio work by Beckett supported by a band of enthusiasts including the French-speaking head of the Script Unit, Barbara Bray, and Cecilia Reeves, the BBC's contact in Paris. Six months later, Beckett's first play for radio, *All That Fall*, was broadcast. The speed of this, from Morris's speculative chat with Beckett in Montparnasse to the broadcast, was remarkable; it would have required not only Beckett to write the script rapidly[31] but also the choice of producer and actors and some difficult decisions about sound effects had to be made. Anthony Cronin places Barbara Bray at the centre of the BBC's dealings with Beckett: 'A highly attractive and vivacious young woman who had come down from Cambridge after the war with a good degree.'[32] Bray was a good example of the intelligent, young but relatively inexperienced producers and editors favoured by Gielgud in what looks like a deliberate policy to keep in touch with developments in the theatre which he himself found repugnant. In addition, Bray was also a reviewer and translator of French literature and would have been able to discuss literary matters with Beckett. Following Morris's visit to Paris, she liaised between Beckett and McWhinnie, exchanging letters and visiting Beckett with McWhinnie on a couple of occasions.[33]

All That Fall[34] was produced by Donald McWhinnie with Mary O'Farrell as the central character, Maddy Rooney, and J. G. Devlin as her husband, Dan; it lasted for seventy minutes. The play is set in rural Ireland close to the fictional Boghill railway station. There is a strikingly odd and unsettling beginning when actors play the parts of farmyard animals, we hear 'sheep, bird, cow, cock, severally, then together'[35] and then a confusing sound which turns out to be Maddy Rooney slowly dragging herself along the road. Then there is the incongruous sound of Schubert's *Death and the Maiden* and Mrs Rooney's voice, 'Poor woman, all alone in that ruinous old house.' In this first part of the play, Mrs Rooney gradually makes her way to the station where she is going to meet her husband. She encounters various rural types on the road while apparently talking to herself in a manner which is both very sad and, in typically Beckettian style, very funny. The first character she meets, Christy, is on a horse drawn cart and offers to sell Mrs Rooney some dung, which she refuses. After he has gone she asks mournfully, 'What have I done to deserve all this? What? What?' Maddy Rooney has some obviously humorous characteristics, one of these is that she is fat: 'Oh, let me just flop down flat on the road like a big flat jelly out of a bowl and never move again. A great big slop, thick with grit and dust and flies. They would have to scoop me up with a shovel.' Another of Mrs Rooney's characteristics which Beckett milks for its humorous effect is her self-pity. She has been destroyed, she claims, 'with sorrow and pining, gentility and church going and fat and rheumatism and childlessness'. The theme of childlessness is returned to and, at the end of the play, when we learn of the death of a child we are left to wonder if childlessness might be the central theme. Mrs Rooney refers twice to 'little Minnie' who we learn was her child, now dead, 'she'd be in her 40s or 50s … girding up her lovely little loins'. Even Mr Tyler, another character she meets on the road, says that his daughter has had an operation which 'removed everything' and so 'I am now grandchildless'.

Beckett was fortunate to have Donald McWhinnie as his producer and *All That Fall* is an aurally rich and adventurous production. Apart from the acted farmyard animals all of the sounds we hear are stylized, so they are identifiable as a car or approaching train but distorted enough to make them have a dreamlike or fantastic quality. The most persistent sound is that of Mrs Rooney feet, given a musical treatment by McWhinnie using a drum and always accompanied by her rhythmic sighing. When she eventually meets Dan and they walk back home, there is a mixture of her feet and his stick and their joint moans and sighs.

Mrs Rooney's next encounter on the road is with Mr Slocum in his very eccentric sounding car. He offers her a lift and much is made of the difficulty she has getting in and even more when they arrive at the station and young Tommy helps Mrs Rooney out of the car. At the station she meets the station master Mr Barrell and Miss Fit. Eventually the train arrives accompanied by echoey, unreal sounds but there is no sign of Dan Rooney. Then we hear the tapping of blind Mr Rooney's stick and Mrs Rooney sounds for the first time almost happy, 'Oh Dan! There you are!' He is a particularly grumpy husband and dismissively informs Mrs Rooney that he had been 'in the men's'. She asks him to kiss her to which he responds 'Kiss you? In public? On the platform, before the boy? Have you taken leave of your senses?' When Mrs Rooney then asks little Jerry, 'How's your father?' he replies, 'They took him away mam.' The scene is the cruellest possible combination of humour and tragedy in which everyone, even little Jerry, plays their part. What follows is the long, slow return home; Mrs Rooney asks Dan, 'Put your arm around me' to which he replies in typically cruel vein, 'Have you been drinking?' They bicker as they make their way and the slow journey is made to sound like a great struggle with the sound of the stick, the drumbeat used to signify Mrs Rooney progress and many sighs and moans. Eventually she stops to Mr Rooney's intense irritation, 'All this stopping and starting is devilish, devilish. I get a little way on me and begin to be carried along when suddenly you stop dead, 200 pounds of unhealthy fat, what possessed you to come out at all?'

The final third of the play features not only the tortuous walk home but Mrs Rooney's interest in why the train was late. The secret lies with Mr Rooney who reveals himself increasingly troubled, even dangerous. Mrs Rooney and Mr Rooney are taunted by two children and he comments, 'Did you ever wish to kill a child? Nip some young bloom in the bud?' He follows this by starting tentatively to explain what happened on the train. He says that he was alone in the compartment, or at least thought he was. Mrs Rooney interjects with a memory of going to see a doctor speak who had a patient, a young girl, who died. The couple then walk on and we hear the sound of the wind and the rain begins to fall. Near the end of the play Mr Rooney asks which text the preacher had chosen for the following day's service and whether he has chosen his text. Mrs Rooney replies, 'The Lord upholdeth all that fall, and raiseth up all those that be bound down.'[36] There is a silence and then the pair burst into a hideous cackle, clearly finding the optimism of the psalm unspeakable funny. Then Jerry appears carrying an object which Mr Rooney may have dropped. It is like a ball but Dan denies any knowledge of it. Mrs Rooney takes the opportunity to ask Jerry about the unresolved lateness of the train:

Mrs Rooney: What was it Jerry?
Jerry: It was a little child mam.
Mrs Rooney: What do you mean it was a little child?
Jerry: It was a little child fell out of the carriage mam, under the wheels mam.[37]

The play then ends with the sound of footsteps and the wind, and the listener is left with the inevitable suspicion that Dan had murdered the child.

The critical reception to *All That Fall* was extensive; indeed given the huge amount of writing about Beckett it probably counts as one of the most discussed and analysed radio dramas of all time. The day after the broadcast, Val Gielgud was full of praise: 'My warmest congratulations on your outstanding success with the Beckett play ... your exceptional casting, your ingenious use of effects, and your extreme sensitivity of approach, combined to do a fascinating script every sort of justice.'[38] Given Gielgud's outspoken dislike of Beckett and original rejection of *Waiting for Godot* it is hard not to find these words disingenuous, but no doubt he was greatly relieved that the Beckett problem had apparently been solved. He would have been even more pleased when the press reviews came out. Roy Walker wrote the following in *The Tribune*:

Please listen! Not to me but to the repeat of *All That Fall* in the Third Programme on Saturday (Jan.19) at five minutes to seven. If you hear the first performance on Sunday you will probably be listening again anyway, as I shall. If not, don't miss this. It has been specially commissioned by the BBC from the Irish author of Waiting for Godot, Samuel Beckett. I don't guarantee you'll like it mind. *All That Fall* is, I insist, the most important and irresistible new play for radio since Dylan Thomas's *Under Milk Wood* three Januaries ago.[39]

The production of *All That Fall* is examined in some detail by Donald McWhinnie[40] who justified the stylized sound effects as a way of avoiding a 'simple realism' in favour of Mrs Rooney's inner world. This point is made more forcefully by the American director Everett Frost who interprets the play as taking place entirely inside her head.[41] McWhinnie also comments on the use of silence in the play and there are throughout the 1957 recording several quite uncomfortable periods of silence. For example, Mrs Rooney's conversation with Christy is interrupted by silences, before her question, 'Why do you halt?' and then a long silence before she asks herself, intimately, 'Why do I halt?' This combination of production elements, the stylized realism of the sound effects and innovative manipulation of sound, the intelligent use of silences and the triumphant performances of the two central characters by Mary O'Farrell and J. G. Devlin, was assembled, according to Clas Zilliacus, in what was virtually a one-take recording session.[42] There is no doubt that the 1957 recording does have a feeling of immediacy, even liveness, which may well be the result of a virtually uninterrupted recording.

In his book *The 101 Greatest Plays*, Michael Billington surprisingly did not include *Waiting for Godot* but instead chose *All That Fall* as Beckett's best dramatic work.[43] For such a notoriously difficult writer, *All That Fall* is a surprisingly accessible work in which Beckett, who had complained about the overly comic interpretations of *Godot*, seemed to have learnt something from that success.[44] The humour in *All That Fall* is genuinely funny while Mrs Rooney herself is a profoundly sad character, and the underlying mystery of the murdered child introduces the darkest aspects of Beckett's writing. Eric Tonning describes the Third Programme as 'mediating modernism' to the British public in order to prove that the BBC, while offering the regular diet of classics, was not 'out of touch' with the avant garde.[45] In *All That Fall* the Third Programme had the perfect Beckett play, funny enough to be enjoyed, even entertaining, but with undercurrents of Beckettian nightmare.

Emily Bloom provides an intriguing analysis of *All That Fall* focusing on the dramas 'archivizing' potential and relating this to the actual problems archiving and playing back the production to Beckett himself.[46] For Bloom, the play serves to preserve the memories of a dying (Protestant) community while also confirming the ephemeral nature of the world. Sounds come into being but are then immediately lost: 'The characters in *All That Fall* recognize that their words vanish in the moment of their utterance, yet they continue talking and talking to stave off the final silence of death. … [Maddy and Dan] are acutely aware that their words are fading in a space that will neither preserve nor remember their utterances.'[47] A dying community, a dying language ineffectively captured by the recording equipment and practices of the BBC. Beckett's experience of trying but failing to hear a satisfactory recording of *All That Fall* directly inspired his stage play *Krapp's Last Tape*. If anything, Emily Bloom's comments on *All That Fall* only add to and burnish its reputation and significance. Not only is it a triumph as a play and as a production but it is also a profoundly important commentary on sound and language and the challenges of their preservation.

The success of *All That Fall* marked a decisive moment in the post-war history of radio drama. It opened the floodgates for Beckett-related broadcasting, including work written by him for radio, adaptations of his stage plays, readings from his novels and innumerable programmes about him. As Erik Tonning put it, 'Beckett became one of the Third Programme's most valued assets.'[48] In addition, after *All That Fall*, Drama Department embraced other plays written for radio which might loosely be called avant garde and especially those written by Giles Cooper, Rhys Adrian and Harold Pinter. One of the other great absurdist playwrights, Eugene Ionesco was also suddenly popular at the BBC; no fewer than four different plays by Ionesco were adapted for the Third Programme in 1957. Finally, *All That Fall* was appreciated by critics for its radiogenic quality, its success as sound drama, at a time when television was emerging as the dominant medium. This made it easier for McWhinnie and Bray to argue for the new Radiophonic Workshop, dedicated to the creation of artificial sounds and mainly for radio drama; McWhinnie's use of actors to 'baa' like sheep and 'cluck' like chickens resulted in the establishment of a unit in the BBC for electronic sound production and manipulation.

Following the triumph of *All That Fall* the obvious course of action to capitalize on the critical success of the play would have been to broadcast an adaptation of *Waiting for Godot*, and it reflects Val Gielgud's decidedly mixed feelings about Beckett that this did not happen. Instead, there was a broadcast in French of the stage play, *Fin de Partie* on 2 May 1957 in the production by Roger Blin. This probably did not satisfy Beckett's admirers, either inside or outside the BBC, and what followed was a curiously old-fashioned BBC device of broadcasting parts of larger works, in this case parts of *Molloy*,[49] *From and Abandoned Work*,[50] *Malone Dies*[51] and *The Unnamable*.[52] This approach is reminiscent of pre-war broadcasts of, for example, scenes from a Shakespeare play or a movement from a symphony. Such an approach would now be seen as anachronistic, but it reflected a 'something is better than nothing' approach to broadcasting major works of literature and classical music. Reading extracts from Beckett's novels was a pragmatic approach to providing more Beckett when there was nothing else available, but it can also be seen as an entirely appropriate treatment of some famously difficult writing. The extracts varied in length from twenty minutes (*From an Abandoned Work*) to one hour fifteen minutes (*Malone Dies*), and they were all read by the Irish actor Patrick Magee, who 'had a harsh, gravelly voice which had little superficial charm but had a hypnotic effect on the listener. With his voice and his light blue eyes went a faint air of menace.'[53] Magee was the perfect reader for Beckett, there was a natural fit, 'There was a sense in which, as an actor, he had been waiting for Beckett just as Beckett had been waiting for him.'[54] Magee's own acting persona and voice were so close to Beckett's requirements that he wrote a play for him provisionally titled 'Magee Monologue', then renamed *Krapp's Last Tape*. In addition, Beckett's nephew, John, composed music for the readings which, importantly, were produced by Donald McWhinnie. Although the readings were clearly a stopgap for the BBC, a way of fulfilling a perceived need for Beckett's work on the Third Programme, they benefitted from excellent production and the best possible actor to read them. For many, the readings would surely have constituted a far more approachable version of the novels than the books themselves.

In the summer of 1958, Beckett sent Barbara Bray and Donald McWhinnie an early version of the play which came to be known as *Embers*. The play contained a story told by the main character about two people, Bolton, a patient, and Holloway, a doctor. Understandably this offer was seized upon by McWhinnie and Bray who began to think of it as Beckett's next radio drama. He was typically reluctant about this idea and protested in a letter to Barbara Bray that it was rather an experiment in writing for which he was requesting their reaction.[55] Needless to say that was not going to put them off, and by February 1959 Beckett had sent a script of *Embers* to the BBC. The play was broadcast on the Third Programme on 24 June 1959 starring Jack MacGowran in the main role who, like Patrick Magee, was an Irish actor who could produce a most disturbing vocal performance, and Magee himself playing two much smaller roles; production was by Donald McWhinnie and the play lasted forty-five minutes.[56]

Embers is about an old man, Henry, walking and sitting by the sea and apparently calling up the voices of the dead including his wife Ada and his daughter Addie. It is evident from the very beginning that this is a drama specifically written for radio and in places is, as Katherine Weiss notes, a self-reflexive comment on radio as a storytelling medium.[57] It starts with the sound of the sea as waves come in and then withdraw on a shingle beach and slow, trudging steps on the shingle reminiscent of Maddy's footsteps at the beginning in the *All That Fall*. There are also two very simple musical notes which slowly repeat themselves, like someone breathing in and out, and these are present for almost the entire play. Then we hear Henry's voice, 'on' which is then repeated, almost as a shout. The same with the word 'stop' spoken twice and 'down' also spoken twice. The first word 'on' suggests Henry is switching on the radio: later he says the word 'hooves' which is followed almost comically by the most clichéd sound effect of horse's hooves, this is followed by Henry saying 'again' and the sound effect is repeated. It is almost as if Beckett is referencing the famous artificiality of sound effects used by McWhinnie in *All That Fall*. Henry then proceeds to talk in a rambling and incoherent manner, partly about the death of his father. In *All That Fall* we experienced the world as imagined by Maddy Rooney and in the same way *Embers* is very much a play about the thoughts and utterances of the central character. Henry is a storyteller, one of the dominant themes of Beckett's later work, whose stories give him his sense of identity. The main story is about Bolton who calls his doctor, Holloway, at night. Towards the end of the play we learn that Bolton wants an injection, presumably to relieve pain, to which the unsympathetic

Holloway responds, 'If you want a shot say so and let me get the hell out of here. We've had this before Bolton, don't ask me to go through it again.'

Henry's wife Ada is another disturbing presence in the play; she talks in an entirely emotionless manner, reinforcing the idea that she is a ghost. Ada asks Henry to laugh and smile and is treated, perhaps predictably, to a hideous cackle. They talk about their daughter, Addie, and we hear her suffering the cruelty of the Music Master (Magee) and then her riding lesson accompanied by nightmarish, distorted sound. Henry walks down to the sea and shouts, 'Darling! Darling!' to which Ada responds, 'You must see a doctor about your talking. It is very bad for the child. There must be something wrong with your brain.' In another reference to recorded sound, Henry, who apparently hates the sound of the sea, says he walks about with a gramophone in the hope of drowning out the sound of the sea, but this fails. For Henry, storytelling, recounting memories or telling tales is a way of existing and having an identity but for Ada it has the opposite effect: 'The time will come when no one will speak to you at all. Not even complete strangers. You will be quite alone with your voice, there will be no other voice in the world but yours.' Towards the conclusion of *Embers* Henry's speech falters, he speaks only in single or pairs of words: 'Ada. Father. Christ. White world. Bitter cold. Old man. Great trouble. No good.'[58]

Writing in *The Listener*, the radio drama critic of the time, Ian Rodger, was harsh in his judgement: 'It had the familiar trademarks of our greatest living obscurantist. Croaking voices once more repeated insignificant words, effects were bizarre, and there were once more the pauses which are intended to provoke meditation but which succeed only in promoting impatient hysteria.'[59] It is certainly the case that *Embers* is a particularly challenging and demanding listening experience. Present-day listeners benefit from half a century of Beckett scholarship which assist us in understanding what Beckett was trying to achieve, but it is interesting to note that two of the more important pro-Beckett commentaries published at or near the time by Donald McWhinnie[60] himself and Martin Esslin[61] barely acknowledge *Embers*. However, Katherine Weiss provides an important commentary which relates Beckett's developing attitude to both speech and sound stating that in *Embers* 'Beckett applies his mistrust of language to sound'.[62] The unreliability of language is a recurring and mounting theme in Beckett's work, but here it is also true of sound: the distorted, repeated sounds of the sea, the hooves and the voices of ghosts. The 'stylized sound' which Donald McWhinnie developed for *All That Fall* not only confirms in both plays the unreality of the drama and the world as a dream or fantasy but also affirms the unreliability of sound. Clas Zilliacus observes that of all Beckett's plays '*Embers* is the most saturated with sound',[63] and it is a sonically powerful if profoundly disturbing experience.

The period following the broadcast of *Embers* up to 1964 saw Beckett far less engaged with radio, although he maintained his close relationship with Barbara Bray and continuing friendship with Donald McWhinnie. He became more interested in film and television as well as writing for the stage. BBC Radio, however, remained keen to capitalize on Beckett's fame and their promotion of him over the previous two and a half years. The strategy, if it can be called that, was to adapt *Waiting for Godot* and then *Endgame* for radio despite considerable resistance from within the BBC. Of these two, the case of *Endgame* is particularly interesting, and so this will form the final element of this discussion of Beckett's plays on radio.[64] In early 1958, there was an intriguing exchange of memoranda about the English translation of *Fin de Partie* which McWhinnie had obtained. The play had been broadcast in French, but it was now ready to be adapted as a radio drama in English. McWhinnie wrote to John Morris and Val Gielgud stating this: 'I would strongly recommend this text for a Third Programme broadcast. It is a brilliant and distinguished piece of writing.'[65] He added that there was a problem because the Lord Chamberlain had refused to grant the play a licence for theatrical performance because of a blasphemous reference to god, 'The bastard. He doesn't exist.'[66] Radio broadcasts were not censored by the Lord Chamberlain but, as McWhinnie put it, 'if we were to broadcast this play in the Third Programme we should almost certainly excite a good deal of publicity'.[67] The usually very conservative John Morris, controller, Third Programme, supported McWhinnie: 'This is difficult and [unreadable] obscure (like all Beckett's works) and where pp 36 and 37 are blasphemous if read out of context the total effect of the play is in my opinion, not.'[68] At the bottom of the same memorandum, 'DSB'[69] has added 'I agree'. In a much longer memorandum McWhinnie argued for broadcasting *Endgame* because of the reputational damage that not broadcasting it would have on the Third Programme. McWhinnie of course knew of the sensitivity around the BBC's reputation, and the fact that both John Morris and Val Gielgud were motivated by the desire to maintain the BBC's reputation, even if it meant broadcasting work which they personally disliked. These words would therefore have had an impact:

> If we were to refuse to broadcast his play in an English version although there would be no wide publicity for this decision it would certainly be known to a considerable number of people whose respect for the intellectual integrity of the Third Programme we value and whose respect would thereby be lessened.[70]

The decision was then passed up the BBC hierarchy and eventually reached the chairman who decreed in February 1958 that the play could not be broadcast. Becket was then asked if he would replace the word 'bastard' with something less offensive but declined. There was then a pause of almost four years before the new controller, Third Programme, P. H. Newby wrote in a memorandum that Beckett had replaced the word 'bastard' with 'swine' and so allowed *Endgame* to be performed at the Royal Court Theatre. Plans for a radio broadcast were immediately resurrected, but as McWhinnie had then left the BBC the producer chosen was Michael Bakewell, and the play was finally broadcast on the Third Programme on 22 May 1962.

As a radio drama, *Endgame* has major strengths and weaknesses. It is easy to agree with McWhinnie's enthusiasm for Beckett's writing in *Endgame* which contains some of his most striking and at times poetic dialogue. However, this is an intensely visual play; interestingly not a problem discussed at all in the memoranda leading up to the decision to broadcast. The script begins with a page and a half of set description and stage directions for one of the characters:

> *Bare interior.*
> *Grey light.*
> *Left and right back, high up, two small windows, curtains drawn.*
> *Front right, a door. Hanging near door, its face to wall, a picture.*
> *Front left, touching each other, covered with an old sheet, two ashbins.*
> *Centre, in an armchair on castors, covered with an old sheet, Hamm.*
> *Motionless by the door, his eyes fixed on Hamm, Clov. Very red face.*[71]

The stage directions at the start of the play are elaborate and involve Clov looking at the windows, fetching a step ladder, opening the curtains then removing the sheets covering the ashbins and the one covering Hamm:

> *He goes to Hamm, removes sheet covering him, folds it over his arm. In a dressing-gown, a stiff toque on his head, a large blood-stained handkerchief over his face, a whistle hanging from his neck, a rug over his knees, thick socks on his feet, Hamm seems to be asleep.*[72]

It is clear from these very precise directions and description that adapting *Endgame* as a radio play would present serious, if not insuperable, problems. Michael Bakewell's solution was to have a narrator read Beckett's directions, but there is clearly no substitute for seeing Hamm or the cruel depiction of his parents, Nagg and Nell, in dustbins. Later in the play, Nagg and Nell try to kiss:

> Nagg: Kiss me.
> Nell: We can't.
> Nagg: Try.
>   *Their heads strain towards each other, fail to meet, fall apart again.*
> Nell: Why this farce, day after day.[73]

While it is true that any adaptation of a stage play will inevitably lose the visual dimension of the drama, in *Endgame* the bizarre imagery is clearly lost in the radio version. Other visual aspects of the play are also lost: the picture on the wall which hangs with 'face to wall' and the alarm clock which Clov places on the lid of Nagg's bin. At the end of the play, Clov enters 'dressed for the road. Panama hat, tweed coat, raincoat over his arm, umbrella, bag.'[74] This is an important visual image but one that is lost in the radio version.

As the play progresses, Hamm and Clov and then Nagg and Nell engage in dialogue which is, in true Becket fashion, both comic and cruel, as in this exchange:

Hamm: Why don't you kill me?
Clov: I don't know the combination of the larder.

In addition there are some long soliloquys delivered by Hamm. One of these (beginning, 'One! Silence!') occupies three pages of the script. These long speeches are particularly effective in the radio version of the play, even if some of the visual dimensions of their setting are missing.

In his review of *Endgame*, Martin Shuttleworth provides a taste of the animosity Beckett could generate. He began with an understandable concern: 'I couldn't see the set for one thing in my mind's eye, even though the narrator read out the stage directions.'[75] He found the play predictable in terms of character and dialogue, 'Beckett characters randomly playing the usual Beckett shove ha'penny with words.' The review ends with these contemptuous words: 'The majority of the play was on the usual long, whining, self-pitying note, the dirty water running out of the birth in which Joyce died.'[76] Recent critical writing, however, helps in the appreciation of one of Beckett's most important plays. Michael Worton, for example, convincingly compares *Waiting for Godot* and *Endgame*: both including pairs of characters, the importance of death and dying, the waiting for something to happen and so on.[77]

The question of whether or not radio adaptations of stage plays were successful was a persistent them in the discussion of radio drama in the post-war period. Philip Hope-Wallace's sustained criticism of adaptations in *The Listener* in the 1940s and the widely held view that Ibsen could be successfully adapted whereas Chekhov was more problematic contributed to the policy of encouraging writers, and especially successful writers, to write specifically for radio. In *All That Fall*, this policy can be seen at its triumphant best, the great playwright producing a genuinely radiogenic drama. *Endgame*, bravely produced by Michael Bakewell, although an intriguing experience as radio was written as Beckett became increasingly concerned with very precise visual imagery and without these clues and symbols arguably too much of the meaning of the play is lost.

Of other absurdist writers, the one who made the most important contribution to BBC radio drama was undoubtedly Eugene Ionesco. Like Beckett, Ionesco adopted Paris as his home and French as his language. Unlike Beckett, Ionesco was not courted by the Drama Department and not commissioned to write radio dramas but his writing was presented in different ways on the Third Programme including full adaptations of stage plays and shorter broadcasts based on the short stories, one of which was read by Ionesco himself.

An unusual feature of his writing was the way he sometimes wrote a short story first which was then turned into a stage play. This was true of two of his most famous plays, *Rhinoceros* and *Victims of Duty*, both of which were subsequently adapted as radio dramas. In 1956, at the very beginning of the absurdist turn in radio drama, Ionesco read his short story *La Photo du Colonel*.[78] It was followed by *The Picture*,[79] a one-act play starring Maurice Denham and Mary O'Farrell (a few months after her performance as Maddy Rooney in *All That Fall*) produced by Michael Bakewell. There were further short stories including *The Horns of the Dilemma*, a twenty-five minute adaptation from a short story, read by Ionesco.[80] Then there were two productions of Ionesco's stage plays; *Rhinoceros*[81] and *Victims of Duty*,[82] the latter produced by the newly appointed replacement for Donald McWhinnie, Martin Esslin, with Harold Pinter as the detective.

Rhinoceros was produced by Michael Bakewell who had already been trusted with some avant-garde drama, including plays by Ionesco and James Joyce. The play begins with some uplifting, even exuberant, piano music[83] followed by the meowing of a cat (performed by an actor), a shopkeeper complaining about the 'stuck up' woman who owns the cat and then a conversation between her and another shopkeeper complaining about the lack of business. There is the sound of a church bell and horses' hooves followed by the sound of an accordion. These sounds are used to suggest a provincial French town which is the setting for Ionesco's disturbing, political play in which all but one character turn into rhinoceroses. The naturalism of the scene contrasts with the absurdity of what is said, for example by the Logician who talks magnificent nonsense, together with the gradual transformation of characters into animals. Also talking in the café are other characters who discuss the rhinoceros phenomenon and try to explain it by blaming the government, the trade unions and anonymous conspirators, among others. At the same time two characters, a drunken and aimless young man, Berenger and his older, bullying friend, Jean, provide a naturalistic quality in their well-observed bickering while the deeper absurd reality gathers pace. This conflict between the play's naturalism and the absurd produces a disturbing and unsettling listening experience. The sound of a rhinoceros, a deep groan and the pounding of hooves is incongruous, but it is either ignored by the characters or incorporated into their nonsensical conversation, for example by wondering if the animal is an Asiatic or African rhinoceros. The scene moves to an office and two men talking accompanied by the hammering of a typewriter. Once again the prosaic naturalism of the scene is about to be destroyed by the absurdity of events. A woman arrives, she was chased all the way by a rhinoceros, and we hear the animal's groaning sound; it tries to climb the stairs but they break. The rhinoceros is in fact Boeuf, her husband, the manager is not unduly concerned: 'I will take this up with the proper authorities.'[84] As the play progresses people start to change, their skin goes green and their speech is deeper and hoarser. Throughout the play the comedy of the situation is sustained: 'What's wrong with being a Rhinoceros? I'm all for change.'

The play gathers pace as more and more people become rhinoceroses, and we hear them thundering through the streets. In the final scene, Berenger declares his love for Daisy, and they talk about their future together and having children. Daisy then declares that she admires the tremendous energy of the rhinoceroses as she watches them dance, and she says she supports them. Berenger strikes her and she walks out; he is alone and declares, 'How I wish I was like them!' He tries to howl but fails and so he decides to take a stand: everyone except him is now a rhinoceros and so he gets his rifle and goes to confront them. He shouts, 'I'm not capitulating! I'm not capitulating!' and we hear two shots and in the background a brass band plays for the dancing rhinoceroses and the play ends.

In his review of the radio drama in *The Listener*, Ian Rodger discusses it very much in terms of the ideas and themes explored by Ionesco rather than as a sound production. He applauds the political message of the play and the inability of the townfolk in the café to provide any explanation for the end of humanity in what is clearly an allegory for the rise of barbarism. He suggests that when Berenger defies the animals at the end, 'he speaks for his author and for all those who believe that the answers to the world's problems are not as simple as self-appointed committed ones think they are'.[85] He concludes his review by stating that '*Rhinoceros* is a major work and a landmark in the work of M.Ionseco'. It is not clear from these words whether he is commenting on the play as a theatrical work or this particular production for radio and what is missing in Rodger's review is an appreciation of the multilayered and highly effective use of sound in Michael Bakewell's production. The contrast between the light-hearted tunefulness of the piano music with the growling rhinoceros sounds and thundering hooves adds to a highly effective and disturbing sonic interpretation of Ionesco's play. In addition, the use of special effects created by the Radiophonic Workshop made this an aurally innovative production.

Rhinoceros raises an interesting question, not one addressed at all by contemporary reviewers, whether such an intensely visual drama, featuring human beings physically turning into wild animals thundering through the streets of a French town smashing up the human environment can be successfully adapted for a non-visual medium. Michael Bakewell's virtuoso production demonstrates convincingly that *Rhinoceros* can be adapted to create a highly effective radio drama which surely bears comparison with the major BBC radio dramas of the post-war era. There is indeed a case for suggesting that even though *Rhinoceros* was written for the stage and then adapted for radio it is a highly radiogenic work, one which works *more* effectively on radio than on the stage. This is because the listener is forced to imagine the transformation of a person into a rhinoceros rather than look at whatever clever use of make-up or prosthetics can achieve. This suggestive transformation is somehow more disturbing, if it is invisible and in addition forces the listener to reflect more on the meaning of Ionesco's allegory. There is more space for the listener to the drama to use their imagination to reflect on barbarism and humanity's propensity to follow the herd than if there is a physical representation of becoming an animal. At the end of *Rhinoceros*, the radio drama, Michael Bakewell's brilliant assembly of the actor's cries, the growling of rhinoceroses and the band playing followed by silence leaves the listener to reflect on a drama which makes a highly effective political point and is surely a play for all times.

This chapter has focused mainly on the work of Samuel Beckett and, to a lesser extent, Eugene Ionesco. There were other important examples of absurdist radio drama including plays written by Arthur Adamov: *En Fiacre*[86] (in English) was written for radio and produced by Barbara Bray and *Living Time*[87] also written for radio was produced by Michael Bakewell. Edward Albee's *The American Dream*[88] produced by John Ginson and Jean Genet's *The Maids*, one of John Tydeman's early productions, were also important adaptations from the stage by playwrights identified by Esslin as part of the 'theatre of the absurd'. Harold Pinter's work is also influenced by absurdism and is discussed in Chapter 8. Giles Cooper, whose work is examined in Chapter 6, had absurdist tendencies but, like all of the writers discussed in this chapter, cannot be encapsulated by that label. The themes of absurdity, of apparently meaningless behaviour conducted by characters unable to communicate with each other, combined with incomprehensible events, all pointing to a deeper philosophical critique and often delivered as humour can be found in all of the radio drama examples mentioned here. There is no doubt that absurdism had a major impact on radio drama and especially in the late 1950s and early 1960s and indeed continued to be important, for example, in the work of Tom Stoppard. The connection between absurdism and radio is not hard to explain, and indeed it could be argued that the absurd is radiogenic, particularly suited to the non-visual medium. The fantastic and irrational worlds created by absurdist writers, often existing only in the minds of the main character, do not always benefit from visual representation. The image of rhinoceroses dancing to a band, from the end of Ionesco's play, may be far more disturbing and arresting if it can only be imagined and not seen. The theatre of the absurd was one of the main achievements of post-war theatre but it also inspired some of the most important radio dramas, either written for radio or adaptations of stage plays.

Notes

1 This chapter is partly based on the research conducted for two earlier articles on Beckett, the avant garde and radio; Hugh Chignell, 'Out of the dark, Samuel Beckett and radio', *Peripeti* 22 (2015): 10–22; Hugh Chignell, 'British radio drama and the avant-garde in the 1950s', *Historical Journal of Film, Radio and Television* 37, no. 4 (2017): 649–64.

2 Esslin, *The Theatre of the Absurd*.
3 Anthony Cronin, *Samuel Beckett, the Last Modernist* (New York: Da Capro Press, 1999), 424.
4 Ibid., 23.
5 John Calder, *The Philosophy of Samuel Beckett* (London: Calder Publications, 2001), 86.
6 Esslin, *The Theatre of the Absurd*, 26.
7 Calder, *The Philosophy of Samuel Beckett*, 17.
8 Ibid.
9 Samuel Beckett, *Endgame* (London: Faber, 1964), 51.
10 Cronin, *Samuel Beckett*, 361.
11 Ibid., 373.
12 Ibid., 380.
13 Dirk van Hulle in David Addyman et al., *Samuel Beckett and BBC Radio* (New York: Palgrave Macmillan, 2017), 44.
14 In French as *En attendant Godot*.
15 Quoted in Cronin, *Samuel Beckett*, 421.
16 Assistant Head of Drama (Sound), Donald McWhinnie.
17 Cecilia Reeves, 17 March 1953. BBC WAC.
18 E. J. King Bull, 15 April 1953. BBC WAC.
19 Val Gielgud, 20 October 1953. BBC WAC.
20 Gielgud quoted in James Knowlson, *Beckett Remembering/Remembering Beckett* (London: Arcade Publishing, 2006).
21 Cronin, *Samuel Beckett*, 447.
22 Tynan, *The Observer*, 7 August 1955.
23 Ibid.
24 Harold Hobson, *Sunday Times*, 7 August 1955.
25 Ibid.
26 Helena Wood, 20 September 1955. BBC WAC.
27 Raymond Raikes, 29 September 1955. BBC WAC.
28 Barbara Bray, 3 November 1955. BBC WAC.
29 Val Gielgud, 23 November 1955. BBC WAC.
30 John Morris, 18 July 1956. BBC WAC.
31 According to Clas Zilliacus it took Beckett less than a month to write the play, from 30 August to 27 September 1956. Clas Zilliacus, *Beckett and Broadcasting: A Study of the Works of Samuel Beckett for and in Radio and Television* (Abo: Abo Akademi, 1976), 29.
32 Cronin, *Samuel Beckett*, 461.
33 Ibid., 462. The relationship between Beckett and Bray grew and deepened until it became 'a close personal one' (p. 462).
34 *All That Fall*, 13 January 1957. BBC Third Programme.
35 Samuel Beckett, *All That Fall* (London: Faber, 1957), 7. All of the quotations from *All That Fall* are taken from the published version.
36 The text is from Ps. 145.14.
37 *All That Fall*.
38 Val Gielgud, 14 January 1957. BBC WAC.
39 Roy Walker, 'Review of All That Fall', *Tribune*, 18 January 1957. Roy Walker also reviewed the play in his column, 'Critic on the hearth', *The Listener*, 24 January 1957.

40 McWhinnie, *The Art of Radio*, 133–51.
41 Everett C. Frost, 'Fundamental sounds: Recording Samuel Beckett's radio plays', *Theatre Journal* 43, no. 3 (October 1991): 361–76.
42 Zilliacus, *Beckett and Broadcasting*, 23.
43 Michael Billington, *The 101 Greatest Plays: From Antiquity to the Present* (London: Faber/Guardian, 2015).
44 Erik Tonning in Addyman et al., *Samuel Beckett and BBC Radio*, 69.
45 Ibid., 60.
46 Emily C. Bloom, *The Wireless Past: Anglo-Irish Writers and the BBC, 1931-1968* (Oxford: Oxford University Press, 2016).
47 Ibid., 131–2.
48 Erik Tonning, 61.
49 *Molloy*, 10 December 1957. BBC Third Programme.
50 *From an Abandoned Work*, 14 December 1957. BBC Third Programme.
51 *Malone Dies*, 18 June 1958. BBC Third Programme.
52 *The Unnamable*, 19 January 1959. BBC Third Programme.
53 Cronin, *Samuel Beckett*, 470.
54 Ibid., 471.
55 George Craig et al. (eds), *The Letters of Samuel Beckett, 1957-1965* (Cambridge: Cambridge University Press, 2014), 184.
56 *Embers*, 24 June 1959. BBC Third Programme.
57 Katherine Weiss, *Plays of Samuel Beckett* (Huntingdon: Methuen Drama, 2012), 75.
58 *Embers*.
59 Ian Rodger, 'Critic on the hearth', *The Listener*, 2 July 1959, 35.
60 McWhinnie, *The Art of Radio*.
61 Esslin, *The Theatre of the Absurd*.
62 Weiss, *Plays of Samuel Beckett*, 78.
63 Quoted in Weiss, *Plays of Samuel Beckett*, 78.
64 In addition there was a problem of access. It was not possible to obtain a copy of *Waiting for Godot* (27 April 1960) but *Endgame* (22 May 1962) was available.
65 Donald McWhinnie, 14 January 1958. BBC WAC.
66 Samuel Beckett, *Endgame* (London: Faber, 1958).
67 Ibid.
68 John Morris, hand written note on Donald McWhinnie, 14 January 1958. BBC WAC.
69 Director, Sound Broadcasting, Lindsay Wellington.
70 Assistant Director Sound Broadcasting to D.S.B., 19 March 1957. BBC WAC.
71 Beckett, *Endgame*, 11.
72 Ibid., 12.
73 Ibid., 18.
74 Ibid., 52.
75 Martin Shuttleworth, 'The critic on the hearth', *The Listener*, 31 May 1962.
76 Ibid.
77 Michael Worton, '*Waiting for Godot* and *Endgame*: Theatre as text', in *The Cambridge Companion to Beckett*, ed. John Pilling (Cambridge: Cambridge University Press, 1994), 67–87.
78 *La Photo du Colonel*, 2 October 1956. BBC Third Programme.
79 *The Picture*, 29 April 1957. BBC Third Programme.
80 *The Horns of the Dilemma*, 23 November 1957. BBC Third Programme.

81 *Rhinoceros*, 20 August 1959. BBC Third Programme.
82 *Victims of Duty*, 21 August 1961. BBC Third Programme.
83 Poulenc, 'L'Embarquement pour Cythère' for two pianos, 1951.
84 *Rhinoceros*, 20 August 1959. BBC Third Programme.
85 Ian Rodger, 'The critic on the hearth', *The Listener*, 27 August 1959.
86 *En Fiacre*, 10 December 1959. BBC Third Programme.
87 *Living Time*, 9 November 1961. BBC Third Programme.
88 *The American Dream*, 8 November 1962. BBC Third Programme.

Chapter 6

GILES COOPER

Giles Cooper was by far the most prolific of all BBC radio dramatists; he wrote twelve plays for the Third Programme, thirty-one for the Home Service and seven for the Light Programme, a total of fifty different dramas.[1] He deserves a special place in the history of radio drama not only because of his considerable output but also because he probably did more than anyone to develop the radio drama written specifically for radio and because his work seems to speak directly to the anxieties and experiences of the post-war listener.

Giles Cooper was born in Carrickmines, a suburb of Dublin, in 1918, just a few miles from the birthplace of Samuel Beckett twelve years earlier.[2] His father was in the colonial service, and he had a conventional upper-middle-class upbringing. He was educated at English boarding schools, an experience which informed one of his most well-known plays, *Unman, Wittering and Zigo*.[3] The family's expectations were that after school and a year at a French university he would go to Cambridge University as preparation for a career in the diplomatic service. Instead, however, in act of rebellion, he attended the Webber Douglas School of Singing and Drama[4] and left with an acting qualification in 1939 at the age of twenty-one. Giles Cooper's wartime experiences had a decisive influence on his writing; he spent the first two and a half years in England before embarking on a troop ship eventually arriving in Mumbai before continuing on to the Burmese jungle where he endured the appalling conditions of jungle warfare for over two years. A number of his most important plays concern military life and the tail end of the British Empire.

Giles Cooper's desire to write developed during the war and notebooks from that period show him experimenting with dialogue and passages of prose.[5] He completed a novel[6] after the war and wrote several short plays for the stage and then in 1949 completed two short radio plays both of which were subsequently broadcast: *Thieves Rush In*[7] and *Never Get Out*,[8] which was originally a stage play running for one week at The Gateway Theatre in June 1950. *Never Get Out* concerns two characters, Harvest and Catherine, who meet in an empty house. The Royal Air Force intends to use the deserted village where the house is as a bombing range but the man refuses to leave. There is a romantic and very touching scene between the two (something entirely missing from his other output), and Harvest delivers this hopeful speech:

> Harvest: Catherine – Catherine (pause). So many thoughts are going through my head like fishes in a stream that I don't know which to look at. I feel all excited and full of life so that my hands are shaking with it when I think what's happening: and part of me feels mad like a funeral going to the cemetery with the black hearses and the rain falling and everybody crying away. But that's only a bit of it. I think of what would happen if we lived here all the time.[9]

Then the bombs drop; the couple survive but she must return to her loveless marriage, 'He wanted a housekeeper who could share his bed with him and that's what he got.'[10] In this very early play there are many of the Cooper's themes and hallmarks: the play starts at London Paddington railway station, trains and railway stations were a common feature of his later plays, the reference to a failed marriage is another important theme, Cooper dramas frequently contain the unhappiest of relationships between men and women. The main male character in *Never Get Out*, Harvest, is also very much a Cooper creation; he dreams of a better life and talks of the future full of hope, but his dreams fail as Catherine returns to her unloving husband.

Following the broadcast of his first two radio dramas, Cooper wrote occasionally and was clearly considered a useful contributor of adaptations of stage plays, especially those filling the matinee slot on the Home Service. Then in 1952 he adapted Charles Dickens's *Oliver Twist* in twelve parts all produced by Charles Lefaux.[11] His adaptation must have been approved of by senior staff in Drama Department because it led to Cooper being given a more permanent position as he wrote in a notebook: 'April Fool's day [1953] was marked by my first appearance as an employee of the BBC. I was sent to a house in Hammersmith Grove which contained three tables, two typewriters and five telephones.'[12] His main task as a BBC writer seems to have been adapting populist drama in long-running serials. He adapted a six-part television serial, *Epitaph for a Spy*, and then Ngaio Marsh's *Artists in Crime*[13] and Dorothy L. Sayer's *The Nine Tailors*.[14] Although he quickly developed his own authorial voice and was clearly brimming with ideas about drama and what he wanted to write, he was forced early in his career to compromise his original creativity to focus on making money. His notebook for 1953 reveals constant money worries and the knowledge that he could adapt long-running detective fictions for radio and later for television must have come as a welcome relief even if it did eventually take him away from radio.

William Golding's first novel, *Lord of the Flies*, was published in 1954 and was broadcast in a two-hour adaptation[15] by Cooper on the Third Programme only a year later. It must have been a great moment for him to be chosen to adapt the book and work with the veteran radio producer, Archie Gordon, but there can be little doubt that Cooper was the ideal person for the job. The story of a group of boys stranded on a Pacific island and the barbarism which follows was ideally suited to his style and themes. The military context includes a non-specific war taking place, naval ships and mention of an atomic bomb. The boys are then organized into a party of hunters under the cruel and authoritarian Jack. One boy, Piggy, is mercilessly bullied and other boys tied up and tortured. The play reaches a climax of violence including a scene with a severed pig's head before the navy arrive and order is restored. The bizarre and disturbing quality of the drama was emphasized by the use of music and special effects to produce what is at times a genuinely frightening piece of radio. J. C. Trewin, writing in *The Listener*, was shocked by the concluding scenes which he found 'powerful and detestable'.[16] While acknowledging the craft of Archie Campbell and Giles Cooper and agreeing that the qualities of terror, evil and savagery were clearly expressed, he was just grateful when the two hours ended. Giles Cooper subsequently explored the theme of school boys as murderers in one of his most successful and well-known dramas, *Unman, Wittering and Zigo*.

Less than a year after *Lord of the Flies*, Giles Cooper collaborated with Donald McWhinnie in a production which confirmed Cooper's position as one of the leading proponents of the play written for radio, *Mathry Beacon*.[17] Cooper had sent a synopsis of the play to the script editor, Barbara Bray, in February 1955 with the words, 'Sorry it's got a military background again, but it's emphatically not a war play.'[18] The work was commissioned three weeks later by Bray who originally thought it should be broadcast on the Home Service. According to Kate Whitehead, Giles Cooper started writing the play in June 1950 and submitted a full script in October or November. Barbara Bray was very pleased with what she read and recommended it for the Third Programme (where it would get a very much smaller but more 'cultured' audience than on the Home Service), she wrote, 'It certainly requires a discriminating audience who can think in terms of texture and distinguish fantasy from fact.'[19]

Mathry Beacon[20] is a play for radio that lasts one hour thirty-five minutes, about a group of soldiers sent to guard a mysterious 'deflector', designed to repel incoming missiles, during the Second World War. Mathry Beacon is the name of the hill on which they are based somewhere in Wales, and at the beginning of the play we hear jazz trumpet and then the voices of the soldiers: two women, a Welshman, a 'West Indian cockney' who plays the trumpet, an 'educated man' and the man in charge, a retired sergeant major, Lieutenant Gann. The soldiers arrive and are addressed by Gann in a parody of military jargon and meaningless barked orders. The characters are all archetypes of army life: the sergeant major talking nonsense (Gann), one naïve woman from the countryside (Betsie) and one more streetwise from the town (Rita), the jazz-playing West Indian (Olim), a crafty Welshman ('Taff') and the 'educated man' (Blick) who is 'very nearly but not quite an intellectual'.[21]

Donald McWhinnie's production includes the sonification of the deflector which makes a variety of deep humming and other more mechanical sounds, a precursor to a Radiophonic Workshop treatment and three years before that was available.

The characters of the soldiers are revealed as the drama develops; in his synopsis of the play Cooper wrote about the Sergeant Major: 'He is delighted to leave the paper-work and the complications of mess life for the simple sort of command which he understands. He is haunted by the dreadful fear that one day he will find himself out of the army and wearing a commissionaire's uniform.'[22] We learn that all of the soldiers have their reasons for wanting to be in the isolated backwater of Mathry Beacon and in fact are perfectly happy with the status quo brought about by war. Olim is avoiding various paternity suits, Taff is keen to avoid fighting and everyone seems content with their lot. *Mathry Beacon* was an opportunity for Cooper to draw on his military experience and especially his ear for army banter. Gann tells Blick, who has been promoted, that the inventor of the Deflector hanged himself because in fact the machine doesn't work. Blick is not concerned even though their mission is pointless and wonders if it might be possible to grow vegetables. Gann also reveals that the war is over, but they conspire not to tell the others because as Gann says, 'Peace don't do me any good.' As time passes the soldiers become self-sufficient and rear chickens and pigs and the relationships between the men and the women develop. Winter comes and the Sergeant Major becomes ill; he is delirious and talks about his time in India before almost comically giving himself his last orders: 'Turn to the right. Face the wall. Expire.' Following Gann's death the years pass, couples have formed and babies are born at Mathry Beacon. The year is 1952 and Blick, the 'educated man', appears to be going mad as jealousies develop between Olim and Evans when Rita has a mixed race baby. Blick reveals the truth about the deflector and the end of the war and also the fact that everyone is owed a lot of money by the army. He is then chased out of the camp and runs through the fog and falls off a cliff to his death. This leaves the two couples who decide it's time to move: 'civilization here we come' and they leave Mathry Beacon accompanied by the sound of Olim's trumpet.

The BBC was clearly pleased with *Mathry Beacon* and, as Kate Whitehead points out, not only was it repeated several times[23] but it was also the Drama Department entry for the Prix Italia.[24] Frances Gray calls the play a 'masterpiece',[25] and *The Times* critic called it a 'near masterpiece';[26] there is no doubt that *Mathry Beacon* established Giles Cooper as a serious and respected playwright whose scripts were welcomed by all three radio networks and BBC television. Frances Gray praised the symbolic use of sound in the play with the sound of the deflector suggesting conformity and discipline, while the jazz trumpet represents a certain type of freedom.[27] Although there has been considerable praise for Cooper's first major radio play, it lacked the radiogenic quality of his later work; to put it differently, *Mathry Beacon* would work very well as a television drama and seems to represent a mid-point in Cooper's transition to becoming a radio specialist. The play is full of action and rounded characters interacting in a largely naturalistic, if rather caricatured, manner, but it lacks the dreamlike inner worlds of much of his later writing for radio. It was very much of its time, expressing not only mid-1950s' British society but also Giles Cooper's writing trajectory at a particular moment in his development. It was written at a time of economic growth which is expressed in the new-found affluence of the soldiers who can now draw on their back pay and are increasingly optimistic for 'civilization' and the future. For Cooper, *Mathry Beacon* also marked a transition to greater economic security, as Frances Gray describes in some detail, with each repeat of the play adding to his income, also augmented by overseas broadcasts.[28] The play also seemed to allow him to move away from military themes, purging himself finally of the army as a dramatic subject.

Giles Cooper's next major work written specifically for radio was *The Disagreeable Oyster*[29] produced by Donald McWhinnie and broadcast a year after *Mathry Beacon*. For several months at the end of 1956 and beginning of 1957, the proposed play 'was bandied about in Drama meetings'[30] before a decision was made about a broadcast. McWhinnie made an experimental recording of the drama in the spring of 1957 and sent it to Val Gielgud for his approval, which he got with the following words written to the controller, Third Programme: 'I heard the recording myself, and I should like to recommend it to you in the strongest possible terms. It seemed to me both amusing in itself and quite first rate as a piece of radio conception and production, and I think it would be a thousand pities if it failed to get its chance on the air.'[31] Gielgud's praise for the play is surprising given his dislike of avant-garde and absurdist drama, and it is tempting to find the reply from John Morris more believable: 'I myself have now heard the recording of *The Disagreeable Oyster* and it would be dishonest for me to pretend that I found any merit in it. ... I feel sure [Donald McWhinnie] will not be offended when I say that I think this is very much below his normally high standard.'[32] Morris reluctantly accepted the play which was then broadcast four months later.

It is not surprising that *The Disagreeable Oyster* divided opinion in the BBC; it is one of Cooper's most experimental plays with the main character divided in two and played by two different actors; Bundy Major is the Mervyn Bundy 'we see walking about the streets'[33] and Bundy Minor is his critical inner voice. It is one of Cooper's most 'absurd' plays and sexually explicit in places so no wonder it was not liked by the culturally conservative John Morris. It begins with Bundy Major describing his office at Craddock's Calculators where he has a job as Head of Costing. His manager, Mr Gunn, tells him there is a crisis which requires Bundy to go immediately to a factory near Leicester; meanwhile the voice of Bundy Minor provides a child-like running commentary: 'Mr Gunn has ginger hair growing out of his ears.' The actor, Hamilton Dyce, speaks with an unusually high-pitched and nervous voice in an attempt to vocalize the downtrodden clerk sent on a mission which terrifies him. Bundy phones home to tell his wife he has to go away:

> Bundy: I haven't slept away from home for twenty-two years but I couldn't tell him that. (*Fade in ringing tone of telephone*)
> Bundy Minor: That's my telephone on the rickety table in my hall. I can hear the sunlight sending a long shaft down from the landing window, I can hear the carpet breathing dust.
> Alice:[34] (*Distort*) Hullo, who's that? My husband's out.
> Bundy: Alice, it's me, Mer.
> Alice: Is something wrong?[35]

The surreal quality of Bundy Minor's comments ('I can hear the carpet breathing') reflects a much more experimental approach by Giles Cooper; the comparative realism of *Mathry Beacon* was left behind and replaced by drama featuring characters and situations that are more bizarre. The fantasy of the drama is emphasized by the rapid changes of scene, the use of sound effects and Bundy Minor's voice; so Alice complains about Bundy's departure and asks who will bring in the coal and buy the bread, and immediately we hear the train's whistle, the sound of the train, a female station announcer and Bundy Minor saying over and over again, 'I've got thirty-four pounds. Thirty-four pounds.' When Bundy arrives at his hotel remarking that 'the world is my oyster', McWhinnie uses the sort of stylized sound effects which were so striking in Beckett's *All That Fall* broadcast six months earlier, so when Bundy goes into a pub the sound of people talking loudly is achieved by someone saying 'jubber, jubber' very quickly then 'swoon' followed by silence. At the bar Bundy meets Peregrine, a man horrified by Stoddeshunt and its cultural philistinism. Bundy eventually flees from Peregrine and goes to a cinema only to realize he has seen the film before; he leaves the cinema and there is a fast-paced exchange between him and Bundy Minor about women and sex. Bundy Major thinks he is alone, but Bundy Minor sees an opportunity, a prostitute: 'Over by the statue in the centre of the square, idling with a handbag, to and fro from the parking sign to the litter basket, let's try her.'[36] This is the beginning of a series of increasingly bizarre adventures with varying degrees of absurdity. Bundy encounters a group of bawdy women with strong northern accents, and he argues with them so they strip him and leave him naked and alone. A café owner takes him to a local nudist colony where he has to fill in a long form; he meets other characters he recognizes, and they play bridge, another opportunity for Cooper to emphasize the absurdity of the drama:

> Bundy: Six no-trumps. (*Pause*)
> Rigg: Seven pineapples.
> Bundy Minor: (*Makes a noise which can only be described as 'Glug'*)
> Receptionist: Eight small owls.

Bundy Minor: No!
Miss Pringle: Double them. (*Pause*)
Rigg: Bundy
Bundy: Twenty-five tortoises.[37]

Other adventures follow in which Bundy attempts to steal some clothes and then encounters a group of bell ringers from whom he at last manages to buy clothes. Finally he goes to a baker's shop and manages to get the bread Alice asked for. He tells the baker the story of his night before running to the train: '*Running feet. Church bells up, jangling and clashing. Some are tinny little tinklers, some massive great Bourdons. They come to a peak and then fade.*'[38]

In her discussion of the play,[39] Frances Gray places it in the broader context of the avant garde: 'It is plain from the shifting universe of *The Disagreeable Oyster* that Cooper has something in common with the Absurdists, and the richness of his radio development in the middle fifties coincides with the impact of Beckett and Ionesco in the British theatre.'[40] Central to Cooper's writing, according to Gray, is someone like Bundy: 'His characters stand on the edge of chaos but surrounded with the concrete realities that brought them there; their desperation is spiritual but grounded in a recognizable world.'[41] Bundy is certainly on the edge of chaos and Cooper allows us to inhabit the nightmare of his trip to Stoddeshunt where his adventures concern his impotence in the face of events in a highly sexualized universe; the apparently predatory Peregrine, the prostitute, the women who strip him, the nudist colony and his prolonged nakedness. Perhaps even more striking about *The Disagreeable Oyster* are the structure and production of the play which add to the play's success and confirm this as a powerful and disturbing journey into mid-1950s' masculine anxieties. By creating two Bundies, Major and Minor, Giles Cooper reveals the outward, conventional 'man in the street' hurrying home to his wife with a loaf of bread and Bundy Minor, the hidden Bundy who expresses his innermost desires, as in this exchange before he meets the prostitute:

Bundy: (*Lingering on the word*) Women—
Bundy Minor: Yes, women. Passionate Bundy, crammed to the gorge with primeval urges. I'm a gorilla, I beat my breast in the jungle, I snort and paw the ground.[42]

The Disagreeable Oyster may be Giles Cooper's most important contribution to the development of radio drama. This was the moment when he moved on decisively from more conventional and realist scripts to the avant-garde world of absurdist drama. The play is highly innovative and is not afraid to examine sexual themes and deep masculine neuroses. To modern ears, the characters might appear too archetypal (Bundy as the cowering and wimpish clerk; Alice his helpless, housebound wife; Olive the saucy, cockney prostitute – 'Hullo dear. Do you want to be a naughty boy?'), but in a rapidly moving fifty-five minute drama they provide the characters needed to make sense of Bundy's world. Not only is the script an important contribution to the genre but the production shows off Donald McWhinnie at his adventurous best, making the most of the artistic licence granted to him by the success of *All That Fall* earlier in the year.

The year 1958 marked the summit of Giles Cooper's radio drama career with three plays for radio broadcast, all produced by Donald McWhinnie. *Without the Grail*[43] begins with a dysfunctional couple, Hazel and a very cold, colonial type called Innes who is contemplating getting married for the good of his career, but not to Hazel whom he casually discards in the first few minutes of the play. The ninety-minute drama is an exploration of colonial themes and characters and features Innes's mission to find a man called Felix Barrington in a remote part of India. He eventually arrives to find Felix, his family and servants living in a colonial time warp where people dress for dinner and men pass the port (or coloured water as there is no port left) after dinner. Felix is a terrible snob and apologizes to Innes for mistaking him for a gentleman; he informs him he will take his meals in his room and until he leaves:

Innes: (*Laughs*)
Felix: Is there a joke?
Innes: there is, and I'm enjoying it very much. You're sacked.
Felix: What?
Innes: Dismissed from the company's service. You will leave here within three days; the Company will pay your fare back to place of residence as per contract. Here's my letter of authority.[44]

It turns out that Felix is the negligent manager of a tea plantation which has failed to make any money. But Felix has no intention of leaving and it turns out that Innes is trapped; he cannot escape from the remote plantation surrounded by the blood-thirsty Nagas who would cut off his head. Felix is a colonial fantasist waiting for India to be conquered again: '(India) is nothing; a hundred thousand villages, a vacuum of stupidity and greed and ox-eyed gentleness waiting for a conqueror. Perhaps from the north, perhaps from the east, perhaps from within, but a conqueror will come, and unless men like me can make our strongholds, everything will go.'[45] Innes befriends Leila, Felix's daughter, who tries to teach him mahjong and reveals that she has friends who are Chinese communists. Siri is a Naga who was adopted by Felix but clearly has mixed loyalties and tells Innes about his father, a 'head-hunter'. Innes plays croquet with Felix's son, Derek who has a highly unrealistic view of England, a place he has never visited. Like his father, Derek is a colonial fantasist who dreams of England and decides the time has come to leave: 'I'm on my way. I shall join White's club and own a Bentley and have a little place in Kent and a bachelor apartment in Half Moon Street.'[46] Derek's plans however come to nothing, and he is found later with his throat slit, as it turns out his father, Felix, was the murderer. The Nagas rebel, Felix's head is cut off, Innes and Leila talk unconvincingly of love and marriage and the play ends.

Roy Walker's review of *Without the Grail* captures some of the experience of hearing it for the first time in 1958: 'A remote tropical setting, a veneer of civilized ways crazily cracking to emit violence and madness, and the implied indictment of our own society.'[47] He describes Felix Barrington's children as all 'personifications of trends in a decaying imperialism'[48] and no doubt Giles Cooper will have known people like Derek, who hankers after a non-existent England, Siri, who wants to return to his ancestral ways, and Leila, who thinks communism is the solution. Walker is critical of Cooper's tendency to create rather archetypal characters which he describes as 'stylised type-masks' although he concludes his review by writing that the Home Service's 'Play for Radio' series in which *Without the Grail* was placed 'has found at least one script that justifies the hopes the Drama Department cherishes of original writing for the medium'.[49] The most positive discussion of the play is, perhaps unsurprisingly, provided by the producer Donald McWhinnie who praises Cooper for the way he uses minimal dialogue to evoke a powerful sense of place. McWhinnie quotes from the play at the point where Innes is trying to make his way to Felix Barrington's plantation:

(*Fade in car running: it slows and stops.*)
Innes: What's the matter?
Indian Driver: Stop to cool engine.
Innes: Okay, you're the driver. (*Pause*). So this is the jungle.
Driver: Yes, all jungle here.
Innes: H'm—very dusty looking.
Driver: The road is making it dusty. Inside is green (*Pause*.)[50]

In this brief exchange, Cooper says lot with a few words, and this quality of his writing is demonstrated again when Innes finds Felix's decapitated head and says simply, 'No head—no head'.[51] Everything, according to McWhinnie, is left to the creative imagination of the listener aided by the use of pauses in the script.

Without the Grail is a far more conventional drama than *The Disagreeable Oyster*, and the Cooper fan listening to both of these plays with only a few months between them must have wondered what direction the playwright was taking. The absurdism and experimental nature of the earlier play was replaced by something much closer to more typical Home Service dramas with straightforward, linear plotting and plenty of post-colonial heat and action. What makes the later play of particular interest is Cooper's developing mastery of radio drama and, as McWhinnie explains, the use of minimal dialogue to stimulate the imagination of the listener. The play is also striking as either an anti-colonialist drama or at least a drama that suggests the different ways the end of empire damaged and destroyed the British who had so much invested in it. Whether Cooper included himself in that category is hard to say.

The BBC's new Radiophonic Workshop was established on 1 April 1958, and it meant that Donald McWhinnie, like Barbara Bray a particular enthusiast for experimental sound, had 'access to a unit dedicated to the creation of radiophonic sound'.[52] Following the critical success of *The Disagreeable Oyster*, McWhinnie was authorized to commission Giles Cooper to write another play for the Third Programme which could benefit from the Radiophonic Workshop. According to Kate Whitehead, Cooper's script, which depicts a man in his bath for the entire play, met with serious misgivings in the Third Programme Committee.[53] However, John Morris, as controller, maintained his pragmatic approach to work; he would have no doubt detested and 'said that Third Programme were not enthusiastic about this script, but as it had been commissioned he agreed that it might be placed'.[54] The play, which is unusually short (forty-five minutes), was broadcast at 5.30 pm on a Sunday. Hamilton Dyce, who played Bundy in *The Disagreeable Oyster*, is once again the male lead and has the task of performing another confused and anxious man.

At the beginning of *Under the Loofah Tree* there is the sound of bath water and a man's voice,[55] 'Toe—ow, no. Ooh. (*One tap runs briefly*) Leg—other leg. All right so far, warm but not agony.'[56] The man is Edward Thwaite, and his wife, Muriel, shouts through the bathroom door: 'Ted. Don't take all the hot' because she has the washing up to do. Edward is one of Cooper's most downtrodden characters, oppressed, as he believes, by his wife and so taking refuge in the one place he is left alone, or so he thought, the bathroom. The play contains two simple elements, Edward's fantasies based on his life and the constant interruptions as different people, even an encyclopedia salesman, try to speak to him through the bathroom door. The play features a variety of radiophonic sound effects throughout including voice distortion and other more creative experiments with sound. Edward's fantasies include being on a television programme, 'This is a man'.[57] The American 'compere' announces that the guest is Edward Thwaite who says, 'I didn't know it was going to be me – after all who am I?'[58] The compere calls the first guest to talk about Edward, his mother. Her memories of the young Edward are cruelly deprecating; the agony of his birth, how he 'didn't look right', was constipated and spotty and couldn't get a 'trade'. This is followed by his failure as a son when she was old and ill and then these words and a moment of pathos: 'And then I died one night and Edward said it was all for the best. (*She sniffs*) But I didn't want to die. It wasn't best for me, I wanted to be there at seven-thirty when the tea came round.'[59] Although the tone of the play is humorous and surreal, there are also moments of anguish and truth. A travelling salesman visits the house and tries to persuade Edward to buy the Shumbles Encyclopedia: 'This is really your last chance of obtaining the position, the money, the power to which knowledge is the key. Shumbles, sir, will open doors to you.'[60] We return to the television programme, and the next guest to talk about Edward is his old headmaster who is full of praise for Edward's leadership quality; he is of course thinking of a different Thwaite. He is then visited by his father and a policeman, Judkin, delivering a document:

> Edward: Push it under the door.
> Judkin: No, sir. I'm afraid it has to be delivered into your hand.
> Voice: (*Disembodied, starting in the distance and spreading he words out so that they end on a shout*) Something to do with the Rates![61]

From here the play becomes increasingly surreal with bizarre situations and sounds; Muriel is thrown out of the window by the mysterious 'brokers', there is a roll of thunder, the howl of the wind and a duck quacks. Edward cannot stand the stresses and demands on him, 'Roll on another bloody war. D'you hear me in the Kremlin? Are you there? Roll on!'[62] The next guest for 'This is a man' is Edward's sergeant from his time as a soldier. The sergeant (who is very reminiscent of the sergeant in *Mathry Beacon*) is full of praise for Edward and especially his great bravery at the battle of Loofah corner. It transpires that Edward had been sent to get reinforcements in a battle with Japanese soldiers but had failed, and all of his comrades, including the sergeant, had perished. Edward reflects on his own failure and how he might die: eaten by a lion, hanged, run over by a train, murdered and asks, 'How can I go on living?' He contemplates drowning himself in the bath and recalls all of the unpleasant and cruel things people have said about him. He then emerges from the bath, 'If I'd stayed under much longer I would have drowned.' The dreams are over, the mysterious visitors have left and Edward returns to the world of normality, and we hear the final sound of the water gurgling down the plughole.

Under the Loofah Tree is clearly the successor to *The Disagreeable Oyster*; experimental, absurdist drama, but with the benefit of the aural creativity of the Radiophonic Workshop. In both plays we encounter the inner world of the central character, a man oppressed and ridiculed by women (principally) but by others as well. In *Under the Loofah Tree*, Edward Thwaite's suicidal fantasies in the bath depict him as a victim of his wife, mother, father, Headmaster, a policeman, salesman and his wartime sergeant. In his discussion of the play, the producer, Donald McWhinnie praises it as 'an impeccable and apparently effortless example of the best kind of "free" radio writing'[63] by which he means unconstrained by the conventions of character and plot, drama in which fantasies and dreams are dominant. McWhinnie describes what he calls the 'realistic core of the play', the man in the bath and the wife complaining through the bathroom door. This everyday quality at the start of the play means that 'audience identification with the main character can seldom have been more quickly achieved'.[64] However, this naturalism is soon punctuated, with the help of stylized sound effects, as we enter Edward's inner world of paranoid and suicidal fantasy. McWhinnie finishes his (five page) discussion of the play with this evaluation:

> Using every shorthand device of imaginative radio, Cooper paints vividly, with a blend of farce and bitter irony, a man's life, his aspirations, hope, frustrations, failures; the 'little man's' triumphant assertion of his own individuality – 'There's always ME' – as he rises from his attempted suicide by drowning, is the com-tragic climax of forty-five minutes of pungent human observation.[65]

Just three months after the August broadcast of *Under the Loofah Tree*, a completely different example of Giles Cooper's writing was heard on the Third Programme, the highly successful story of a schoolmaster[66] terrorized by his pupils, *Unman, Wittering and Zigo*.[67] The play is the story of John Ebony who arrives at Chantrey, a conventional, old English boarding school where he attempts to teach form Lower 5b following the sudden death of Pelham, Ebony's predecessor. Ebony is accompanied by his highly critical young wife, Nadia, who is not only appalled by the apartment by the noisy railway line but also by her husband's choice of career. Cooper's script captures the word play between the boys (or 'men' as they insist on being called) and their new, hesitant teacher, and as result this is a very naturalistic record of the boarding school world. When Ebony tries to discipline his form the truth about Pelham is revealed:

> Ebony: Stop! (*Silence*) Very well. You have had your warning. The form will stay in this afternoon from half-past two until I am satisfied with your behaviour.
> Cloistermouth: It's not a good idea, sir.
> Ebony: No, Cloistermouth? Tell me why not?
> Cloistermouth: Well sir, Mr Pelham did it once.
> Cuthbun: The week before last, sir.
> Cloistermouth: And that was why we killed him. (*Dead silence*).[68]

In the recording of Donald McWhinnie's production of the play, the silence after Cloistermouth's shocking revelation lasts a full ten seconds. Ebony soon realizes that he is trapped by the boys, and his attempts to tell the Headmaster met with complete disbelief. He finds some comfort telling everything to the wonderfully cynical old art teacher Cary, and every evening is spent drinking in the Green Man. The boys propose a deal with Ebony whereby they will be compliant in the classroom and in return Ebony will place bets for them at the local betting shop. As his job becomes a nightmare of blackmail and barely concealed violence, Ebony's relationship with Nadia is frosty in the extreme. They are invited to dinner at the Headmaster's house, and she enjoys shocking her hosts by saying she was a waitress in a coffee bar and that was where she met her husband. After dinner they have a row:

> Ebony: You know I've always wanted to teach. You knew when you married me.
> Nadia: There was a hell of a lot I didn't know when I married you.
> Ebony: For instance?
> Nadia: That those who can do, do, and those who can't teach. Not only in the classroom either ….[69]

The suggestion of Ebony's sexual inadequacy (a typical Cooper touch) adds to the sense of him as yet another male beset with failure and especially in relation to women. Ebony decides to talk to some of the boys individually to ascertain who their ringleader is. He corners a boy called Terhew, and in the interrogation they struggle, and Terhew threatens Nadia; when Ebony tells Cary in the pub that the boys have threatened his wife, he adds, 'I think he meant it too. But I don't care.'[70] He adds that he would be indifferent if they pushed her over the cliff, as they did with Pelham. The Headmaster then informs him that his job will end that term as the school prefers to employ 'old boys'. In the classroom there is the usual chaos and Ebony, who has lost interest, lets the boys take over completely. In ensuing the chaos they bully Wittering and we hear the pathetic sound of his cries as they assault him. Later in the pub, Ebony tells Cary of what happened:

> Ebony: And I sat there and watched them, and the boy's comb fell out of his pocket, and his pen and all his letters from home and they kicked them round the room.[71]

Meanwhile two of the boys go to see Nadia. She is very friendly and offers them cigarettes and beer and calls them by their first names, unaware of their true intention. The boys seem to lose heart and leave in a hurry and as they do one of them drops a knife and Nadia remarks, 'Oh, John, what a dangerous looking knife to keep up your sleeve' then adding, 'It looks terribly sharp. You want to be careful.'[72]

The play ends when a policeman arrives at the school, and Ebony is called to see the Headmaster. Wittering has committed suicide and thrown himself off the cliff where his former teacher had died. He has left a letter to his parents confessing that the murder of Pelham was his idea, designed to make the other boys like him, a plan which had completely failed. In his final conversation with Cary, Ebony wonders what made the boys behave in the way they did as murderers and bullies. Cary replies that it was their schoolmaster, as the figure of authority, which had bound them together into a murderous unit, and Ebony cries out 'for god's sake, Cary, no!' when she realizes that he has become an authority figure too.

Unman, Wittering and Zigo is one of Giles Cooper's most conventional plays; it has the qualities of convincing characters, with some character development, and a strong narrative structure while being set in a very well-observed boys boarding school complete with memorial cloisters. Perhaps because this was such a conventional play, one of Giles Cooper's most accessible works, it became a success in other media. There was a television version broadcast on BBC 2 in 1965, and it was then performed on the stage before the film version of 1971 starring David Hemmings.

Clearly, *Unman, Wittering and Zigo* was influenced by Golding's *Lord of the Flies*, adapted by Cooper just three years earlier. Golding's novel is also about the brutality and violence of uncontrolled adolescent boys and the cruel bullying of one individual; in *Lord of the Flies*, Piggy is murdered, and in Cooper's play, the target of merciless bullying Wittering commits suicide. The play contains some of Giles Cooper's most persistent themes; the inadequate and frustrated man surrounded by those who would do him harm and unable to do the one thing he wants to do, like Bundy searching for some clothes in *The Disagreeable Oyster* or Edward wanting some peace and quiet in his bath, in *Under the Loofah Tree*, Ebony has a modest wish, to be a successful school teacher, but everything conspires against it. Another Cooper theme is the failure of marriage or indeed any romantic relationship. Nadia Ebony has utter contempt for John's ambition, or lack of it, and also for their apartment, the town and her dreary life; she is also dissatisfied with her husband. In the play, Nadia's solution to her various frustrations is to get a job as an usherette in the cinema where she will have a uniform and the manager is a 'lambie'. Ebony himself is so completely alienated from Nadia that he would be 'indifferent' to her death.

Despite the obvious connections between Golding's novel and Cooper's play, *Unman, Wittering and Zigo* is arguably the more politically radical. At the end of *Lord of the Flies*, salvation comes in the form of the naval officer who rescues the remaining sobbing boys with reassuring words, and so authority returns in place of chaos. At the end of *Unman, Wittering and Zigo*, however, John Ebony is horrified by the realization that it is authority itself which turned the boys into murderers. For Cooper there is no solution to this, the final words spoken are Cary's desperate attempts to get a final drink. This was the last of seven of Cooper's plays written for radio which were produced by Donald McWhinnie, and although the producers who took on Cooper's writing after that were all successful in their way, none of his later radio dramas captured the assurance and aural brilliance which McWhinnie provided.

Following the comparative realism of *Unman, Wittering and Zigo*, the next Cooper play on the Third Programme was the far more experimental and absurdist, the forty-five minute *Before the Monday*.[73] The beginning of the script is indicative of the play as a whole:

(*The voices are quiet, separate, secret*)
Jane: Saturday before—
Desmond: August.
Jane: Before the Monday. Hot.
Desmond: Quiet.
Jane: Holiday, holiday, hollidee.
Desmond: All gone away.
Jane: Gone away.
Desmond: Left it all to me.[74]

The play basically has two characters, Jane and Desmond, with a third, Alfred, making a brief appearance. At the start of the play, Jane delivers some flowers to Desmond's apartment. He is a completely aimless young man thinking of his own death while she is far more sensible and practical. While he reflects on his own mortality, she comments that he could do with a shave and a haircut. We learn that Desmond's wife has gone to Cromer with the two children, and the practical Jane performs various tasks for Desmond; she shaves him and shops for food and cigarettes. A character called Alfred, a 'one-man-band', appears, and they invite him into the apartment. Alfred is strongly reminiscent of a Harold Pinter character, the strange outsider who arrives to disrupt whatever harmony exists. Eventually, Desmond drives Arthur out of the flat. The play ends with Desmond apparently more energetic and with plans to go to church while Jane is left behind to her thoughts.

Before the Monday was praised by the anonymous reviewer in *The Times* who marvelled at its radiogenic quality and the wit, fun and compassion of the play. The reviewer described it as a duet in which the fiercely intelligent man, ridden with existential angst, is saved by the 'simple, earthy and limited' Jane.[75] Although there is something undeniably experimental and unusual about Cooper's script, it also suffers from his tendency to write archetypal characters. Jane's apparent stupidity and inability to comprehend the world about her, combined with her maternal qualities, no doubt reflected not only the misogyny of the time but also the less attractive side of Cooper's character.

October 1959 was a busy time for Cooper as it marked the beginning of his new job for BBC television dramatizing Georges Simenon's *Maigret* stories. This was a major undertaking; between December 1959 and December 1963 he adapted twenty stories, each lasting fifty minutes and was script editor for a number of others. This new commitment clearly had an impact on his radio writing; although he continued to write for radio, this was no longer the central part of his professional work. However, the radio drama *Pig in the Middle*[76] was produced by the experienced H. B. Fortuin and subsequently transferred to television. The play features a family on the beach including a little boy Angus and an old Uncle Arthur who appears to be still living in the First World War. An interesting aspect of the play is Cooper's return to war themes, Uncle Arthur talks it all the time and even Angus's father reminisces about the Second World War. At the end of the play, Uncle Arthur and Angus find some landmines on the beach and then return to the house where the family is staying and lay the mines around the building. In a rather confusing ending the older man dies.

The following year, deep into his commitment to the Maigret series, Giles Cooper's major post-colonial play *The Return of General Forefinger*[77] was broadcast on the Third Programme produced by Michael Bakewell who had by that time replaced Donald McWhinnie as the main producer of avant-garde drama. The play features a very strange and amusing old Irish woman, Augusta, played by Mary O'Farrell (who played the part of Mrs Rooney in Beckett's *All That Fall*). This is a distinctly absurdist drama in which Aunt Augusta pays a man called Quentin to go in search of statues of her distinguished colonial husband, mounted on horseback, from different parts of the British empire. Augusta is visited by her Australian nephew George who thinks his aunt is wasting her money sending Quentin around the world. Later in the play, George accompanies Quentin to London and discovers that he is in fact a sculptor, making George wonder if Quentin is in fact making the statues he brings Augusta. Quentin then admits that he has indeed made the statues and that they are fakes so George says he will tell the police. The plot is complicated, and there are a number of amusing, archetypal characters: an artist's model who only speaks to repeat exactly the words of the artist and a policeman who was once an army sergeant and can only speak in lists. Various adventures follow in which George and Quentin go to India to find a statue, and Quentin is crushed beneath it as a result of George's incompetence.

The play is clearly an opportunity for Cooper to indulge his considerable ability as a comic writer and revisit his understandable fascination with India and the empire. The play was reviewed enthusiastically in *The Times* where the critic noted in particular, 'the art of the cartoonist applied with wit and subtlety to the writing of dialogue'.[78] Frances Gray has also commented on the cartoon quality of the play and made comparisons to the iconic BBC radio comedy *The Goon Show*. She provides an interesting analysis of the play comparing the surreal comedy of the Goons, a comic universe where nothing really matters, with *The Return of General Forefinger*, a far darker, critical representation of empire. As in some of his other plays, Cooper combines bizarre or absurd events with a very well-observed naturalism. He knew a lot about the British Empire and India and also of human suffering so, for example, when Quentin dies because a statue falls on him,

> we hear him suffering in a monologue intercut with scenes of caste-ridden Indians shifting the statue and recalling the good old days of the juggernaut; he speaks, as he dies of thirst, in naturalistic tones which force us to see the whole farcical action in the cold light of reality, to appreciate the full implications of George's Empire-building ambitions.[79]

Gray adds that the eccentric Aunt Augusta is an essentially harmless relic of colonial days, tending the symbols of a former but extinct glory, whereas George is a dangerous young man, corrupted by the myth of empire and a warning of the lethal potential of imperialist fantasies.

As the 1960s progressed, Giles Cooper wrote more for television. Following the success of *Maigret* his television output included an adaptation of *Madame Bovary*, three one-off plays for BBC 2, two four-part adaptations of novels by Earnest Hemingway, and less than a year from his death in 1968, he co-wrote a ten-part adaptation of Victor Hugo's *Les Miserables*. Despite this focus on television, Cooper managed to produce some radio drama of which one of the most important was *All the Way Home*[80] produced by Charles Lefaux. The fifty-minute play is another 'two hander' which, like *Before the Monday* features a man and a woman and their relationship and is one of Cooper's most important and powerful radio dramas with its relentless pursuit of frustration. It starts with a very familiar Cooper sound effect, a train's whistle and a stylized station announcer's voice. It is clear that Ellis, the man, and Una, the woman, are having an affair and on their way to a hotel. The play is the story of how, at every turn, they are frustrated in their attempts to be intimate together. The couple both work for the same company and are anxious not to be spotted by anyone who would recognize them so they have to get away from their home town. They catch a train to another town, but when they get off it they realize they are at the wrong station, in the middle of nowhere and there are no taxis. They are lost but find a house and knock on the door to ask for a room. The strange owner offers them 'my upstairs front' where they find a stuffed dog, 'that was our doggie, run over by a motor cycle'.[81] Ellis and Una decide not to stay and they leave. They then meet a policeman and ask him for a lift. He asks if Una is Ellis's wife and also asks them for a means of identity, and he tells them to open their suitcases before driving off and leaving them stranded again. Una says she thinks Ellis was weak in his dealings with the policeman and not a real man, so they argue. The unfortunate couple have various other encounters during the night, each one adding to their frustration and a sense of the modern world conspiring against them: insolent teenagers at the bus stop and a vending machine which spurts out soup. At last, as dawn arrives they find the town, but as they approach it they realize all they have done is to walk all the way back home; Una cries out in frustration.

All the Way Home was not only one of Giles Cooper's last radio plays but also one of his darkest. The mood of unbearable frustration builds throughout the play coming to a climax with the final, terrible realization that they were back where they started. Once again the theme of a man frustrated by his inability to get what he wants is central to the drama: this time together with his frustrated female friend who, almost inevitably for a Cooper play, turns against him. The play is an interesting snapshot of attitudes to sex in the early 1960s. Although the 'swinging sixties' is associated with more liberal attitudes, these existed alongside very traditional ideas which are voiced in the play by the first man with a room, the policeman and even the teenagers at the bus stop.

Giles Cooper's contribution to radio drama is substantial, and he probably did more than any other playwright to establish drama written specifically for radio. Before Cooper became a regular contributor of radio dramas in the mid-1950s, most plays heard on radio were adaptations of stage plays or novels. In the week of the first broadcast of *Mathry Beacon* in June 1956, for example, the Third Programme had a Proust 'reconstruction', an adaptation of a story by L. P. Hartley and of a novel by David Lindsay and an adaptation of a stage play by Ibsen. The Home Service in the same week had two drama adaptations, one of *The Count of Monte Cristo* and the other of a play by George Farquhar. Under Val Gielgud's direction and despite the arrival of new producers like McWhinnie and Bray, BBC Drama's output was heavily based on work written for another medium. With *Mathry Beacon* and then with a series of other highly successful plays written for radio, Cooper helped establish drama written for radio. He achieved this by writing plays which worked better on radio than anywhere else, that were 'radiogenic'. Of course it was the case that other writers, including Samuel Beckett, Louis MacNeice and Harold Pinter, also wrote successful radiogenic drama, but it was the sheer volume and accessibility of Cooper's output that made him so influential.

Giles Cooper's writing for radio included an ability to write very spare dialogue in which complex emotions are expressed with few words. In addition, he was a playwright who clearly thought in terms of sound. So the first page of the script for *All the Way Home* has these sound directions:

> *Fade in a train drawing up at a station. A voice is heard saying something over a public address system. Whatever it is seems to consist entirely of vowels. A carriage door slams, further away another door slams. A whistle blows and the train moves out of the station and fades into the distance. Two pairs of footsteps, a woman's and a man's on the platform approaching. They stop.*[82]

These detailed directions suggest a keen awareness of sound and the way sounds can be used to convey meaning. The distorted speech of the station announcer here suggests the non-realist character of the play; the footsteps of a man and a woman when the train has left suggest a couple, alone. Cooper's interest in the use of sound and willingness to experiment with it made him an ideal collaborator for Donald McWhinnie who was the most creative radio drama producer at the time. Cooper's most sonically creative dramas are usually the ones which feature the inner world of the main character, especially *The Disagreeable Oyster* and *Under the Loofah Tree*, the latter benefitting from the effects created by the new Radiophonic Workshop.

During Cooper's career as an active radio playwright, there were two main innovations in dramatic writing, absurdism and realism. Cooper's plays do not fit easily into either category, although his writing often has explicit absurdist qualities (the soldiers who carry on soldiering when the war is over in *Mathry Beacon*, the widow who collects sculptures of her husband from around the empire in *The Return of General Forefinger*). Cooper was clearly no realist in the mould of John Osborne or even Harold Pinter, but he did adopt a naturalism in his plays, a very well-observed record of speech in particular which resulted in dramas containing unnervingly believable elements; the school in *Unman, Wittering and Zigo* and even the plantation settlement in *Without the Grail* benefitted from Cooper's own experiences. *Pig in the Middle* begins as a naturalistic play about a family on holiday with all of the typical trappings: the bad weather, the lack of privacy and the annoying old relative before descending into a nightmare of death and planted explosives.[83] The naturalistic world is undermined by the bizarre and absurd events that follow. This disturbing transition into nightmarish confusion is often structured as a series of encounters; *The Disagreeable Oyster*, *Under the Loofah Tree* and *All the Way Home* are all episodic as the main character meets increasingly strange and always obstructive people.

The various descriptions of Cooper's radio dramas in this chapter have included an attempt to identify his main themes: the end of empire, failed marriages, suicide, the frustrated man, among others. Some of these were important aspects of 1950s' culture as Britain continued to be influenced by military life and values, as the empire declined and fell and as men, perhaps more than women, found themselves lost without the structure of military life, no longer able to benefit from the colonies and facing an increasingly consumerist modern world which was alien to them. There are clear similarities here between the work of Giles Cooper and Terence Rattigan. Rattigan was born in 1911, seven years before Cooper, and they both came from Anglo-Irish diplomatic or colonial backgrounds and went to English boys boarding schools. Both fought in the war and included war themes in their plays. Rattigan was a successful writer before the war and a very popular theatre dramatist working for H. M. Tennent, so he inhabited a far more glamorous and affluent world than Cooper, still 'worried to death about money'[84] in 1953. Michael Billington describes Rattigan as 'a traditionalist drawn to classical structures and reticent understatement'.[85] Rattigan wrote beautifully crafted and understated stage plays, while Cooper was drawn to experiment and the absurd. Despite their very different writing, Cooper and Rattigan explored similar themes. In Rattigan's *The Deep Blue Sea*, Freddie is a former RAF pilot who has never been happy since he left the air force; Cooper has a number of similar characters and especially Gann in *Mathry Beacon*, the sergeant who is terrified that the war will end. *The Deep Blue Sea* is about the inequality of love between a man and a woman, and there are similarities here with Cooper whose depiction of marriage and relationships is almost always unbalanced and negative. Cooper's women are often hectoring, unsympathetic characters, often dissatisfied, like Hester in *The Deep Blue Sea* and Nadia in *Unman, Wittering and Zigo*. In their very different ways, Cooper and Rattigan responded to the world after the war in their writing. Both were psychologically complex men, Rattigan a closet homosexual, Cooper a victim of dark moods, both contained within a defiance of convention and authority as well as being solid members of the British upper-middle class and both had the ability to use drama to express the crisis of identity brought about by a post-war world.

Notes

1. Includes both original dramas written for radio and adaptations. Multi-part serials count as one.
2. This account of Giles Cooper's life is based on 'The playwright and the paradox', an unpublished 'introduction to the life and work of Giles Cooper' believed to be by his son Ric.
3. *Unman, Wittering and Zigo*, 23 November 1958. BBC Third Programme.
4. There is an interesting comparison here with Harold Pinter, most of whose friends from Hackney Grammar School went to university while he chose acting.
5. The Giles Cooper Papers, Box 34. Rare Book and Manuscript Library, Columbia University in the City of New York.
6. Giles Cooper, *But Not Magnificent* (unpublished), 1947. The Giles Cooper Papers. Rare Book and Manuscript Library, Columbia University in the City of New York.
7. *Thieves Rush In*, 29 March 1950. BBC Home Service. In 'The playwright and paradox' (see footnote 2) the author suggests that Giles Cooper was encouraged to submit the play to the BBC by Lance Sieveking.
8. *Never Get Out*, 3 July 1950. BBC Home Service.
9. *Never Get Out* draft script, The Giles Cooper Papers, Box 18. Rare Book and Manuscript Library, Columbia University in the City of New York.
10. Ibid.
11. *Oliver Twist*, 6 January 1952 to 30 March 1952. BBC Home Service.
12. The Giles Cooper Papers, Box 33. Rare Book and Manuscript Library, Columbia University in the City of New York.
13. *Artists in Crime*, from 10 August 1953, in five parts. BBC Light Programme.
14. *The Nine Tailors*, from 24 August 1954 in four parts. BBC Light Programme.
15. *Lord of the Flies*, 28 August 1955. BBC Third Programme.
16. J. C. Trewin, 'The critic on the hearth', *The Listener*, 1 September 1955.
17. *Mathry Beacon*, 18 June 1956. BBC Third Programme.
18. Quoted in Whitehead, *The Third Programme*, 37. Cooper's comment probably means that although the characters and situation are military, the play is not about war but about broader themes.
19. Ibid., 39.
20. *Mathry Beacon*, 18 June 1956. BBC Third Programme.
21. *Mathry Beacon* Synopsis, The Giles Cooper Papers, Box 33. Rare Book and Manuscript Library, Columbia University in the City of New York.
22. Ibid.
23. *Mathry Beacon* on BBC Third Programme, 18 June 1956 (original broadcast); 21 June 1956; 21 August 1956; 25 November 1962; then on the Home Service, 29 October 1956.

24 Whitehead, *The Third Programme*, 40.
25 Gray, 'The nature of radio drama', 64.
26 'Questions of value much too close for comfort', *The Times*, 12 September 1964.
27 Gray, 'The nature of radio drama', 65.
28 Ibid., 40.
29 *The Disagreeable Oyster*, 15 August 1957. BBC Third Programme.
30 Whitehead, *The Third Programme*, 149.
31 Val Gielgud to John Morris, 19 March 1957. BBC WAC.
32 John Morris to Val Gielgud, 26 March 1957. BBC WAC.
33 Giles Cooper, *Giles Cooper: Six Plays for Radio* (London: BBC Publications, 1966), 84.
34 Bundy's wife.
35 Ibid., 87.
36 Ibid., 98.
37 Ibid., 111.
38 Ibid., 124.
39 Frances Gray, 'Giles Cooper: The medium as moralist', in *British Radio Drama*, ed. John Drakakis (Cambridge: Cambridge University Press, 1981), 142–5.
40 Ibid., 145.
41 Ibid.
42 Ibid., 97.
43 *Without the Grail*, 13 January 1958. BBC Home Service. Adapted for television, 13 September 1960 starring Sean Connery. As there is no existing recording of this play these comments are based on reading the script in Cooper, *Giles Cooper: Six Plays for Radio*.
44 Ibid., 141.
45 Ibid., 144.
46 Ibid., 163.
47 Roy Walker, 'Critic on the hearth', *The Listener*, 23 January 1958.
48 Ibid.
49 Ibid.
50 Giles Cooper's *Without the Grail* quoted in McWhinnie's *The Art of Radio*, 52.
51 Ibid., 57
52 Niebur, *Special Sound*, 67.
53 Whitehead, *The Third Programme*, 149.
54 John Morris in ibid., 149.
55 Edward and Muriel Thwaite both speak with northern English accents; Thwaite is the name of different places in north-east England.
56 Cooper, *Giles Cooper: Six Plays for Radio*, 185.
57 A pastiche of the popular television series, *This Is Your Life* which began in the United States as a radio series in the late 1940s.
58 *Under the Loofah Tree*, 3 August 1958. BBC Third Programme.
59 Cooper, *Giles Cooper: Six Plays for Radio*, 191.
60 Ibid., 193.
61 Ibid., 199. The Rates are a locally payable tax in the United Kingdom.
62 *Under the Loofah Tree*.
63 McWhinnie, *The Art of Radio*, 158.
64 Ibid., 159.

65　Ibid., 163.
66　The term 'master' is an old-fashioned term for a schoolteacher.
67　*Unman, Wittering and Zigo*, 23 November 1958. BBC Third Programme.
68　Cooper, *Giles Cooper: Six Plays for Radio*, 219.
69　*Unman, Wittering and Zigo*.
70　Cooper, *Giles Cooper: Six Plays for Radio*, 251.
71　Ibid.
72　Ibid.
73　*Before the Monday*, 4 June 1959. BBC Third Programme. As there is no existing recording of this play, these comments are based on reading the script.
74　Cooper, *Giles Cooper: Six Plays for Radio*, 265.
75　'A play to be heard', *The Times*, 23 June 1959.
76　*Pig in the Middle*, 4 October 1960. BBC Third Programme. As there is no existing recording of this play, these comments are based on reading the script in The Giles Cooper Papers, Rare Book and Manuscript Library, Columbia University in the City of New York.
77　*The Return of General Forefinger*, 15 July 1961. BBC Third Programme. The play is described in the *Radio Times* as a 'comedy of motives.'
78　'Intricately written fantasy', *The Times*, 26 July 1961.
79　Gray, 'Giles Cooper: The medium as moralist', 153.
80　*All the Way Home*, 13 September 1963. BBC Third Programme.
81　Ibid.
82　*All the Way Home*, The Giles Cooper Papers, Box 2. Rare Book and Manuscript Library, Columbia University in the City of New York.
83　Gray, 'Giles Cooper: The medium as moralist', 146.
84　Workbook 1956, The Giles Cooper Papers, Box 33. Rare Book and Manuscript Library, Columbia University in the City of New York.
85　Billington, *State of the Nation*, 38.

Chapter 7

FEATURES DEPARTMENT DRAMATISTS

The majority of radio dramas broadcast between 1945 and 1963 were, unsurprisingly, produced by members of the Radio Drama department under Val Gielgud. But, to Gielgud's intense irritation, the Features Department produced a type of 'literary' feature which was to all intents and purposes, radio drama. By far the most important features department dramatist was the poet and radio producer Louis MacNeice, whose *The Dark Tower* is discussed in Chapter 3. Most of this chapter is concerned with MacNeice's contribution to radio drama, both as a writer and a producer, but another influential and much respected features producer and poet Henry Reed also features here. Other features producers also crossed the boundary between 'proper' factually based features into drama production. Rayner Heppenstall was a prolific writer who also worked as a features producer.[1] In addition to his many literary features, for example, on poetry or features titled *Imaginary Conversations* or *Dialogues from Plato*, Heppenstall also adapted and produced dramas, some of which used characters from famous literary works and placed them in new, original writing. *The Fool's Saga*[2] was a reworking of the story of Hamlet, and *Swann in Love* was a 'Proust reconstruction' by the prolific English novelist Pamela Hansford Johnson produced by Heppenstall.[3] A version of George Orwell's *Animal Farm*[4] was closer to drama than features, and an adaptation of André Gide's *The Return of the Prodigal*[5] and *Morel*[6] was a substantial one-hour-twenty-five-minute production with this billing in the *Radio Times*: 'If Proust's long novel, A La Recherche du Temps Perdu, can be said to have a villain, it is the young violinist, Charles Morel. Yet he was clearly very gifted, and after the First World War he was regarded with universal respect. It is conceivable that Marcel's view of him was biased and even vindictive.' It is clear that Heppenstall's interpretation of the radio feature allowed him to produce programmes which were often derivative of other, often important, work. He saw radio as an opportunity to augment literature and the theatre by reconstructing scenes or re-imagining established characters. Perhaps Heppenstall's intriguing approach to the appropriation of characters for the purposes of writing new drama influenced the young Tom

Stoppard whose *Rosencrantz and Guildenstern Are Dead* (1966) is based on the appropriation of two minor characters from Shakespeare's *Hamlet*.

Turning now to the doyen of Features Department dramatists, Louis MacNeice was born on 12 September 1907 in Belfast, Northern Ireland (a year after Beckett), the son of the rector of the local church. He attended English boarding schools before going to Oxford to study classics. His first job was as a lecturer in classics at Birmingham University, but his main passion in life was writing poetry.[7] In 1936 he moved to a new job in London and went on two remarkable trips: to pre-Civil War Spain with an old school friend, the art historian and soviet spy, Anthony Blunt, and then to Iceland with the Irish poet W. H. Auden. In the years before the war, MacNeice was part of literary London, and he published poetry, including *The Earth Compels* which contains some of his finest love poems,[8] and the *Autumn Journal* in 1938 about which one commentator wrote, 'If anyone wants to know what it was like to be a young, very intelligent, sensitive man in the autumn of 1938, this is the book to read.'[9] The *Autumn Journal* contains a personal story set against world events, the coming war in Europe, and is full of well-observed detail; it is suggestive of verse drama, of the use of verse to describe a world and tell a story, which would become MacNeice's technique in his later contribution to radio drama. MacNeice was in Galway in Ireland when the war broke out in September 1939, playing golf and writing poetry. He departed for America where some contemporaries, including Christopher Isherwood and W. H. Auden, remained for the war; MacNeice, however, eventually sailed for Britain at the end of 1940. A few months later he wrote to the director general of the BBC, F. W. Ogilvie, and also to Archie Harding, the features producer, offering his services.

The phenomenon of the verse drama is often traced back to *The Fall of the City* in 1936 for the American network CBS by Archibald MacLeish, which although certainly not the first verse play alerted 'serious writers to the opportunities of the medium'.[10] Earlier in the same year, D. G. Bridson produced *The March of the '45*,[11] a verse play about the Jacobite rebellion of 1745 led by 'Bonnie Prince Charlie' which ended disastrously at the battle of Culloden. By the beginning of the war a number of poets and musicians, including Benjamin Britten and William Walton, were contributing to radio, but MacNeice was not required to write grand verse dramas in the style of MacLeish or Bridson; the war required the BBC to produce propaganda features and in particular those aimed at encouraging America to enter the war. MacNeice's first assignment for the BBC, therefore, had little to do with his literary qualities and poetic skills; *The Stones Cry Out* was a weekly fifteen-minute programme on the BBC's North American Service and also on the rest of the Overseas Service.[12] The first of these programmes, 'Doctor Johnson takes it', was a dramatized visit to Johnson's former home in London's Gough Square where he had famously written his dictionary.[13] At the BBC, MacNeice the poet was learning the skills of communicating directly with an audience which would influence his later dramatic work for radio. This was not confined to radio, however, as this extract from a magazine article titled 'The morning after the blitz' demonstrates:

> There was a voice inside me which kept saying, as I watched a building burning or demolished: 'Let her go up!' 'Let her come down'. Let them all go. Write them all off. Stones do not a city make. Tear all the blotted pages out of the book; there are more books in the mind than have ever got upon paper.[14]

The experience of living in London during the war, writing for the BBC and publication, clearly helped MacNeice develop communication skills which would contribute to his writing as a radio dramatist, not in the literary verse style of *The Dark Tower* but in his other more prosaic and surprisingly accessible dramas.

Some of the BBC's wartime output was designed to reach out to allies, including the Soviet Union and America in a statement of solidarity. MacNeice had a pivotal role in two of these large-scale productions. *Alexander Nevsky*[15] was based on the film by the Russian director Eisenstein. The producer, Dallas Bower, who had transferred to BBC radio following the closure of the television service, asked MacNeice to provide the script.[16] This grand and symbolic production featured the original music by Prokofiev with Robert Donat in the starring role and an opening announcement by the Russian ambassador. In a similar vein was one of MacNeice's most important wartime scripts, the verse drama *Christopher Columbus*.[17] It was a sign of the BBC's great confidence in him that within two years of the start of his broadcasting career, he was entrusted with one of the most spectacular wartime productions. October 1942 was the 450th anniversary of Columbus's arrival in America and, as gratitude for America's participation in the war deserved recognition, the BBC wanted to mark this anniversary. The task of writing the script was given to MacNeice, and the final production, performed live in the relative safety of Bedford's Corn Exchange, had forty-nine speaking parts, music by William Walton performed by the BBC Symphony Orchestra conducted by Sir Adrian Boult and an impressive cast led by Laurence Olivier. Douglas Cleverdon described the play as 'a major creation for radio',[18] and Asa Briggs wrote that it was a 'sensation in artistic circles on both sides of the Atlantic'.[19]

Immediately after the war, MacNeice's great verse drama, *The Dark Tower* (see Chapter 3), added to his stature as a radio dramatist, but the ambition and scale of the two verse dramas, *Christopher Columbus* and *The Dark Tower*, were not to be repeated and, instead, MacNeice's career as a radio playwright was to be marked by experimentation and a willingness to try very different styles; to put it differently, his post-war output 'included work of tremendous breadth'.[20] MacNeice's work as a scriptwriter and producer was characterized by an abiding interest in classical writing, and this was particularly true of his work during the war and in the 1940s so, for example, his translation of *Agamemnon*[21] was the Third Programme's first new production of a Greek tragedy.[22] Soon after that *Enemy of Cant*[23] offered 'fresh translations of substantial extracts from eight of

Aristophanes' comedies'.[24] Other classically inspired drama included *Trimalchio's Feast*[25] and *Carpe Diem*[26] which features a dying man who is a follower of the Roman poet Horace and includes extracts from Horace's work as well as more modern 'Horation' poetry. MacNeice had developed an interest in Icelandic sagas while at school and wrote two violent and murderous dramas based on them: *The Death of Gunnar*[27] and *The Burning of Njal*.[28] Despite this academically inspired approach to radio drama as an opportunity to visit different forms of classical literature, no doubt inspired by some of the exciting work produced by the drama department, MacNeice also wrote contemporary drama for radio, some of which resonates with the adventurous approach of Giles Cooper and also acknowledges the absurdist trend in the theatre and this work is considered later in this chapter. As a features producer, MacNeice continued to produce more factually based documentary features including three programmes following a visit to India in 1948, more about Athens, where he was based for eighteen months in 1950–1. He wrote and produced other documentary features on the birth of Ghana in 1957, the city of Oxford and even the World Health Organization in 1958. A different and much more literary style of radio feature produced by MacNeice was his adaptation of Virginia Woolf's *The Waves*.[29]

The Death of Gunnar and *the Burning of Njal* were broadcast on consecutive nights and are parts one and two of MacNeice's adaptation of Njal's saga. The play starts with orchestral music and a presenter, an old man, who is the 'chronicler'. Gunnar is played by the deep-voiced character actor Francis de Wolff, whose rich and sonorous delivery is a particular quality of the radio drama. In the fast-paced action of the play, Gunnar marries Hallgerda, despite the reservations of his friend and adviser Njal and feuds develop resulting in various killings and the payment for atonement. The drama describes the complicated and mysterious Icelandic blood feuds in an entertaining action-based drama in which Gunnar is a decent and brave warrior, and Hallgerda is a devious and scheming wife. She thinks up a rude name for Gunnar's friend Njal and encourages others to be rude about Njal and his sons. Njal's sons kill Sigmund who had abused their father, and Hallgerda wants Gunnar to take revenge but Gunnar and Njal remain friends and declare their friendship. The drama becomes increasingly dramatic and violent, and Gunnar accuses and then slaps his wife which is followed by the sounds of fighting, screams and music. A blood feud has begun, and Gunnar is accused of man-slaughter. After further fighting and accusations Gunnar is made to leave Iceland for three years.

MacNeice first read the Icelandic sagas as a schoolboy, and this production would surely have appealed to a child wanting a proper adventure on radio with murders, feuds and plenty of rapid action. It is testimony to MacNeice's range of styles that he should produce such a comic book radio drama containing fast-paced action and rapid changes of scene reminiscent of the radio dramas of L. du Garde Peach who pioneered rapid action in the 1930s. It is unlikely (but possible) that MacNeice was influenced by the very successful radio action serial *Dick Barton – Special Agent*,[30] but his adaptation of the Njal saga was exciting and entertaining, and testimony to the remarkable versatility of a man usually characterized as a classicist and a poet.

Trimalchio's Feast[31] is a fascinating example of MacNeice combining his classical background with a determination to make classical literature accessible and entertaining. The play is based on a story in the *Satyricon* of Petronius concerning a freed slave called Trimalchio who has become both wealthy and vulgar. The former slave demonstrates the worst possible excesses of the nouveau riche and is hosting a lavish dinner party. The play was written and produced by MacNeice with music by Alan Rawsthorne, and the cast included the Yorkshire comic and broadcaster Wilfred Pickles as Trimalchio and Dylan Thomas as Agamemnon. The play opens with this announcement:

> We are taking you into a world founded on the institution of slavery but largely run by freedmen – that is by ex-slaves. These people, who come from all parts of the Roman Empire, were the *nouveaux riches* of the day; Trimalchio, the prince of big business and giant of vulgarity, is merely an outsize member of the species.[32]

After a long orchestral introduction we hear people arriving at Trimalchio's house for the feast. They see their corpulent host, and we hear the slaves singing their dialogue accompanied by the sounds of jazzy music and the voices of people at a party. Trimalchio speaks and Wilfed Pickles clearly had directions to emphasize his Yorkshire accent. The excess and vulgarity of the feast are indicated by the use of wine to wash peoples' hands, and the lavish quantity and bizarre variety of food is described. The dialogue is spoken with a variety of regional accents including Yorkshire, Scottish and Irish which appears to denote their lower social status, as Wrigley and Harrison explain: 'Petronius' careful characterization of Trimalchio's fellow freedmen as lower-class is thus perhaps reproduced for the contemporary Third Programme listeners to MacNeice's version by traces of regional dialects.'[33]

The play is surprisingly 'indecent' by the standards of the time. Trimalchio talks about his bowels and ostentatiously visits the toilet returning to talk about it further. There are also explicit references to homosexuality, and Trimalchio insists on having a boy on his lap to his wife Fortunata's disgust:

> Giton: Oh now, there *is* a looker. That little boy on Trimalchio's lap.
> Fortunate: Will you leave off that!
> Trimalchio: What's that you say dear? Ah you curly-headed rascal!
> Fortunata: Listen now, I'm not going to stand for this in front of my guests. You may be richest man in Italy but you behave like a—like a—I don't know what to say—a dog.
> ...
> Trimalchio: I was petting this lad here not because he's good looking but because he's bright at arithmetic. Why should a wife object to that?[34]

Research by Barry Baldwin in the BBC archive has shown the consternation expressed in the BBC at the 'indecency' of *Trimalchio's Feast* and there were attempts by the head of Features, Lawrence Gilliam, to dissuade MacNeice from going ahead, but, in the end, the Third Programme controller, Harman Grisewood, justified the inclusion of indecency as an essential part of the *Satyricon*.[35]

The ensuing dialogue serves to emphasize the ignorance and superstition of the characters; a former slave tells a story in an Irish accent about a werewolf and Trimalchio tells another story about witches. Later in the play Trimalchio announces that when he dies all of his slaves will be freed, and this is followed by a song sung by a slave. Trimalchio says he wants a monument in which he will be represented sitting on a throne. Eventually the party comes to an end, the fire brigade arrives and Trimalchio announces that he is dead. The final music is a funeral march.

In his brief review of *Trimalchio's Feast*, Philip Hope-Wallace wrote that the extract from the *Satyricon* had been 'daringly transposed into terms of our day's hypersensitive accent consciousness'.[36] He added that 'on the whole this succeeded, though it must have seemed a very private joke to many of its hearers'.[37] The accusation that the play was a 'private joke' rings true, and indeed there is something of the senior common room sneer about MacNeice's play, encouraging us to laugh at the nouveau riche: undeservedly rich, vulgar, stupid and speaking with regional accents. Fortunata talks about make-up, clothes and jewellery with her female friends:

Scintilla: *Oh ma petite cocotte!* That wonderful bracelet! May I try it on?
Fortunata: You're welcome—and while you're at it, try this one too, it's antique. Here—and this one—and this one—and this one. And here's a nice pair of anklets and if I get off my hair net.[38]

The humour here is identical to that in contemporary reality programmes in which the audience is positioned as a critic of the excess and lack of sophistication of nouveau riche women. It is not surprising that the product of an English public school and Oxford who was a part of London's cultural elite, writing at a time when social class differences were so pronounced, should harbour such supercilious views but they are certainly expressed without constraint in *Trimalchio's Feast*.

Further evidence of MacNeice's great versatility as a writer came with the broadcast of *One Eye Wild*.[39] The play is both contemporary and subjective, if not autobiographical. It concerns a sports journalist, a man obsessed by sport who is married to a disapproving woman and fantasizes about another. He seems highly educated in the classics and modern languages and has a drinking problem and also has a son. The similarities with MacNeice himself are clear: he was a great lover of sport, especially rugby and cricket. He was a heavy drinker,[40] and when he was writing *One Eye Wild*, although married to

Hedli, he was falling in love with the actress Cécile Chevraux[41] and in addition MacNeice was father to a son, Dan.

One Eye Wild begins with a man, Roger, a sports journalist, who is dreaming and the dream is full of references to Homer, gambling and rugby. He wakes and his wife Margaret complains about his behaviour the previous night. He starts work and types as his wife takes their son Timothy to school. He quotes to himself in Latin and German and sings about a fantasy woman, Heliodora. He claims that he is 'just a hack yoked with a nag' and wonders if Heliodora would nag. Margaret says she wants to live in the country and decides to leave Roger who then has to go to Lords cricket ground to do a commentary for radio. Roger is then run over in a car accident, and what follows are Roger's dreams and fantasies in his concussed state. The next part of the play has the excited Timothy on his way to the country with his mother listening to his father on the radio providing a cricket commentary. Roger then tries to phone Margaret, unsuccessfully, and we hear Timothy speaking words to copy the rhythm of the train, 'soup, fish, pudding, cheese, Julius Caesar, Shakespeare, Hamlet'. Then Margaret's words, 'I hate you, you're horrible, you never make love to me, not anymore—I hate you, I hate you.' Our attention then turns to Roger, and in the 1961 recording this is given a radiophonic treatment[42] as he meets a man after his broadcasting duties and they arrange to go somewhere quiet; this is followed by special effects, a very discordant screeching and speeded up vices intercut with sports commentary. They arrive at a zoo and in a decidedly absurdist moment speak to a parrot who says 'one eye wild'. It turns out that the man is the joker in a pack of cards. Following a strangely surreal conversation with the joker, Roger fantasizes about heroic deeds. He goes back in time and is a medieval knight on a horse: 'In brave pursuit of honourable deed, there is I know not what great difference between the vulgar and the noble.'[43] A jousting tournament follows and also a commentary on the tournament.[44] A scene with Roger and his wife is intercut with Roger the jouster and Heliadora. The joker and Roger discuss classical literature and then Roger and Heliadora are together in classical times and he takes part in a wrestling competition at Olympia. Roger then wakes up in hospital; it has all been a dream. He buys a gift for Margaret when he leaves the hospital and returns home. There is no one there but the joker reappears mocking him for his failure in the war (no medals) and with Heliadora. They fight. When Margaret and Timothy return home, they find Roger lying on the floor. He is delirious. There is a reconciliation which MacNeice called a 'more-or-less happy ending',[45] and finally Roger dreams of a game of rugby, he scores a try and the crowd roars.

In his lukewarm review of the 1961 production of the play, Ian Rodger acknowledges that the play reflected 'improvements in technique' and recognizes the important fact that in 1952 MacNeice was 'writing expressly for the medium'.[46] He also sees the play as a response to the zeitgeist: 'The day of heroes is past, Mr. MacNeice suggests, and in this he speaks for that generation which began by adoring the idealisms only to find them hollow and fake.'[47]

Rodger makes no mention of the self-referential nature of the play although Coulton does when she writes that it is 'too subjective to be a comedy'.[48] It is tempting to see *One Eye Wild* as an honest and highly self-critical play in which MacNeice cruelly represents some of his own personal weaknesses. It is also highly innovative and an early and successful attempt to write specifically for radio. The slightly surreal and dreamlike quality of the play made it perfect material for a later production making full use of radiophonics and further evidence that this was writing for radio well ahead of its time.

MacNeice's next drama written for radio was *Prisoner's Progress*[49] described by Christopher Holme as 'a more decided attempt at naturalistic characterization and psychology than any other MacNeice play'.[50] MacNeice himself claimed that his play was a 'fable of imprisonment and escape'[51] and concerned the 'Browns' (men) and the 'Greys' (women) in segregated sections of a prison campy. They are both plotting their escape, and their escape tunnels meet. One man, Waters, is then chosen to go with one woman, Alison, and they reach a mountain that lies between the camp and freedom. They discover that they are in love before the sound of pursuing dogs, then automatic gunfire and the play ends 'with the ghostly strains of "Lavender's Blue", on the accordion of a fellow-prisoner killed earlier in the play'.[52] *Prisoner's Progress* was deemed a success at the BBC and won the 'Premier Italiano' prize, the second award at the Prix Italia.

MacNeice's 'famous adaptation'[53] of Virginia Woolf's *The Waves*[54] is not strictly speaking radio drama, but it is an intriguing production based on a novel which could almost have been written for radio.[55] MacNeice suggested the adaptation to the features producer Douglas Cleverdon in September 1954: 'There are, as you know, six main characters who alternatively speak their thoughts from childhood up to middle age, and what one would need therefore is very careful casting and judicious cutting, no "dramatisation" or frills.'[56] MacNeice was true to his word and the production is remarkable for having no music or special effects and being based entirely on vocal performance. The characters do not engage in dialogue but rather express their thoughts in alternating stream of consciousness. MacNeice warned that it had to be one programme and not a serial so would inevitably be long, the final production ran from 8.40 pm to 10.50 pm, a full two hours and ten minutes with a ten-minute interval. The programme is important as a demonstration of how voice alone can be the basis of a drama and also as a demonstration of the way that radio can help clarify the meaning of a difficult novel; MacNecie's production of *The Waves*, despite its great length and lack of the usual aural stimuli, is a dramatic and arresting adaptation.

In the mid-1950s, approximately from 1955 to 1959, MacNeice produced only one drama for radio, *Also among the Prophets*,[57] about the biblical character Saul. MacNeice used the bible story to explore themes of power and corruption. Then, after a period of time when he produced mainly documentary features, he adapted the old Norwegian fairy tale *East of the Sun and West of the Moon*[58] in a production with music and 'specially devised sounds'⁵⁹ by Tristram Cary. The play reflected MacNeice's persistent interest in Scandinavian folklore and starts with the sound of a woman singing, people talking and some radiophonic sound. A husband and wife are arguing (she with a strong Irish accent); they have a daughter, Helga, who should get married. There is a knock on the door and in comes a white bear who offers to make them rich in return for their daughter. The haggling which takes place between the parents and the bear is written in a demotic style:

> Bear: I will give you a house as large as you want and as many servants as you want and tapestries on the wall and swansdown beds in the bedrooms and for Sundays a dinner service of gold—
> Mother: What about weekdays?
> Bear: Gf! Another for weekdays.
> Mother: In that case—
> Helga: No, mother, stop it! I've said no and I mean no. That bear may be as white as snow but look at his size and his jaws and his paws—
> Mother: Ssh! Don't take offence mister. You just come back here next Thursday. She'll have changed her tune by then maybe.⁶⁰

The bear takes Helga away and great wealth is magically bestowed on her parents. Helga finds herself in the bear's palace surrounded by opulence; she is dressed in silk, and when she goes to bed she is visited by a mysterious man in the dark who tells her she is dreaming. Helga goes back to her parents and despite the bear's request talks alone to her mother who tells her to light candles so she can see her night time visitor. This she does and the bear then confesses he is a bear in the day and a prince at night but now he must return to his wicked stepmother who is a troll and he must marry her troll daughter. The following day the bear or prince has gone, and Helga goes off in search of him. She embarks on a quest which involves asking various people for help to find the stepmother's castle and then she asks the east, west, south and north winds whose advice brings her the castle. Further adventures follow in which the prince is drugged by his troll fiancé, but then when the wedding approaches he declares that he will only marry the woman who can clean the candle wax from his shirt; the troll princess fails (as she isn't a Christian) but Helga can and when the north wind blows the castle down, Helga and the prince are together.

In his review of the play, Ian Rodger wrote that MacNeice has 'showed his old mastery'⁶¹ adding that what was frightening about the drama was the combination of a child's fairy tale with much darker and more horrible themes. There is much to commend in the play which is, like some other MacNeice productions, surprisingly fast-paced with an experienced team of actors and clever use of music and special effects. (Ian Rodger thought there was some 'wonderful icicle and troll music'.⁶²) In his discussion of the play, Jon Stallworthy comments that MacNeice in 1959 was a reluctant radio producer but one for whom 'the claims of the BBC could not be indefinitely ignored'.[63] He added that 'the programme had its charm but lacked the intensity of MacNeice's best work, no doubt because his imagination was elsewhere'.[64] Just a few days after the broadcast of *East of the Sun and West of the Moon*, he finished his verse 'Prologue' (for the abandoned book *The Character of Ireland*) which was clearly a major effort and a distraction from radio drama.

From MacNeice's adaptation of a Norwegian fairy tale in July 1959 to the experimental and absurdist radio drama *The Administrator*[65] in March 1961 is a considerable journey. The play was, as usual, written and produced by MacNeice and this was one of his original plays written for radio which utilized the resources of the Radiophonic Workshop. The one-hour play features a nuclear physicist, Professor Jerry King, who is offered the job of director of a research institute. His 'pushy' wife Martha wants him to take the job, and the action that follows begins late one evening and ends early the next morning mainly in the form of a dream. The dreams in *The Administrator* are not like those in Giles Cooper's *Under the Loofah Tree* or MacNeice's own *One Eye Wild*, so not Walter Mitty fantasies but rather suppressed memories of events in the past which have been released. There is a house-warming party, suggesting he has taken the job, but it turns out this is Martha's dream. Jerry says to her that he won't take the job and just be an administrator, she pleads with him. He dreams and we hear a distorted sound and what appear to be the sounds of future events, including an unveiling ceremony, a speech and then his death. In the intermingling of their dreams we encounter a traumatic episode in which his old friend, Robert, was killed in a road accident; we learn that Martha was in love with Robert. There are other dreams about hunting in South Africa; Jerry on trial accused of being anti-establishment, a crossword puzzle, Jerry with the prime minister, a court case in which an administrator is asked about 'creative work' followed by laughter. The absurd content of the play accelerates towards the end as different people are charged in a court case. Martha is charged and this is linked to the car crash in which Robert dies, then on a boat with animals who drown, and there are references to the sinking of the Titanic. Following this hectic passage the phone rings; it is the 7.30 am alarm call, and the play draws to an inconclusive end.

Frederick Laws described the play as a drama about decisions and judgements[66] and thought it's entirely successful. He approved of the 'echoey' acoustics of the courthouse and the presence of unjust judges who might represent Nazis, psychiatrists or even 'one's nearest and dearest' or the dead. Professor King was faced with the dilemma of becoming a successful administrator 'or remaining at his own game – which is what selfish creative types are known to prefer'. Laws also points to the presence of the (atomic) bomb in the background which he felt gave the play a nightmarish quality. The reviewer in *The Times* was also positive about the play calling it a 'virtuoso' production and 'exciting, vivid and memorable'.[67] *The Administrator* could be described as a drama influenced by Giles Cooper's more experimental writing with the extensive exploration of dreams and use of sound effects. As in so many of Cooper's plays, in *The Administrator*, the main male character is unable to make decisions and is out of control. Perhaps what makes the play so interesting as an example of post-war radio drama is the combination of personal and political themes: the man and his wife struggling with a dilemma set against the threat of nuclear war.

Following broadcast of *The Administrator*, MacNeice produced the second version of *One Eye Wild* in November 1961, then a contemporary drama about journalism *Lets Go Yellow* in December 1961 and in April 1962, *The Mad Islands* which, according to Barbara Coulton, was MacNeice's response to being pestered for a decade to write another *The Dark Tower*;[68] the play was based on Irish legends and an attempt to write a 'modern morality'. Then, in February 1963 MacNeice wrote to the controller, Third Programme, Howard Newby, saying how pleased he was that his proposal for a new drama about a distracted artist had been accepted for production.[69] *Persons from Porlock*[70] is the story of a painter who is deflected from his work by various temptations: commercialism and fashion as well as drink and women. This was to be MacNeice's last production. In August 1963 he went with sound engineers to the caves at Ingleton in the Yorkshire Dales and while there he was caught in heavy rain and soaked through, he became ill, eventually going to hospital where on 3 September he died slightly before his fifty-sixth birthday.

The play, which is set in the 1930s at the time of the Spanish Civil War, begins with three art students, Sarah and Hank, a couple, and their friend Peter. They disagree about Picasso in the pub. Peter is going to explore some caves and encourages Hank to join him. The scene changes to the caves where we meet another character, the eccentric, Mervyn. There is another rapid scene change to Peter and Sarah back in London and then again to their apartment where there is a knock on the door, and Peter enters to announce that Russia had signed a pact with Germany.[71] There is another very rapid scene change to Sarah talking to her mother-in-law about Peter who had been sent to fight in Burma. The war years are covered swiftly as the action moves from Hank talking to a sergeant about caving and then directly to the sound of a V2[72] exploding while Peter is on leave. The war is over and Peter and Hank are reunited:

Peter: Hank!
Hank: Peter!
Peter: Well, you old so-and-so! You're looking terribly well, Burma must be healthy.
Hank: You should try it some day.[73]

The war and his experiences in Burma have affected Hank's ability to paint, so he accepts Peter's offer of another weekend of caving. On his return to London, Hank not only decides to accept commercial work but also starts to drink heavily. Sarah leaves Hank who then tries lecturing but is drunk and the students laugh at him. Hank, who appears increasingly drunk agrees to meet a man from television to get work drawing cartoons for commercials. A year passes during which time Hank has painted a lot for an exhibition. Peter and Sarah assess his work: almost all of the paintings are of caves. The exhibition takes place but makes very little money, and there is another rapid scene change to a knock on the door and a bailiff enters from the court to get Hank to pay his debts. Hank once again gets drunk, and Sarah, who has reunited with him, is involved in a car accident and goes to hospital. Hank agrees to get medical help to cure his drinking, and he visits a psychiatrist. There is another change of scene to the cave, and Hank is once again with Mervyn and Donald. The caving is getting increasingly dangerous, and the men are caught underground when the water level suddenly rises while Mervyn is trapped. Despite the danger, Hank decides to try and rescue Mervyn:

> Donald: Good luck, Hank.
> (*violent splash*)
> (*calling*) Good luck, Hank!
> (*cross-fade to telephone ringing: receiver lifted*)
> Police Officer: Yes, this is the police station—What! Two men cut off in a cave! And the entrance is flooding rapidly![74]

Hank is now alone and cut off in the cave and starts to hallucinate. He has conversations with his doctor, a character from Jules Verne's *Journey to the Centre of the Earth*, Mrs Beeton and the bailiff among others. The exchanges refer back to earlier events and memories and finally the 'person from Porlock' appears:

> Doctor: A Person—
> (*Hank stops screaming*)
> A Person ... from Porlock.
> Hank: Not another!
> Person: Another—yes. But the last one.[75]

The Person commends Hank for some improvements in his behaviour, his attempt to rescue Mervyn and better behaviour towards Sarah and adds that this will help sell his pictures, implying that the improved sales will be posthumous.

Any analysis of *Persons from Porlock* is inevitably influenced by the fact that making it contributed to MacNeice's death and that he died just four days after it was broadcast. David Wade, writing three years later, admired much about the economy of the writing but added, 'I cannot help feeling that of all the scripts I have heard, this and others like it with an explicitly realistic and contemporary setting, have been the least satisfactory.'[76] His judgement was based on what he felt was inadequate development of character, lacking depth and insight. In his foreword to the published version of the play, W. H. Auden praised *Persons form Porlock* as an essential radio drama; he explains how the final scene in which Hank is visited by different people in his hallucinations could not work in any other medium. Auden did not mention another radiogenic characteristic of the play: the extremely rapid changes of scene, with no pauses in between. MacNeice had demonstrated his ability to include fast-changing scenes in *The Death of Gunnar*, and it works just as effectively in this contemporary play.

Like *One Eye Wild*, originally broadcast eleven years earlier, *Persons from Porlock* contained strong autobiographical elements; Hank is, like MacNeice, an artist who struggles to stay focused on his art and is lured by commercial temptations. Also like MacNeice, Hank's creative work is interrupted by drink and his troubled relationships with women. MacNeice was never tempted by the riches of the commercial media, but his long association with the BBC was at times a distraction from his more 'serious' poetry. Hank would only achieve greatness as an artist after his death, whereas MacNeice achieved fame and admiration in his lifetime as a poet and radio producer. He must have thought a lot about how what he called 'hack work' interfered with the higher art of poetry, but he made an important contribution to the art of radio drama and was responsible for one of the masterpieces of the genre and also for some highly creative and innovative dramas which at their best are almost cruel self-examinations.

The other important and prolific Features department radio dramatist was Henry Reed, born in the same year as Dylan Thomas and a student and friend of MacNeice's at Birmingham University.[77] He is probably most well known for his wartime poetry, in 1942 three of his poems under the title 'Lessons of War' were printed in the *News Statesman and Society*, one of these was 'Naming of parts' arguably the most anthologized of all the Second World War poems which made its way onto the school curriculum. After the war, Reed was an extremely prolific writer and critic, a profession which inevitably brought him to the BBC and programmes like *The Poet and His Critic*,[78] as a book reviewer for the Home Service and the radio critic on the Home Service Sunday lunchtime programme, *The Critics*.

Given Reed's capacity as a writer it is not surprising that soon after he started contributing to BBC programmes as a critic that he would contribute as a writer. Like a number of other future writers and producers, he was greatly impressed by MacNeice's immediate post-war drama *The Dark Tower*, and wrote to MacNeice after hearing it:

> Dear Louis, Forgive a fan-letter. ... I found I was listening with an intentness I had never been forced to give to anything except music on the wireless. ... I am sure yours is the way radio must go if it is to be worth listening to; I have always thought your claims for its potentialities to be excessive; I now begin, reluctantly, to think you may be right.[79]

By 'your way' Reed was probably referring to at least two aspects of MacNeice's approach: the play written specifically for radio and the use of verse. Reed's first contribution to radio drama was his adaptation of Herman Melville's *Moby Dick*.[80] This was a major production for the new Third Programme for which he had adapted the substantial novel as a two-hour-fifteen-minute drama.[81] The play starred Ralph Richardson as Captain Ahab, and the music was composed by Antony Hopkins. Reed then wrote his first original play for radio, *Pytheas: A dramatic speculation*,[82] produced by Rayner Heppenstall. His two 'dramatic studies' of the life of the poet, Giacomo Leopardi, *The Unblest*[83] and *The Monument*,[84] were both produced by Rayner Heppenstall and repeated a further six times on different networks up to 1970. Reed describes these verse features as aspiring to the verse drama of T. S. Eliot's *The Cocktail Party*,[85] but as dramatic interpretations of the past they appear closer to orthodox radio features than radio dramas. The following year, 1950, saw the broadcast of Reed's six-part adaptation of Thomas Hardy's *The Dynasts*[86] which at a total of nine hours of radio must have been a major undertaking. *The Streets of Pompeii*[87] was a 'dramatic poem' produced by Douglas Cleverdon and starring Marius Goring and Flora Robson which won the 1953 Prix Italia prize. Robert Savage offers this description, 'in *The Streets of Pompeii*, where ideas of fecundity and sterility, imagination and pedantry, love and death are woven together through the patterning of the experiences of a dozen Pompeian natives and visitors'.[88] It was followed by another 'dramatic speculation' *The Great Desire I Had*[89] in which Shakespeare travels to Italy in the 1590s which was also produced by Douglas Cleverdon and once again was a radio feature with at least some factual basis. Another of Henry Reed's significant contributions to post-war radio drama was his translation of the plays of the Italian playwright, Ugo Betti. The first of these, in 1954, was *The Queen and the Rebels*,[90] and this was followed by another six Betti plays up to 1961. Although Reed was mainly associated with Features department, these adaptations were produced mainly by Donald McWhinnie, Val Gielgud's deputy in the Drama department: McWhinnie produced five, John Gibson and Raymond Raikes one each.

In his discussion of Henry Reed's career, Roger Savage states that he was celebrated in three different roles: as a poet, a translator (and adapter) and finally as a radio dramatist. This last category mainly concerns Reed's authorship of a group of seven radio dramas commonly referred to as the 'Hilda Tablet' series.[91] The plays are all set in the 1950s and concern a deceased novelist, Richard Shewin, and his surviving family and friends. These are all highly eccentric and comic characters, for example, the cat-obsessed Connie, the rather dotty and bell-obsessed General Gland and Miss Alice Gland who practices 'creative sleep'.[92] The most formidable of the friends of Shewin is the composer, Hilda Tablet who has her own circle of eccentric friends. One of these friends is the earnest scholar Herbert Reeve (a slightly mischievous play on Reed's own name) who embarks on Robert Shewin's biography only to be hijacked by Hilda Tablet and persuaded to write a twelve-volume biography of her instead.

A Very Great Man Indeed is a satirical drama which begins with a narrator full of admiration for the deceased Richard Shewin. The script is genuinely funny as we follow Herbert Reeve to Shewin's brother's house; the brother clearly despised Richard (who he describes as 'bitter, aggrieved and depressed').

Eventually the brother gives Reeve the names of two women who he suspects knew Richard very well; he visits them and they are clearly prostitutes, the ensuing the dialogue is full of *double entendre*. Reeve then meets Shewin's 'valet' who is only able to answer questions with the words 'yes, I did'. Reeve then interviews another novelist who is wonderfully dismissive of Shewin's talent, doubts very much that Shewin is worth a biography and claims that one of Shewin's books was based on his own. He suggests that Reeve might consider writing a biography about a living author (in other words, himself). An interview with the very deaf Lady Blackley follows in which the titles of Shewin's books are mentioned: 'The Top and the Bottom', 'The Head and the Heart, 'The Hot and the Cold', 'The Arse and the Elbow'. Finally Reeve meets Hilda Tablet, and we hear her sing some of her modernist music. She tells a funny story about herself and 'Dick Shewin'. There are various other unsuccessful attempts at writing the story of Shewin's life; it is clear that Shewin was certainly not a 'very great man' and that Reeve's chances of writing his biography are non-existent.

J. C. Trewin clearly loved Henry Reed's satire on literary life; 'It came to us as an endearing joke at the expense of critics and biographers who are given to mumbling too solemnly about Motives and Periods.'[93] The humour could probably be described as esoteric and particularly amusing to those who knew something about the social world that Reed lampoons. This presumption on Reed's part that the listener should share his attitudes and knowledge is reminiscent of Savage's suggestion that anyone wanting to understand some of Reed's poems should have a 'decent knowledge of Sophocles'[94] and the observation that Reed 'requires considerable knowledge of half a dozen Shakespeare plays in his listeners if they are fully to savour *The Great Desire I Had*'.[95] Reed was one of those who fully embraced the Third Programme as a justifiably elitist network commenting that 'some listeners are fools and some are not, and ... we cannot wait for the fools to catch up with their betters'.[96]

The success of what might be called 'features drama' owed a lot to the relative freedom which the more innovative and self-consciously experimental department under Lawrence Gilliam gave writers and producers, until Drama began to catch up after the appointment of Donald McWhinnie as Gielgud's deputy in 1953. Henry Reed's whimsical seven-part Hilda Tablet cycle is an example of a respected writer being allowed to pursue his own creative impulse; similarly, MacNeice's highly variable, even erratic, output as a dramatist could be seen as Features granting one of their favourite writers considerable licence. The continued involvement of Features in drama production was also probably due to Drama department's rather restricting, continued belief in the importance of the adapted stage play, and especially adaptations of what was perceived as a theatrical canon. Producers like Gielgud and Raymond Raikes in Drama department remained fixated on the concept of the national theatre of the air whereas Features valued the original play for radio and as a result made a significant, if uneven, contribution to post-war radio drama.

Notes

1. Rayner Heppenstall, *Portrait of the Artist as a Professional Man* (London: Peter Owen, 1969).
2. *The Fool's Saga*, 1 August 1949. BBC Third Programme.
3. *Swann in Love*, 3 March 1952. BBC Third Programme. This was the first of six such reconstructions written by Hansford Johnson and produced by Heppenstall.
4. *Animal Farm*, 14 January 1947. BBC Third Programme.
5. *The Return of the Prodigal*, 2 June 1952. BBC Third Programme.
6. *Morel*, 13 October 1957. BBC Third Programme.
7. Coulton, *Louis MacNeice in the BBC*, 23. The account of MacNeice's life here is largely based on this book.
8. Ibid., 32.
9. Quoted in ibid., 33.
10. Rodger, *Radio Drama*, 31.
11. *The March of the '45*, 28 February 1936. BBC regional programme, Midland.
12. There were thirty-five editions of *The Stones Cry Out* which ran from 26 May 1941 to 29 December; America entered the war on 7 December, the day after the Japanese attack on Pearl Harbour. MacNeice wrote and produced nine of these; see Coulton, *Louis MacNeice in the BBC*, 204.
13. Jon Stallworthy, *Louis MacNeice* (London: Faber and Faber, 1995), 295.
14. Louis MacNeice, 'The morning after the Blitz', *Picture Post*, 3 May 1941.
15. *Alexander Nevsky*, 8 November 1941. BBC Home Service.
16. Christopher Holme, 'The radio drama of Louis MacNeice', in *British Radio Drama*, ed. John Drakakis (Cambridge: Cambridge University Press), 39.
17. *Christopher Columbus*, 12 October 1942. BBC Home Service.
18. Quoted in Coulton, *Louis MacNeice in the BBC*, 62.
19. Asa Briggs, *The History of Broadcasting in the United Kingdom*, Vol. 3 (Oxford: Oxford University Press, 1970), 529.
20. Wrigley and Harrison (eds), *Louis MacNeice*, 24.
21. *Agamemnon*, 29 October 1946. BBC Third Programme.
22. Wrigley and Harrison, *Louis MacNeice*, 21.
23. *Enemy of Cant*, 3 December 1946. BBC Third Programme.
24. Wrigley and Harrison, *Louis MacNeice*, 22.
25. *Trimalchio's Feast*, 22 December 1948. BBC Third Programme.
26. *Carpe Diem*, 8 October 1956. BBC Third Programme.
27. *The Death of Gunnar*, 11 March 1947. BBC Third Programme.
28. *The Burning of Njal*, 12 March 1947. BBC Third Programme.
29. *The Waves*, 18 March 1953. BBC Third Programme.
30. *Dick Barton – Special Agent*, from 7 October 1946 to 30 March 1951. BBC Light Programme.
31. *Trimalchio's Feast*, 22 December 1948. BBC Third Programme.
32. *Trimalchio's Feast* script in Wrigley and Harrison, *Louis MacNeice*, 334.
33. Wrigley and Harrison, *Louis MacNeice*, 332.
34. *Trimalchio's Feast* script in Wrigley and Harrison, *Louis MacNeice*, 360–1.
35. Baldwin's research is quoted in Wrigley and Harrison, *Louis MacNeice*, 330.
36. Philip Hope-Wallace, 'Critic on the hearth', *The Listener*, 6 January 1949.

37 Ibid.
38 *Trimalchio's Feast* script in Wrigley and Harrison, *Louis MacNeice*, 356.
39 *One Eye Wild*, 9 November 1952. BBC Third Programme. There was a second production of the play broadcast on 14 November 1961, and it is this version for which there is a recording.
40 In 1952 when *One Eye Wild* was broadcast, MacNeice was a regular drinker with Dylan Thomas, W. R. Rodgers, Jack Dillon and others, and his heavy drinking persisted during the 1950s until, according to his biographer, John Stallworthy, in the last three years of his life he lost control of his drinking and for days on end he was 'living on alcohol'.
41 Stallworthy, *Louis MacNeice*, 407–8.
42 The *Radio Times* billing for the 1961 production states 'special effects by the BBC Radiophonic Workshop'.
43 A quotation from Edmund Spenser's *The Fairy Queen*, Canto IV Book II.
44 There are clear similarities here with Giles Cooper's *Under the Loofah Tree* in which Edward Thwaite fantasizes about past heroic deeds.
45 Quoted in Coulton, *Louis MacNeice in the BBC*, 132.
46 Ian Rodger, 'The critic on the hearth', *The Listener*, 23 November 1923.
47 Ibid.
48 Coulton, *Louis MacNeice in the BBC*, 132.
49 *Prisoner's Progress*, 27 April 1954. BBC Third Programme. The comments here are based on secondary sources as no recording is available.
50 Holme, 'The radio drama of Louis MacNeice', 66.
51 Stallworthy, *Louis MacNeice*, 407.
52 Ibid., 407. Stallworthy goes on to tell the story of Louis MacNeice and the woman playing the part of Alison, Cécile Chevreau; after a rehearsal he took her for a drink where he told her he loved her.
53 Lewis, *Radio Drama*, 8.
54 *The Waves*, 18 March 1955. BBC Third Programme.
55 Lewis, *Radio Drama*, 8.
56 Louis MacNeice to Douglas Cleverdon, 20 September 1954. BBC WAC.
57 *Also among the Prophets*, 5 February 1956. BBC Third Programme. No recording of this play was available but there is a very useful discussion of it in Coulton's *Louis MacNeice in the BBC*, 153–5.
58 *East of the Sun and West of the Moon*, 23 July 1959. BBC Third Programme.
59 *Radio Times*, 7 August 1959, 23.
60 Louis MacNeice, *Persons from Porlock and other plays for radio* (London: BBC, 1969), 47.
61 Ian Rodger, 'The critic on the hearth', *The Listener*, 30 July 1959.
62 Ibid.
63 Stallworthy, *Louis MacNeice*, 432.
64 Ibid., 433.
65 *The Administrator*, 10 March 1961. BBC Third Programme.
66 Frederick Laws, 'Critic on the hearth', *The Listener*, 16 March 1961.
67 *The Times*, 11 March 1961.
68 Coulton, *Louis MacNeice in the BBC*, 182.
69 Ibid., 188.

70 *Persons from Porlock*, 30 August 1963. BBC Third Programme. The title comes from the story of the poet Samuel Taylor Coleridge who was disturbed while writing a poem by 'persons from Porlock' (a small village in the county of Somerset). The expression has come to refer to the distractions encountered by artists.
71 German – Soviet non-aggression pact, 23 August 1939.
72 The German V2 rocket was a weapon fired at Allied cities, including London, in the final year of the Second World War.
73 Louis MacNeice, *Persons from Porlock and Other Plays for Radio* (London: BBC, 1969), 118.
74 Ibid.,140.
75 Ibid., 143.
76 David Wade, 'Dying Fall', *The Listener*, 2 February 1967.
77 This account of Henry Reed's career is based on Roger Savage, 'The radio plays of Henry Reed', in Drakakis, *British Radio Drama*, 158–91.
78 *The Poet and His Critic*, from 26 October 1946. BBC Third Programme.
79 Quoted in Coulton, *Louis MacNeice in the BBC*, 83.
80 *Moby Dick*, 26 January 1947. BBC Third Programme.
81 According to Roger Bickerton the adaptation of *Moby Dick* was written during the war while Reed was working at the Government College and Cypher school as a translator, 'Henry Reed, the Hilda Tablet Plays', accessed 11 May 2018, www.suttonelms.org.uk/hreed.html
82 *Pytheas: A Dramatic Speculation*, 25 May 1947. BBC Third Programme.
83 *The Unblest*, 9 May 1949. BBC Third Programme.
84 *The Monument*, 7 March 1950. BBC Third Programme.
85 Savage, 'The radio plays', 170.
86 *The Dynasts*, six parts, each one hour thirty minutes, first episode 3 June 1951. BBC Third Programme.
87 *The Streets of Pompeii*, 16 March 1952. BBC Third Programme.
88 Savage, 'The radio plays', 171.
89 *The Great Desire I Had*, 26 October 1952. BBC Third Programme.
90 *The Queen and the Rebels*, 17 October 1954. BBC Third Programme.
91 *A Very Great Man Indeed*, 7 November 1953; *The Private life of Hilda Tablet*, 24 May 1954; *'Emily Butter' – An Occasion Recalled*, 14 November 1954; *Through a Hedge – Backwards*, 29 February 1956; *The Primal Scene, As It Were …*, 11 March 1958; *Not a Drum was Heard*, 6 May 1959; *Musique Discrete*, 27 October 1959. All of the 'Hilda Tablet' plays were broadcast on the Third Programme and produced by Douglas Cleverdon.
92 Savage, 'The radio plays', 164–5.
93 J. C. Trewin, 'The critic on the hearth', *The Listener*, 17 September 1953.
94 Savage, 'The radio plays', 168.
95 Ibid.
96 Quoted in John Drakakis, 'The essence that's not seen: Radio adaptations of stage plays', in Drakakis, *Radio Drama*, 112.

Chapter 8

REALIST RADIO DRAMA

One of the persistent features of the work of the radio dramatists considered so far in this book is detachment from the world of the majority of the British population at the time. The abundance of absurdism and fantasy, of historical, classical and epic writing with only occasional departures into the lives of artists, adventurers, people not unlike the playwrights themselves, meant that the voice of the working class was largely absent. This was, of course, true of culture more generally and in particular the intensely middle-class phenomenon of the London stage with the preponderance of 'Loamshire'[1] plays depicting weekends in country houses. As the previous chapters have shown, radio drama on the Third Programme offered a proliferation of adaptations of classic stage plays including those based on the literature of ancient Greece and Rome, adaptations of the theatrical canon (and especially of course Shakespeare and other Elizabethan and Jacobean playwrights) as well as European writers such as Ibsen, Chekhov, Strindberg and the more contemporary Anouilh and Betti. Radio dramas which were set in contemporary Britain were seldom if ever about working-class characters and certainly did not address themes of class and power.

The shock waves sent through British theatre and culture by John Osborne's *Look Back in Anger* which opened on 8 May 1956 at the Royal Court Theatre (and quickly labelled 'kitchen sink drama') reflected only part of the more general tendency in film, the novel, theatre, television and even radio towards working-class and lower-middle-class voices, experiences and opinions. The new social realism was about representation: 'It is a term that resonates throughout the late fifties and early sixties, party because it suggests a range of ambitions (in the plays, the writers and the companies) that are not simply theatrical but are political and social as well.'[2] The advent of social realism or the 'New Wave' reflected not only a greater concern with the working class as the subject of cultural production but also greater numbers of working-class actors and writers contributing to the theatre and culture more generally. There is little doubt that there was a proliferation of social realist output across different media in the late 1950s and early 1960s. The plays of Arnold Wesker and Bernard Kops (e.g. *The Hamlet of Stepney Green*, 1958) and Shelagh Delaney

(*A Taste of Honey*, 1958); the novels of John Braine (*Room at the Top*, 1957), Alan Sillitoe's *Saturday Night and Sunday Morning* (1958) and Stan Barstow (*A Kind of Loving*, 1960); television drama series like *Armchair Theatre* and *The Wednesday Play* and long-running serials like *Z Cars* and *Coronation Street*, to name just a very few examples, all contained representations of working-class life and included working-class voices with accents and regional dialects. The new attention to working-class culture was supported by the highly influential academic intervention of Richard Hoggart whose *The Uses of Literacy* (1958) praised the authenticity of working-class culture and Raymond Williams's *Culture and Society* which also pays attention to working-class culture and experience.

There was a gulf between the esoteric offerings of the Third Programme and the realist revolution taking place outside the walls of Broadcasting House. In the first week of May 1956 which coincided with the first performance of *Look Back in Anger*, the Third Programme broadcast *The Death of Vivien* (an adaptation of 'Chanson de Guillaume'); an early-seventeenth-century Spanish play, *Punishment without Vengeance*; Jack B. Yeats's experimental, modernist drama *In Sand* and R. C. Scriven's play about an eye operation *A Single Taper*. There was a lot to admire in the ambition of Third Programme drama in that week, but it was completely removed from the 'new wave' and especially from any interest in working-class culture or the social realist tendency. For BBC radio drama to reflect the new realism so dominant in other cultural production, it would require contributions from playwrights with distinct realist inclinations; although commentators have hesitated to label him a realist, Harold Pinter does at least reflect some of the ambitions of social realism and was from a working-class background. Another radio dramatist with realist inclinations was the far less well-known writer Rhys Adrian.

Harold Pinter was born in Hackney in the East End of London in 1930 to Jewish parents, his father was a tailor and his mother a housewife.[3] He attended Hackney Grammar School, and despite being an academic high achiever, decided against university and instead went to drama school. Compared to many who contributed to BBC radio drama in the 1950s as writers or producers, Harold Pinter was authentically working class and his experience growing up in the poorest and most ethnically diverse part of London made a vital contribution to his writing. He was also a man of strong anti-establishment political convictions which expressed themselves in his refusal to be called up to perform National Service in 1948 instead declaring himself a 'conscientious objector'. He was repeatedly threatened with prison and fines but seems to have evaded punishment.

Like Giles Cooper, Pinter was drawn to the stage after school and initially attended the prestigious drama school RADA and then the Central School of Speech and Drama before commencing his career as an actor. He toured Ireland assuming the stage name David Baron and then worked in repertory companies in English towns including Torquay, Bournemouth and Colchester. Acting in the very unglamorous and badly paid repertory theatres was his principal activity until the end of the 1950s when he finally achieved critical approval for his plays. Pinter began writing in the early 1950s with an autobiographical novel, *The Dwarfs*, which was subsequently dramatized for BBC radio in 1960 and contains references to Pinter's boyhood friends, the 'Hackney gang' exploring themes of loyalty, friendship and betrayal. In addition, *The Dwarfs* is a novel about language; the characters speak to each other in a sort of private language full of jokes and the 'rat-a-tat dialogue of a Jewish music-hall double act'.[4] It is significant that Pinter discovered Beckett before the success of *Attendant au Godot*; he found a fragment of Beckett's *Watt* in a magazine while touring in Ireland and later stole a copy of *Murphy* from Westminster library. Although he was never an absurdist writer in the Ionesco or Beckett sense, indeed less influenced by absurdism than Giles Cooper, he does feature in Martin Esslin's *The Theatre of the Absurd* where alongside Beckett, Adomov, Ionesco and Genet there is a whole chapter dedicated to him.

In his early writing, Pinter developed some of the themes which would persist in later more successful work. His first stage play, *The Room*, was written for the Bristol University drama department in 1956 while performing in Rattigan's *Separate Tables*. The play takes place in a bedsit with a rocking chair, a gas stove and a sink. Rose makes breakfast for a silent man, and we wonder about his silence and what he is frightened of. Pinter was to develop these themes in his later work; the confines of a room, an anxious recluse frightened of the outside world. For Billington, a feature of *The Room* 'is its social accuracy: in particular, its portrait of a walled-in isolationism and paranoid xenophobia that was to become a feature of English life in the late 1950s'.[5] In addition *The Room* has that persistent Beckettian trope, the failure of language to communicate.

Later in 1957, Pinter wrote *The Party* (later known as *The Birthday Party*), the play which would, eventually, launch his career as a playwright. The story of *The Birthday Party* is important as a commentary on Pinter's eventual move into radio, but it also reveals the ongoing tension between the London metropolitan elite and, specifically, the Cambridge-based opposition. Pinter wrote *The Party* in the dressing rooms of provincial and theatrical digs[6] while on tour with *Doctor in the House*.[7] Themes from 1950s' repertory theatre abound in the play including cliché speaking working-class characters, the lonely lodger, the ravenous landlady, the quiescent husband and an air of menace or threat personified by the two men, Goldberg and McCann, who eventually remove Stanley, an occupant of the digs. At the beginning of the play there is dialogue between Meg, the landlady, and Petey, a guest:

The living room of a house in a seaside town.
Meg: You got your paper?
Petey: Yes.
Meg: Is it good?
Petey: Not bad.

Meg: What does it say?
Petey: Nothing much.
Meg: You read me out some nice bits yesterday.
Petey: Yes well I haven't finished this one yet.[8]

This short extract is revealing; in the confines of a room in a boarding house two characters engage in 'demotic and desultory'[9] dialogue which communicates little between them, but to the audience reveals Meg's neediness and Petey's lack of interest and also suggests that Meg cannot read or at least is not inclined to. The hapless Stanley tortured and brainwashed by Goldberg and McCann is reminiscent of so many of Giles Cooper's male characters: trapped, alone, weak and ineffectual in the face of social pressure, convention and expectation.

The Birthday Party was well received in Oxford (*The Oxford Mail* drew comparisons with T. S. Eliot and Ernest Hemingway[10]) and then on 28 April 1958 made its first performance at the Arts Theatre, Cambridge.[11] This would have been to a very discerning audience including George Rylands, the chairman of the Arts Theatre as well as many future actors and directors studying at Cambridge at the time. The future radio drama producer John Tydeman, an undergraduate at Cambridge at the time, was in the audience and remembers his response to *The Birthday Party*: 'It was so fresh and it was so extraordinary. The audience rose as one and applauded.'[12] *The Cambridge Review* was rather more ambivalent but thought Pinter was a 'lively and assimilative new talent', owing much to Ionesco, while also stating that it was 'nihilistic, for no rich areas of significant human experience seem to exist between the sterile level of reality at the opening (cornflakes, fried bread and the stock question "Is it nice?") and the subsequent gaping horror and claustrophobia of a neurotic's world.'[13] Pinter was to pay tribute to the positive reception he received in Cambridge by writing an article explaining his dramatic beliefs for the *Cambridge University Magazine* published in October 1958.[14]

On 19 May 1958, *The Birthday Party* opened at the Lyric Theatre, Hammersmith. Press reviews were unanimously negative including Milton Shulman in the *Evening Standard*, 'Its appeal is based upon … irreverent verbal anarchy. But the fun to be derived out of the futility of language is fast becoming a cliché of its own. And Mr Pinter just isn't funny enough.'[15] *The Manchester Guardian* critic wrote this: 'What all this means, only Mr Pinter knows, for as his characters speak in non-sequiturs, half-gibberish and lunatic ravings, they are unable to explain their actions, thoughts, or feelings.'[16] Derek Grainger in the *Financial Times* wrote, 'The message, the moral, and any possible moments of enjoyment, eluded me. Apart from a seaside ticket-collector and a bare-legged floozy, all the characters seemed to me to be in an advanced state of pottiness or vitamin deficiency, and quite possibly both at once.'[17] Five days later on 24 May, *The Birthday Party* closed at the Lyric. Fortunately for Harold Pinter, the influential theatre critic of *The Sunday*

Times defended the play claiming that 'Mr Pinter ... possesses the most original, disturbing and arresting talent in theatrical London'. His review was exceptionally perceptive and still provides an important means of interpreting Pinter, and it was worth quoting at length, not only as criticism but also for the striking Cold War references:

> Mr Pinter has got hold of a primary fact of existence. We live on the verge of disaster. One sunny afternoon, whilst Peter May is making a century at Lords against Middlesex, and the shadows are creeping along the grass, and the old men are dozing off in the Long Room, a hydrogen bomb may explode. ... There is something in your past – it does not matter what – which will catch up with you. Though you go to the uttermost parts of the earth, and hide yourself in the most obscure lodgings in the least popular towns, one day there is a possibility that two men will appear. They will be looking for you and you cannot get away. And someone will be looking for *them*, too. There is terror everywhere.[18]

The critical reaction to the play in London, with the exception of Harold Hobson, was markedly different from the more positive response it had received before outside the metropolis, and this rejection shocked John Tydeman: 'When it received those notices from the London critics, it seemed to me that the world had ended, I couldn't believe that this thing called "the Establishment" ... had said no.'[19]

The reactions to *The Birthday Party* are a revealing survey of different perceptions of Pinter's work. In the more critical reviews there is the traditional and familiar frustration at the uncommunicative dialogue and also the difficulty interpreting the play. More positively he was likened to Ionesco and compared to other absurdist writers. For the young John Tydeman, an important voice given his subsequent role as Head of Radio Drama at the BBC, Pinter was an exciting and innovative playwright, welcomed for the 'freshness' of his writing.

Just two days after *The Birthday Party* had opened in London, Pinter, who now realized that 'the play has come a cropper', wrote to Donald McWhinnie at the BBC thanking him for his support.[20] According to Esslin, the BBC finally commissioned a sixty-minute radio play, *A Slight Ache*, from Pinter in July 1958 following an earlier unsuccessful attempt with a play titled *Something in Common*.[21] In Michael Billington's account of Pinter's life and work he explains that Pinter had been the beneficiary of the well-established McWhinnie–Bray partnership which specialized in identifying and then supporting struggling new writers. His play may have flopped at the Lyric but that had happened at the right time: 'Pinter was ... lucky in coinciding with a golden age in radio drama when a BBC producer like Donald McWhinnie and a script editor like Barbara Bray – later a distinguished producer and translator – were actively encouraging innovation.'[22] He quotes Barbara Bray as saying: 'After the failure of *The Birthday Party*, we were able to help Harold keep body and soul together.'[23]

After Pinter had submitted the first draft of *A Slight Ache* in the summer of 1958, there was the almost inevitable exchange of memoranda about the play in a remarkable repeat of the battles fought over Beckett by exactly the same people just a few years earlier. As Billington describes, 'What is striking is how most of the senior producers seemed to have very dogmatic opinions about it: Pinter became a living issue within Broadcasting House.'[24] Archie Campbell thought that 'by no standards could this work be judged a play' and that 'its implications are vaguely repellent'.[25] Charles Lefeaux was full of praise, and D. G. Bridson wrote a one-page memorandum invoking Ionesco, Ibsen and Melville and praised its integrity, strenuously recommending its acceptance. John Morris, controller, Third Programme, was his typical conservative self, expressing his negative views about Pinter in a manner almost identical to his earlier scorn for Beckett: 'Personally I am not at all convinced of Pinter's ability to construct a good play[26] either for the stage or radio and I know H.D. (Head of drama, Val Gielgud) has no great opinion of him.'[27] Meanwhile McWhinnie, Bray and Bakewell championed Pinter's first play for radio and eventually, no agreement having been reached, the progressive radio manager, R. D. A. Marriott, then Assistant Director of Sound Broadcasting ruled in favour of the play: 'Surely, when dealing with any kind of contemporary work, inclusion in our programmes does not indicate faith in the discovery of a literary masterpiece but merely the belief that it is of sufficient interest for the audience to have the opportunity of making up their own minds.'[28] It is striking how the differences in the response to Pinter in the press were reproduced in the BBC itself. The fact that it proved necessary to ask Marriott to make a final decision illustrates how profound and intractable these divisions were.

A Slight Ache[29] was finally broadcast on 29 July 1959 and was produced by Donald McWhinnie. It was one of three radio dramas commissioned by the BBC from Pinter, the other two being *A Night Out*[30] and *The Dwarfs*.[31] The first of these three plays starred the highly experienced film, television and radio actor Maurice Denham as Edward and Pinter's wife, Vivien Merchant, as Edward's wife Flora. The play includes a third character who doesn't speak, Barnabas, and in the *Radio Times* listing for the play the part of Barnabas is played by David Baron (Pinter's stage name). It begins with a middle-class couple sitting in their garden; the production is very spare and there is no music or sound effects.

> Flora: Have you noticed the honeysuckle this morning?
> Edward: The what?
> Flora: The Honeysuckle.
> Edward: Honeysuckle? Where?
> Flora: By the back gate, Edward.
> Edward: Is that honeysuckle? I thought it was—convolvulus, or something.
> Flora: But you know it's honeysuckle.
> Edward: I tell you I thought it was convolvulus.[32]

8. Realist Radio Drama

These opening lines establish the class of the couple, the tension in their relationship and the disagreement about the meaning of words (which quickly become an argument about whether wasps 'sting' or 'bite') is a reference to the familiar critique of language. The couple continue bickering about the names of flowers and then about whether wasps bite or sting. Edward then perks up and appears full of joy about the sun and the flowers, 'It's a good day. I feel it in my bones. In my muscles.' But his exuberance is shattered by the arrival of a blind match seller at the garden gate, Barnabas. Edward is furious while Flora is unperturbed. Edward retreats into the house followed by Flora who realizes that Edward is frightened of the match seller. He then decides to call Barnabas into the house in order to confront him. Flora's reaction to Barnabas is quite different, and she offers a cup of tea and then, 'come and have lunch with us'. The match seller enters Edward's study where he is offered a drink, and Edward explains what he does: 'I write theological and philosophical essays.' Edward attempts to impress Barnabas with his social status: 'I entertain the villagers annually, as a matter of fact. I'm not the squire, but they look upon me with some regard.' As Barnabas won't speak and, annoyingly for Edward, won't sit down, there is a long rambling speech by Edward (lasting eleven minutes in the original recording) which includes his thoughts about Africa: 'Do you by any chance know the Membunza Mountains? Great range of Katambaloo. French Equatorial Africa, if my memory serves me right. Most extraordinary diversity of flora and fauna.' Edward continuously asks Barnabas if he wants a drink, at one point in a moment of pure comedy listing a bizarre selection including 'what do you say to a straightforward Piesporter Goldtropfschen Felne Auslese (Reichsgraf von Kesselstaff)?' He also repeatedly asks Barnabas to sit down and is concerned by his sweatiness, 'You look a trifle warm. Why don't you take off your balaclava?' Finally, having failed to get Barnabas to talk or accept a drink but eventually getting him to sit down, Edward, now exhausted, calls for Flora and retreats to the garden. Then it is Flora's turn to speak uninterrupted to Barnabas. She begins in an innocuous manner similar to Edward's initial comments, 'It's the longest day of the year today, did you know that?' But quickly her comments relate to sex; she tells the story of being raped when 'out riding on my pony' and becomes increasingly intimate with Barnabas, 'I say, you are perspiring aren't you? Shall I mop your brow? With my shiffon?' She asks him if he has a woman and what he thinks about sex. Flora is clearly both repelled by the match seller and attracted to him; she decides he needs a bath, 'All you need is a bath. A lovely lathry bath. And a good scrub. A lovely lathery scrub. Don't you? It will be a pleasure.' Edward then becomes furious with Flora, perhaps because he is aware of the shift in her affections away from himself to Barnabas 'you lying slut, get back to your trough'. There is another long, rambling speech by Edward in which he asks Barnabas if he played cricket at school and whether he knew Cavendish who 'bowled left arm over the wicket'. The more Edward talks the more nonsensical he is. He offers to show Barnabas the garden but is barely able to complete a sentence, 'I would like to join you—explain—show you—the garden—explain—the plantswhere I run—my track—in training.' Flora enters as Edward asks in a whisper 'Who are you?'

> Flora: Barnabas? Ah Barnabas. Everything is ready.
> I want to show you my garden, your garden. You must see my japonica, my convolvulus ... my honeysuckle, my clematis.
> The summer is coming. I've put up your canopy for you.
> You can lunch in the garden, by the pool. I've polished the whole house for you.
> Take my hand.
> Yes. Oh, wait a moment.
> Edward. Here is your tray.[33]

Ian Rodger's review of the play was far from enthusiastic resorting to the familiar complaint, 'It was hard to know ... what the play was really all about.'[34] In her long discussion of the play, Elissa Guralnick attempts to interpret entirely in terms of differing perceptions. Edward's initial perception of the flowers in the garden, of the wasp (as a threat) and then of Barnabas, place him at odds with Flora. In the ensuing battle, Flora's views prevail even though Edward was right in his opinion that the match seller was a threat. For Guralnick the play depicts two very different, male and female, attitudes to the world; Edward who writes (or does he?) philosophical essays, and though fascinated by Africa has never been there, contemplates life at several removes: 'Edward is not there, no matter where he is.'[35] Flora on the other hand is the opposite, out in the garden relishing the plants and enjoying the weather; she was active in her youth. The different outlooks of Edward and Flora are then transferred to Barnabas; Edward despises him and finds him a threat; Flora is fascinated with him and desires him. Guralnick also describes the match seller as Flora's creation: 'Flora has created the match-seller in three easy steps.'[36] She has given him traits which comply with her own needs, dismissed Edward's negative perception of him and finally given him a name. Billington's own assessment of *A Slight Ache* draws parallels with other Pinter plays in which the occupants of a room project their fears on to an unwanted guest. He described Edward's attempts at 'bourgeois assimilation' as an attempt to assimilate the match seller to his own values and ways of life; the offers of a drink, the questions about cricket, references to school days.[37]

Placed in the context of developments in radio drama in the late 1950s, *A Slight Ache* is for a variety of reasons a particularly important play. Like Beckett's *All That Fall* it demands to be performed on radio without any visual imagery which would undermine the central dilemma. Barnabas's silence raises the question of whether he exists at all or is simply a projection, a dilemma which only works if the play is invisible, and so Pinter's first radio drama is profoundly radiogenic. Central to the play are three long speeches in which Edward (twice) and Flora (once) conduct one-sided conversations with the silent match seller. Despite the length of Edward's main speech, the extraordinary range of emotions and verbal strategies make it hold the listener's attention: the offers of a drink, the ridiculous references to Africa and also to the weather and Edward's wife as well as requests for Barnabas to sit and the eventual desperate call, 'Flora!' The speech is not a soliloquy; it is a desperate attempt to communicate which completely fails. The script for the play contains thirty directions to 'pause' in Edward's long speech and demonstrates Pinter's use of silences. This is partly the result of the realism of his writing, based as it is on careful listening to actual speech; as Esslin has commented, 'If we try to listen, with an ear unburdened by an age-old tradition of stage dialogue, to the real speech of real people, we shall find that there are more silences, longer pauses than those allowed by stage convention.'[38] In his long, pause-ridden speech, Edward tries a variety of hopeless strategies to get Barnabas to speak, but in the end they are both speechless. *A Slight Ache* is in no sense a social realist play although it does address the question of social class and can be seen as a harsh and penetrating critique of bourgeois ways: 'Anyone familiar with the English class system will instantly recognize the tone of patronizing absorption.'[39]

Jacob Stulberg sees *A Slight Ache* as a deliberate challenge to the conventions of radio drama claiming that Pinter 'rethought, or even flouted, a range of guidelines that the BBC had laid down for its playwrights'.[40] Guides for radio dramatists written by Gielgud, Sieveking and others emphasized the importance of clarity and coherence in radio drama which as Stulberg correctly observes are largely lacking in the play. Interestingly, he argues that even in Giles Cooper's decidedly obscure *The Disagreeable Oyster*, the two sides of the main character (Bundy and Bundy Minor) are made quite clear in the production. In a persuasive contribution to the discussion about *A Slight Ache*, Stulberg provides an important corrective to the orthodox guides for radio writers, both historic and contemporary, by showing how confusion and misunderstanding are central to one of the most successful radio dramas.

Pinter's second radio play, *A Night Out*,[41] is a far more orthodox social realist drama which was first broadcast on radio, produced by Donald McWhinnie, and then a month later a television production on ABC's 'Armchair Theatre'. Harold Pinter and his wife Vivien Merchant appeared in both versions. Mary O'Farrell played Mrs Stokes, the Mother in the radio version. The existing recording for the play includes an introduction by Donald McWhinnie who says the following:

Within the last four years something like a bombshell has hit the London theatre. He's a young man of 29 and his name is Harold Pinter.
His upbringing in the east end of London with its vivid community life and racy speech idioms mixed with his practical experience as an actor undoubtedly explains Pinter's superb command of dialogue and characterization.[42]

The play starts with a woman (mother) calling for Albert who is cleaning his shoes and looking for his tie; he is going out. Mother is a controlling woman who is suspicious of Albert's night out, 'You're not messing about with girls?' she asks. The next scene is of men in a café with pronounced working-class accents. The men's speech is demotic with deliberate use of 'mate', 'half a dollar', 'booze', Fulham (football club) and a typical conversation about football:

> Seeley: Well, when you couldn't play, Gidney moved Albert to left back.
> Kedge: He's a left half.
> Seeley: I know he's a left half. I said to Gidney myself, I said to him, look, Why don't you go left back, Gidney? He said, no, I'm too valuable at centre half.
> Kedge: He didn't did he?
> Seeley: Yes. Well you know who was on the right wing, don't you? Connor.[43]

Pinter fully exploits the clichéd working-class male obsession with football and the ability to discuss it in great, technical detail, and by doing so gives the play a solid foundation in London male working-class culture. Eventually Albert arrives in the café but says he doesn't feel like going out because he has a headache. The 'lads', however, try to persuade him to stay saying that there will be 'girls'. The occasion is a goodbye party for Mr King, and at the party some of the women notice Albert, 'he's quite nice when you get close'. Mr King makes a speech but then a woman screams 'someone touched me', and Albert feels he is being accused. He leaves but Gidney, who manages the local football team, follows him and there is a fight. Albert goes home. He encounters his mother, 'What have you been doing? Mucking about with girls?' She adds, 'I wouldn't mind if you find a nice girl and brought her home and introduced her to your mother.' In a long speech she complains about her son, his failure to replace the bulb in 'Grandma's' room, that he doesn't tell his mother he loves her, how he has let his father down and is 'mucking about' with girls. We hear a shout from the mother, and then there is a change of scene: later that night Albert is talking to a woman who is clearly a prostitute. She takes Albert back to her room. The conversation which follows is full of deception as both characters, Albert and the prostitute, deny their working-class identities. 'The Girl' (as she is called in the script) claims to have a daughter at boarding school, that her father was a 'military man' and that she is well educated. She wonders if Albert 'has breeding' and tells him off for swearing. She is clearly very class conscious. Albert claims to work in films as an 'assistant director'. The long one-sided conversation in which the Girl does almost all of the talking is strongly reminiscent of Flora and Edward's attempts to communicate with Barnabas in *A Slight Ache*. The Girl then starts to assess Albert:

> Girl: You amuse me. You interest me. I'm a bit of a psychologist, you know. You're very young to be – what you said you were. There's something childish in your face, almost retarded. [*She laughs.*] I do like that word. I'm not being personal, of course—just being psychological.[44]

Albert then becomes very angry and stubs his cigarette out on her carpet. Then he grabs her hand and tells her not to scream: 'Be quiet. I told you to be quiet. Now you be quiet.' His fury at the Girl expresses his deep frustration with women and his sense of powerlessness:

> Albert: You're all the same, you see, you're all the same, you're just a dead weight round my neck. What makes you think—what makes you think you can—tell me—yes—it's the same as this business about the light in grandma's room. Always something. Always something. My ash? I'll put it where I like! You see this clock? Watch your step. Just watch your step.[45]

He barks instructions at the Girl telling her to fetch his shoes and put them on his feet. At last he feels better, 'That's—more like it! Good. Lace them! Good.' Triumphantly he walks out of the room and returns home. Mother hears his return and calls out his name. She begins by criticizing him, and it is clear he had threatened her earlier, 'To threaten your own mother.' But she forgives him. The last words of the play are hers. (Albert doesn't speak at all in this final scene.)

> Mother: It's not as if you're a bad boy—you're a good boy—I know you are—it's not as if you're really bad, Albert, you're not—you're not bad, you're good—you're not a bad boy, Albert, I know you're not—
> [*Pause*]
> You're good, you're not bad, you're a good boy—I know you are—you are aren't you?[46]

The review of the play by Frederick Laws is titled 'New Classic' and he describes Pinter as a radio dramatist of the first quality.[47] He uses the term 'pure radio' for the play but notes that its quality is in the writing, and in the use of pauses and hesitations, rather than the usual battery of effects. Laws is horrified by the character of the mother who uses the full range of emotional blackmail, guilt, sarcasm, misunderstanding and 'maudlin appeals for love' to keep her 'hooks in her son'. He adds that the lads talking about football are ritually boring as well as very funny. Not all of the press reviews were positive, however, and Paul Ferris in the *Observer* claims that 'it lacked the final and only true merit of somehow interfering with the listener'.[48] Michael Billington describes *A Night Out* as 'more realistic in tone than anything Pinter had written before'.[49] He adds that it has a traditional structure and that the theme of the play, the way male inadequacy turns into violent rage, is merely 'Freud for the mass market'.[50] In the broader context of radio drama at the very beginning of the 1960s, *A Night Out* seems more significant than critics have allowed. As a classic social realist play about working-class life and gender politics, it heralded radio's very late arrival in this cultural movement. The long one-sided conversations between Mother and Albert and between Albert and the Girl are as effective and revealing as in *A Slight Ache*. This is a play about working-class life, the 'mates' talking about football are both funny and realistic, but it is also about some desperate working-class attempts to be more respectable and to disavow working-class culture: both Mother and the Girl are highly class conscious and make constant references to their own respectability while criticizing Albert's poor behaviour. Albert is an ineffectual clerk dominated by women, this was also one of Giles Cooper's most successful characterizations, and the contrast between Cooper's and Pinter's versions of the impotent male are revealing. Cooper was strongly influenced by the absurdist tradition and in *The Disagreeable Oyster* and *Under the Loofah Tree* dreamlike explorations of the inner world are supported by the use of special effects and radiophonics. Pinter's depiction of Albert's night out is radically different, a realist play based on closely observed working-class culture including language and devoid of artificial added sound. The fact that *A Night Out* so quickly, and successfully, transferred to television is unsurprising as realist dramas are conducive to visual representation while absurdism and exploration of the inner world often work particularly well on radio.

That *A Night Out* was broadcast again eight months later on the Home Service[51] was something of a vote of confidence, and this followed an episode of *People Today* also on the Home Service in which Pinter was interviewed by Kenneth Tynan.[52] In December 1960, Pinter's adaptation of his unpublished novel, *The Dwarfs*, was broadcast in a production by Barbara Bray.[53] The book on which this radio drama was based was an autobiographical novel based on Pinter's adolescence in Hackney, East London, and in particular the friendship of three boys (Mark, Pete and Len) and one girl (Virginia). In the novel, Virginia is Pete's girlfriend but when he abandons her she immediately starts a relationship with Mark. At the same time Mark discovers that Pete thinks he is a fool. The perceived betrayal leads to the break-up of the male friendship group. The radio play only has the three male characters, and Virginia is omitted which inevitably lessens the sense of rivalry between Mark and Pete.

The Dwarfs, as a radio play, consists of obscure and highly elliptical exchanges between the three young men. They engage in word play, the sort of aimless convoluted dialogue which clever young men with too much time might have enjoyed.

> Len: Where's the milk?
> Pete: You were going to bring it.
> Len: That's right.
> Pete: Well, where is it?
> Len: I forgot it. Why didn't you remind me?
> Pete: Give me the cup.
> Len: What do we do now?[54]

Len's speeches are far more strange and he claims that there are dwarfs 'back on the job'. Len's dwarfs are going to keep a very close eye on Mark and Pete. In the novel version of *The Dwarfs* Len is haunted by hallucinatory dwarfs which are banished at the end of the book. He also feels oppressed and used by Mark and Pete: 'You're trying to buy and sell me. You think I'm a ventriloquist's dummy. You've got me pinned to the wall before I open my mouth.' Len's speeches are increasingly strange, even absurd: 'Pete walks by the – gull. Slicing gull. Gull. Down. He stops. Rat corpse in the yellow grass.' Len tells Mark that Pete thinks he is a fool which appears to shock him. Mark then confronts Pete:

> Mark: You've been wasting my time. For years.
> Pete: Don't push me boy.
> Mark: You think I'm a fool.
> Pete: Is that what you think?
> Mark: That's what you think. You think I'm a fool.
> Pete: You are a fool.[55]

The play ends with a speech by Len in which he states the yard has been scrubbed and cleaned, it was foul and disgusting: 'The alleys a whirlpool of piss, slime, blood, and fruit juice.' Now all is clean and there is a shrub and a flower. Pinter explained what was going on in Len's imagination when he directed a stage version of the play; he sees a predatory and disgusting world which is his perception of the relationship between the three young men, but when this is finally broken he feels clean, purified and stronger.[56]

The review of *The Dwarfs* in *The Times* was full of admiration for Pinter's third commissioned radio drama: 'A striking extension of his talent, but yet remained true to the qualities we have come to expect of him.'[57] The critic sees Mark and Pete as straightforward Pinter types engaging in banter and jostling, 'sinister-comic inconsequentialities', but is fascinated by the character of Len. For the first time it is suggested we are inside the head of a Pinter character, we hear what is going on in his mind, 'where on the brink of insanity he lives with … the dwarfs'.[58] The end result is that the play contains 'some of the most subtly effective writing he has produced'. The next Pinter broadcast on radio was Michael Bakewell's production of *The Caretaker* in 1962.[59] Later that year, as Pinter's fame was increasing, his television play *The Collection*[60] was broadcast on radio in a production by Cedric Messina[61] starring Harold Pinter as Harry and Vivien Merchant as Stella. The radio broadcast went out at the same time as the opening of *The Collection* at the Aldwych theatre which for Michael Billington was a defining moment in Pinter's burgeoning career.[62]

Like *A Slight Ache*, the characters in *The Collection* are taken from the affluent middle class and not the working class which was his more familiar territory.[63] As Pinter, Vivien Merchant and their child Daniel moved out of their tiny flat and into more comfortable accommodation, he wrote a play about two couples living in London's more prestigious neighbourhoods. Harry and Bill are a couple living in Belgravia, and James and Stella live in Chelsea. The drama centres around a simple question did Bill and Stella sleep together in a hotel room in Leeds as she claims they did? James believes that they did and goes to Bill's house to confront him. He arrives and accuses Bill, 'Did you have a good time in Leeds last week?'[64] He describes in detail what he thinks happened, the intimidated Bill falls over a pouffe, 'You made me spill my drink! Are you going to let me get up?' there is a tangible feeling of menace in this exchange, but Bill denies there was an affair; they kissed but 'nothing happened'. When James returns to Stella he implies an intimacy with Bill, he taunts her and there are suggestions of sexual attraction. Later in the play, Bill and James play a game with knives and Bill is cut. At this point Harry arrives and announces that Stella had confessed to him that she had made the whole story up. Harry is furious with Bill: 'Bill's a slum man, he's got a slum mind.' 'He crawls all over the walls and leaves slime'; 'a filthy, putrid slum slug'. James returns to Stella now thinking that the affair was a fantasy; the final words of the play are from James checking with Stella that this was correct, 'That's the truth – isn't it?'

As an adaptation from a television play, *The Collection* appears to suffer more from basic intelligibility than other radio dramas of the time. In his critical review in *The Listener*, Martin Shuttleworth thought the ambiguities and confusion were deliberate: 'Too often he [Pinter] exploits the difficulties and limitations of the medium, not in order to surmount them but to mystify.'[65] Billington is far more positive and sees *The Collection* as 'one of Pinter's most misunderstood works'.[66] For Billington this is a drama about the nature of truth and the way it can be manipulated as well as sexual desire and how men who are attracted to the same woman may be attracted to each other. In many ways *The Collection* is classic Pinter. James is the uninvited guest who bursts into a domestic setting full of threat (a familiar Pinter trope). The dialogue is fractured and communication is confused between characters and also heavily demarcated by silences. Social class is once again an important theme: the 'cockney' taxi driver, Stella's constant references to olives and especially Harry's description of Bill as a 'slum man' and the self-consciously bourgeois lifestyle of the two couples. In this radio version of the play sound is used creatively and particular sounds, the telephone ringing, the front door bell, jazz music are all poignant and significant. The play is, like so many of Pinter's best dramas, also a statement about gender and sexual politics. Stella (like Flora in *A Slight Ache*) emerges at the end of the play triumphant. She may or may not have fabricated the story about the affair but she did so to exercise control over her husband. Both Stella and Flora emerge at the end of the play victorious, if alone.

For the growing number of Pinter enthusiasts in the summer of 1962 the Third Programme production of *The Collection* would have been an extremely welcomed and important opportunity to hear more of the new writer's work. As radio drama, however, it clearly suffers because of the importance of visual clues in the original play. As Billington comments, 'A lot of Pinter's meaning always emerges from the physical choreography of the action: he thinks visually as well as verbally. On stage, the dominant image was of Stella's cool, manipulative independence.'[67] When James asks the final question at the end of the play, 'that's the truth ... isn't it?' the stage directions in the printed version tell us, 'Stella looks at him, neither confirming not denying. Her face is friendly, sympathetic.'[68] Clearly this enigmatic but somehow victorious look is vital but entirely missing from the radio version.

There are obvious similarities in the contribution to radio drama made by Beckett and Pinter. Both wrote extensively for other media, in Beckett's case novels, stage plays, television and film and in Pinter's case stage plays and screen plays. Both were Nobel-Prize-winning giants of literature who wrote a few, highly significant radio plays, among the most important radio dramas written in English. Pinter's three commissioned radio dramas, broadcast over a period of just seventeen months, were varied in terms of subject: a middle-class couple whose lives are disrupted by a match seller, the working-class young man oppressed by women and the three young men engaging in emotionally charged word play. Perhaps Pinter's most important influence on the development of radio drama, apart from the mere fact that such an important writer wanted to use the radio medium, was to demonstrate a form of realism which had hitherto been missing. The contemporary issues of class, gender and power at the beginning of the 1960s were present in all of these plays, and Pinter signalled a decisive move to more realist dramas and a move away from adaptations of the theatrical, literary and classical canon or the cerebral world of the absurd.

Other radio dramatists contributed to the realist turn in the late 1950s and perhaps the most important of these was Rhys Adrian. Between 1956, the date of his first broadcast play, and 1964, the end of the period covered by this book, there were seven original plays for radio by Adrian of which only two (*Betsie*[69] and *Too Old for Donkeys*[70]) are accessible as recordings. Adrian, despite the importance of his contribution as a radio dramatist, he was one of very few British winners of the Prix Italia[71] and won two Giles Cooper awards[72] in a career which lasted from 1956 to 1988, has been largely forgotten. There is no critical account of his work and in the standard commentaries he gets very short shrift indeed.[73] He does, however, represent an extremely interesting development in late 1950s' and early 1960s' radio drama and was clearly well thought of at the time as the regular commissioning of his work and the available contemporary commentaries suggest. In this history of radio drama, Rhys Adrian is placed alongside Harold Pinter whose life and work is the subject of industrial scale analysis and commentary; Adrian, however, may have been writing in a similar realist manner and may, like Pinter, Cooper and Beckett, have had a decisive influence on the genre.

Rhys Adrian's first play for radio, *The Man on the Gate*,[74] was produced for the Third Programme in 1956 by Archie Campbell, despite being described by John Morris (controller, Third Programme) as 'cheap' and 'vulgar'.[75] It was followed in 1957 by *The Passionate Thinker*[76] produced by Donald McWhinnie and was the subject of the same intriguing and highly revealing memorandum from John Morris. Morris had heard Giles Cooper's *The Disagreeable Oyster* and with considerable reluctance agreed to broadcast it. At the same time he had reviewed[77] *The Passionate Thinker*, his response to the latter is an excellent illustration of the persistent conservatism in the BBC towards experimental drama. Morris thought that the play might have 'got by' twenty years earlier as something 'mildly experimental' but the characterization was 'superficial and obvious'. Morris goes on to compare Adrian with Samuel Beckett of whom he wrote, 'however one may personally dislike his work' was a 'near-genius' whereas Rhys Adrian 'seems to me to lack even a modicum of talent'.[78] Despite John Morris's rejection the play was broadcast but on the Home Service and is about a married couple, lying awake in bed having their own separate and private thoughts: 'The thought-patterns approach each other, weave, blend, cross, separate; they are strangely similar, yet ultimately private – and they could never be voiced.'[79] For McWhinnie, the play was an example of what he called 'pure radio', in other words radiogenic drama, only fit for the invisible medium: 'The words whispered in the minds of the actors, the whole an expression in voices of something which cannot be exteriorized. The only words which are actually spoken are trivial in the extreme: "Are you asleep?" And all the more poignant for that.'[80] It is striking how strong the disagreements were about Rhys Adrian, as they were over the work of Harold Pinter two years later; the controller, Third Programme, thought his play was worthless and Adrian himself without talent whereas the assistant head of Radio Drama praised it as 'pure radio'.

There was then a gap in Rhys Adrian's radio career during which time he changed his writing name form L. R. Adrian to Rhys Adrian. His next radio play, *Betsie*,[81] was produced by Michael Bakewell. The play begins with two men, Lucas and, an older man, Jack. There is an absurdity in their conversation as they argue about whether or not they had been to the pub before; Jack asks a series of disconnected questions: 'Ever been in a fight?' 'Have you studied the law?' He asks Lucas (who he insists on also calling Jack) if he has a girlfriend and claims that everyone in the pub is a brigadier as his talk becomes increasingly nonsensical. At this point Betsie arrives and strikes up a conversation with Lucas; she is a very depressed character who visits the pub weekly. The gulf between Lucas, an educated man who writes poetry, and Jack, the uneducated heavy drinking pub bore, becomes increasingly evident. An Irishman appears and starts singing and all the while Lucas tries, unsuccessfully, to leave the pub. Betsie has a conversation with Lucas in which he expresses his inadequacy and failure to impress a nurse that he liked. Betsie then reveals that she and Jack are married. The three male characters move out of the pub where they argue until Lucas eventually manages to leave; Jack shouts, 'Come back, you're a poet' and then 'I don't want to be left on my own.'[82] The play ends with Jack and Betsie still in the pub as the landlord calls 'last orders'.

In his review of the play, Frederick Laws was extremely positive, 'the most interesting and original broadcast for some time'.[83] He found it comic and pathetic and a 'faithful imitation of the rhythms of commonplace conversation'. He noted the realism of the play and compared the writer to Pinter. Laws wondered why realism had become such a popular feature of contemporary drama and traced it back, with some justification, to *Waiting for Godot* stating that 'demotic speech has broken out in a big way'.[84] He also praised the producer Michael Bakewell who 'let the patches of rich talk and deep emotion in a complex and subtle play make their full impression. We must certainly hear more from Mr Rhys Adrian'.[85] In a later review of radio drama in *The Listener*, Ian Rodger described it as 'brilliant'.[86] It is certainly true that there are similarities between Adrian and Pinter and these are clear in *Betsie*. We encounter three people trapped in a room (in this case a pub) and, as in Pinter, their conversation seems to act as a barrier between them or as a means of domination. In *Betsie*, characters engage in a Pinteresque struggle for power in which themes of class (between Jack and Lucas) and gender (between Betsie and the men) are prominent. Unsurprisingly, Rhys Adrian was clearly also influenced by Giles Cooper and especially in the depiction of the frustrated lower-middle-class man apparently powerless in his relationships with women and other, more assertive men.

Rhys Adrian, like so many of his contemporary writers, also wrote for television drama and especially commercial television. The television play *The Protest*[87] was favourably and perceptively reviewed in *The Times* where it was described as 'the rebellion of a "little man" against the anonymity and dreariness of his life'.[88] The connections between Rhys Adrian and Harold Pinter were mentioned in this review; Adrian's writing was described as having 'Pinteresque overtones' and the play starred Pinter's wife Vivien Merchant. Adrian was praised in the review for his 'cruel mastery of our slipshod, contemporary idioms'.[89] His next radio play, *The Bridge*,[90] was produced by Michael Bakewell and featured a middle-aged husband and wife, intensely bored with each other, who fail to communicate with their small son, standing alone on a bridge looking down into the stream below.[91] By this stage in his career Rhys Adrian was writing highly naturalistic representations of working-class speech and producing plays which conveyed a sense of boredom and frustration with the world at the end of the 1950s.

Too Old for Donkeys[92] was produced by Michael Bakewell and takes place on Euston Station, London, at night. The characters, Arthur, an older man and Henry, a young man of seventeen, have working-class accents. They are waiting for two other men, both called Charlie, who both have strong northern working-class accents and one of whom is very drunk. Henry starts a conversation with a woman at the station eventually buying her coffee and chocolate. She is distressed: 'I just want to sit here and wait for my train and not be bothered.'[93] Henry talks to one of the men called Charlie about the woman, 'She's different, it's not like picking up some tart at a dance.' As the play develops various conversations occur on the station platform revealing aspects of the lives of the characters. Arthur had married Henry's widowed mother after the war but his relationship with her was now 'awful'. The young woman is separated from her husband and Henry tries, unsuccessfully, to persuade her not to go home. Eventually the train is ready, they embark, the whistle goes and the train departs.

The review of *Too Old for Donkeys* in *The Times* once again focused on the naturalism of the writing.[94] The critic thought that Adrian was engrossed in 'the precise study of habits of speech' adding that 'he observes minutely and compassionately' and that there was in the play 'extremely precise exploitations of modern, provincial working-class English'. Once again, Adrian's naturalistic approach to depictions of working-class life and especially language are notable as is his representation of aspects of working-class life: the pub, drunkenness, railway stations, the influence of the war, deep gender differences. However this is more than a sociology of working-class culture; the depiction of the relationship between Henry and the young woman and the obstacles that stand in their way are also central to the drama as is the sense of the pointlessness of life. A far more critical review was provided by Martin Shuttleworth in *The Listener*, 'Adrian is a naturalist rather than a realist and I always find his work flat, drawn out and lusterless.'[95] He added that Adrian's radio plays were a bit like 'tapes that sounded fascinating enough[96] when I was getting them but which I know, when I play them back, needed to be edited right down'. This is an interesting and not entirely unfair criticism and perhaps goes some way to explain Adrian's modest success as a playwright. However, it is his meticulous rendition of everyday speech which stands out in an important contribution to the radio drama canon, and he remained an active playwright for many years to come.[97] Following Shuttleworth it could be argued that the naturalist, precise and brilliantly observed reproduction of everyday speech was the defining feature of his plays and not the deeper realist representation of power structures and social divisions.

Harold Pinter and Rhys Adrian, in their different ways, helped develop a realist and naturalist approach to radio drama in which working-class speech, culture and experiences were expressed. However, both writers produced plays which, with the notable exception of Pinter's *A Slight Ache*, focused on a male view of the world and a misogynistic view of women. Radio drama on the Third Programme in the 1950s had previously failed to address issues of social class and inequality and both Pinter and Adrian put working-class characters and the very issue of class itself at the heart of their plays. It is possible to detect in both writers other influences and interests (absurdism included) but both wrote radio plays which turned their attention to Britain in the early 1960s and away from constant references to the past, both the near-past of the Second World War and the distant-past of earlier centuries and classical antiquity. Both writers signalled the possibility of radio drama as a way of interpreting contemporary Britain including the culture and experiences of the male working class.

Realist radio drama thrived after the period covered by this book, and it is worth mentioning one very important example. Joe Orton had a remarkable but short-lived career as a playwright in the mid-1960s before his untimely death in 1967. He wrote one radio drama and its success launched his career. *The Ruffian on the Stair*[98] was produced by the rising star of radio drama production John Tydeman. The play is a classically social realist tale concerning working-class characters, an ex-boxer and a former prostitute, living in a bed sit in London. They are visited by a young thug called Wilson, seeking revenge for the death of his much loved brother. The similarities between this drama and the work of Pinter are striking; themes of violence, squalor, working-class London, claustrophobia and the arrival of a mysterious and dangerous stranger are all typical of Pinter. *The Ruffian on the Stair* is an important indicator that the realist tradition of radio drama, launched in particular by Pinter and Adrian, was to thrive in the years to come.

Notes

1 The term coined by Kenneth Tynan; see Chapter 1.
2 Stephen Lacey, *British Realist Theatre: The New Wave in Its Context, 1956-1965* (London: Routledge, 1995).
3 This account of Pinter's life is based on Michael Billington, *The Life and Work of Harold Pinter* (London: Faber and Faber, 1996) and Martin Esslin, *Pinter, the Playwright* (London: Methuen, 1970).
4 Billington, *The Life and Work of Harold Pinter*, 62.
5 Ibid., 70.
6 'Digs' refer to lodgings or accommodation for travelling people including actors.
7 Ibid., 74.
8 Harold Pinter, *The Birthday Party* (London: Methuen, 1960).
9 Jonathan Bignell, '"Random dottiness": Samuel Beckett and Harold Pinter in 1958', in *Beckett Influencing / Influencing Beckett*, ed. N. Johnson, A. Rokoczy and M. Tanaka (Budapest and Paris: Károli Gáspár University Press/L'Harmattan, forthcoming), 3.
10 Ibid.
11 For a full account of the reception of *The Birthday Party*, see Paul Elsam, 'Harold Pinter's the birthday party: The "lost" second production', *Studies in Theatre and Performance* 30, no. 3 (2010): 257–66.
12 John Tydeman interview, 23 November 2017.
13 Quoted in Bignell, 'Random Dottiness', 2.
14 Billington, *The Life and Work of Harold Pinter*, 94.
15 Quoted in Esslin, *Pinter the Playwright*, 8.
16 Ibid.
17 Quoted in Bignell, 'Random Dottiness', 4.
18 Quoted in Esslin, *Pinter the Playwright*, 9.
19 John Tydeman interview, 23 November 2017.
20 Esslin, *Pinter the Playwright*, 8.
21 Ibid., 10.
22 Billington, *The Life and Work of Harold Pinter*, 95.
23 Ibid.

24 Ibid., 100.
25 Ibid.
26 Ironically, the conventional structure of *The Birthday Party* is frequently noted.
27 Quoted in Billington, *The Life and Work of Harold Pinter*, 96.
28 Ibid.
29 *A Slight Ache*, 29 July 1959. BBC Third Programme. Quotations taken from Harold Pinter, *A Slight Ache and Other Plays* (London: Methuen, 1961).
30 *A Night Out*, 1 March 1960. BBC Third Programme.
31 *The Dwarfs*, 2 December 1960. BBC Third Programme.
32 *A Slight Ache*.
33 Ibid.
34 Ian Rodger, 'Critic on the hearth', *The Listener*, 6 August 1959.
35 Elissa S. Guralnick, *Sight Unseen* (Athens: Ohio University Press, 1996), 112.
36 Ibid., 116.
37 Billington, *The Life and Work of Harold Pinter*, 99.
38 Esslin, *Pinter the Playwright*, 37.
39 Ibid., 98.
40 Jacob Stulberg, 'How (not) to write broadcast plays: Pinter and the BBC', *Modern Drama* 58, no. 4 (2015): 503.
41 *A Night Out*, 1 March 1960. BBC Third Programme. Quotations from Pinter, *A Slight Ache and Other Plays*.
42 Donald McWhinnie, introduction to *A Night Out* recording available on the British Library Soundserver, accessed 6 March 2017.
43 *A Night Out*.
44 'A Night Out', in Pinter, *A Slight Ache and Other Plays*, 81.
45 *A Night Out*.
46 'A Night Out', in Pinter, *A Slight Ache and Other Plays*, 87.
47 Frederick Laws, 'The critic on the hearth', *The Listener*, 10 March 1960.
48 Quoted in Billington, *The Life and Work of Harold Pinter*, 111.
49 Billington, *The Life and Work of Harold Pinter*, 111.
50 Ibid., 112.
51 *A Night Out*, 8 November 1960. BBC Home Service.
52 *People Today*, 28 October 1960. BBC Home Service.
53 *The Dwarfs*, 2 December 1960. BBC Third Programme. No recording of this production was available so this rather truncated account of the play is based on reading the script in Pinter, *A Slight Ache and Other Plays*.
54 'The Dwarfs', in Pinter, *A Slight Ache and Other Plays*, 92.
55 Ibid., 116.
56 Billington, *The Life and Work of Harold Pinter*, 61.
57 'Mr Pinter at his most subtle', *The Times*, 3 December 1960.
58 Ibid.
59 *The Caretaker*, 20 March 1962. BBC Third Programme.
60 *The Collection*, 11 May 1961. Associated Rediffusion.
61 *The Collection*, 12 June 1962. BBC Third Programme.
62 Billington, *The Life and Work of Harold Pinter*, 140.
63 Esslin, *Pinter the Playwright*, 114.
64 *The Collection*.
65 Martin Shuttleworth, 'The critic on the hearth', *The Listener*, 21 June 1962.

66 Billington, *The Life and Work of Harold Pinter*, 137.
67 Ibid., 140.
68 Quoted in Billington, *The Life and Work of Harold Pinter*, 137.
69 *Betsie*, 3 August 1960. BBC Third Programme.
70 *Too Old for Donkeys*, 14 January 1963. BBC Third Programme.
71 In 1969 for the radio play, *Evelyn*.
72 Awards for plays written for BBC radio between 1978 and 1992.
73 For example, Drakakis, *British Radio Drama*; Lewis, *Radio Drama*; Rodger, *Radio Drama*; Tim Crook, *Radio Drama, Theory and Practice* (London: Routledge, 1999).
74 *The Man on the Gate*, 19 November 1956. BBC Third Programme.
75 John Morris to Val Gielgud, 26 April 1957. BBC WAC.
76 *The Passionate Thinker*, 27 September 1957. BBC Home Service.
77 Morris had probably read the script, not heard a recording of the play.
78 John Morris to Val Gielgud, 26 April 1957. BBC WAC.
79 McWhinnie, *The Art of Radio*, 58.
80 Ibid., 59.
81 *Betsie*, 3 August 1960. BBC Third Programme.
82 Ibid.
83 Frederick Laws, 'The critic on the hearth', *The Listener*, 21 August 1960.
84 Ibid.
85 Ibid.
86 Ian Rodger, *The Listener*, 27 August 1961.
87 *The Protest*, 27 September 1960. ITV Play of the Week.
88 *The Times*, 29 September 1960.
89 Ibid.
90 *The Bridge*, 19 July 1961. BBC Third Programme.
91 'Author scores with a study of boredom', *The Times*, 20 July 1961.
92 *Too Old for Donkeys*, 29 January 1963. BBC Third Programme.
93 Ibid.
94 *The Times*, 9 February 1963.
95 Martin Shuttleworth, 'The critic on the hearth', *The Listener*, 28 February 1963.
96 I assume this is a reference to tape recordings of speech or an interview.
97 The year 1963 was very productive for Rhys Adrian as a radio dramatist and alongside *Too Old for Donkeys*, the radio dramas *Room to Let* (19 May) and *A Nice Clean Sheet of Paper* (16 October), both produced by Michael Bakewell, were broadcast in that year.
98 *The Ruffian on the Stair*, 31 August 1964. BBC Third Programme.

Chapter 9

THE 1960s

The beginning of the 1960s at the BBC was marked by the arrival of arguably the most radical and dynamic of all director generals, Hugh Carleton Greene. He has written about his shock at the conservatism of the BBC as a 'pillar of the establishment'.[1] He mocked the 'corporation official' who was 'a bowler-hatted gentleman in striped trousers and black coat, entering the hushed precincts of Broadcasting House with tightly rolled umbrella'.[2] In his tirade against the BBC's conservatism and that of its audience he mocked those who complained about the closure of that great broadcasting institution, the radio news at nine o'clock, citing the remarkable uproar and accusations of his betrayal of trust.[3] Greene was also withering in his criticism of BBC news (under the very conservative and notoriously cautious Tahu Hole[4]) and especially its failure to report on general elections in news bulletins prior to 1959. The start of the new decade under the radical Greene might appear to be fairly momentous for radio drama, but in fact it was not. The reason for that was Greene's focus on television and the development of news and current affairs. His radicalism was expressed in the early 1960s by his support for the iconic satirical television programme *That Was the Week That Was* (1962–3) and by breaking down the barriers between news and current affairs, not by any changes to radio networks or output. For the first few years of the 1960s, Radio Drama Department under Val Gielgud would remain impervious to Greene's change agenda.

The story of BBC radio drama at the beginning of the 1960s is in many ways similar to that of classical music on the BBC at the same time. For Tony Stoller, classical music broadcasting in 1960 was 'relatively conservative';[5] the Home Service provision of classical music was 'firmly middle-brow', while the Third Programme 'still demonstrated its belief that it was catering for listeners of a level of music education and discernment which would have been highly exclusive'.[6] He cites the five-and-a-half-hour broadcast of Berlioz's *The Trojans* on the Third Programme as an example of its output adding that the audience would not have reached more than 47,000 at any one time. For Stoller, Val Gielgud's production of Sophocles's *Electra* might have been worthwhile for the 'Fellows of Balliol' but the 1960s' revolution in popular culture was clearly not happening on the Third Programme.

Despite this justifiable pessimism, 1960 was a year in which a lot happened in radio drama both in terms of personnel and dramatic output. For the radio drama listener, and especially those interested in innovative and challenging dramas, 1960 was a particularly rich year. There were two new dramas by Pinter, a play by Giles Cooper, an adaptation of Beckett's *Waiting for Godot*,[7] Rhys Adrian's *Betsie*,[8] a repeat of Michael Bakewell's production of Ionesco's *Rhinoceros*[9] and Martin Esslin's production of Ionesco's *Victims of Duty*.[10] In the same year there was a repeat of MacNeice's *East of the Sun and West of the Moon*[11] and a remarkable six radio dramas adapted from Ibsen's plays.[12] For those wanting to hear radio adaptations of Shakespeare there were broadcasts of five plays.[13] In addition there was the new drama series 'British Drama 1600-1642' which included among many others Webster's *The White Devil*[14] and Thomas Middleton's *The Changeling*.[15] In the same year there were other radio dramas by Arthur Adomov, Arthur Miller,[16] an adaptation of William Golding's *Free Fall*,[17] a play by him written for radio,[18] Bill Naughton's *On the Run*,[19] Sartre's *La Nausée*[20] and N. F. Simpson's *A Resounding Tinkle*.[21]

By the early 1960s, radio drama was increasingly scheduled in drama series which provided a thematic framework for programming. *Saturday Night Theatre* was the most long-running drama series and began in 1943 with a play by Dorothy L. Sayers. With the launch of the Third Programme in 1946, *Saturday Night Theatre* continued as a very regular fixture on the Home Service (and then Radio Four) and continued up to 1998. The plays' broadcast reflected the perception of the Home Service's audience as mainly 'middle-brow' and so the emphasis was very much on well-structured, entertaining and traditional drama. *From the Fifties* was broadcast on both the Home Service and the Third Programme and began in 1961 with Eliot's *The Cocktail Party*.[22] Among the playwrights to be heard in this series were Sartre, Rattigan, Anouilh, Arden and adaptations of novels by Golding and Amis among many others. This strand ended, significantly, with the first radio broadcast of Pinter's *The Caretaker*[23] on the Third Programme and, on the Home Service, with a double bill of John Mortimer's *The Dock Brief*[24] and N. F. Simpson's *A Resounding Tinkle*.[25] Another very important drama series was *The National Theatre of the Air* (see Chapter 2). This began in 1961 on the Home Service with John Gay's ballad opera of 1728, *The Beggar's Opera*,[26] and ended at the beginning of 1964, immediately after Martin Esslin took over as head of Drama, with Shakespeare's *Twelfth Night*[27] in a production by Val Gielgud and Cedric Messina. As mentioned previously, *The National Theatre of the Air* was largely a project run by Gielgud and Raymond Raikes who represented the most conservative wing of the Drama Department. There was a great deal of sixteenth- and seventeenth-century English drama and an odd mix of Somerset Maugham, Oscar Wilde and medieval English mystery plays. Arguably even more eclectic and again an expression of Gielgud and Raikes's conservatism was the series on the Third Programme, *British Drama 1600 to 1642*. This began at the beginning of 1959 with Thomas Dekker's *The Shoemaker's Holiday*,[28] adapted and produced by

Raymond Raikes, and there were eight plays in total. *World Theatre* started in 1949 and by 1960 was providing on the Home Service occasional adaptations of stage plays with an emphasis on foreign playwrights. In 1960 *World Theatre* included three plays by Chekhov as well as Ibsen and Shakespeare; in 1961 there were three plays by Strindberg as well as Sophocles and Tolstoy among others. Perhaps of all the radio drama series, *World Theatre* was the most didactic, the best example of an attempt to provide an educational experience for listeners by broadcasting adaptations of the theatrical canon.

By the early 1960s, after the various internal disputes in Radio Drama over the merit of Beckett, Cooper, Pinter and Adrian, the department appeared to have reached an uneasy compromise in which producers allied to Gielgud's view of drama, most notably Raymond Raikes, busied themselves producing for series which reflected their specific, and arguably rather eccentric, tastes. Meanwhile, the more radical wing of Radio Drama that clustered around McWhinnie, Bray and Bakewell focused their energies on a strand like *From the Fifties* which celebrated innovative and intellectually demanding writing. This arrangement would not last long, however, as, for various different reasons, key producers began to leave the BBC. Donald McWhinnie, whose contribution to British radio drama was so significant, produced his last play in August 1960. He was replaced as Gielgud's assistant by Martin Esslin whose first production was just eight months later in April 1961. Barbara Bray left at the same time as McWhinnie and her last production was in December 1960. Gielgud himself, after thirty-five years as head of Radio Drama, left in early 1964, his last production being March of that year; he was replaced by Martin Esslin. Michael Bakewell did not continue for long under Esslin, and his last radio drama production was in March 1965. At that time John Tydeman's career had barely begun and he went on to be head of Radio Drama. Raymond Raikes also had many more years in the Drama Department producing his last play in 1975. It is hard to measure the precise impact of these changes, but given the absolutely decisive influence of McWhinnie, Bray and Bakewell on post-war radio drama, it is hard not to conclude that without that powerful and inspirational presence, radio drama would become less important and less culturally significant.

Any account of radio drama in the early 1960s needs to acknowledge the improvements in the quality of television drama from the early 1950s. Developments in technology were obviously an important part of this story, and improvements in television sets and the quality of the image as well as major developments in production technology produced far more satisfactory results. In the 1950s and early 1960s most television programmes were broadcast live,[29] and the increased use of recording technologies, both 35 mm film and videotape, introduced new opportunities for creating and recording television drama. In particular, the use of film inserts in live studio-based drama 'provided a way of furthering the action and drama'.[30] This was demonstrated in iconic early BBC television dramas such as *Quatermass*[31] and *Nineteen Eighty-Four*.[32] The launch of ITV in 1955 had added to the variety and quantity of television drama and especially in the series *Armchair Theatre* (ABC, 1956–69). In 1960 Armchair Theatre presented *Lena, O My Lena*, a much-cited example of realist, studio-based television drama[33] and an adaptation of Pinter's radio play, *A Night Out*.[34]

As television drama improved in quality in the late 1950s and early 1960s, so writers and producers of radio drama were tempted to work in the visual medium. Harold Pinter, after writing three radio dramas (*A Slight Ache*, *A Night Out* and *The Dwarfs*), concentrated on the theatre, television and film. Donald McWhinnie, the most important producer of innovative radio drama in the 1950s, moved to a highly successful television career in 1960. Michael Bakewell, who for a while replaced McWhinnie in importance as a radio drama producer for the Third Programme, also moved to television production as the BBC's first 'Head of Plays'. Unusually he retained an interest in radio and contributed to several episodes of the twenty-six-part *Lord of the Rings*[35] in the role of 'adaptor'. Most significantly, however, in the exodus of radio drama talent to television was Giles Cooper. His dramatizations of Georges Simenon's *Maigret* stories began in 1959, and he wrote original plays for television and made adaptations of his own radio plays as well as a number of multi-part adaptations up to his death in 1968 (see Chapter 6).

The end of the 1950s and the beginning of the 1960s, marked as it was by the irrepressible rise of quality television drama, was also an opportunity for some women to make highly distinctive contributions to radio drama. As Cooper, McWhinnie and Bakewell looked longingly at the opportunities offered by television, so others seized an opportunity. Barbara Bray has already featured in this book, but it is worth paying particular attention to the last few years of her BBC career. Originally, Bray was appointed to head the new radio drama script unit (see Chapter 2), towards the end of the 1950s; however, she was increasingly used as a producer and also continued to translate contemporary French writing. In 1958 she translated, adapted and produced two novels by the French writer Marguerite Dumas.[36] She produced Arthur Adomov's *En Fiacre* in 1959[37] and Alfred Jarry's *Ubu Roi*.[38] Towards the end of 1960 and immediately prior to her departure from the BBC and her move to Paris (to be closer to Samuel Beckett and her other many French literary friends, including Marguerite Dumas), Barbara Bray produced three particularly important radio dramas: *The Old Tune*[39] by Robert Pinget was translated by Beckett; Pinter's *The Dwarfs*[40] was the last of his three plays commissioned by the BBC and Sartre's *La Nausée*[41] which she translated and produced. As already described, it was Bray's close association with the Paris literary scene and a number of writers based in Paris as their translator and friend that not only made a major contribution to the promotion of Beckett's work on the BBC but reinforced the BBC's avant-garde credentials. Despite the obvious resistance of Radio Drama's old guard, led by Val Gielgud,

French avant-garde writing had a direct influence on BBC radio drama and so internationalized Third Programme output and prevented it from being merely the 'National Theatre of the Air' of Shakespeare, Renaissance dramatists and a few mystery plays. No doubt the diametrically opposite views of Gielgud and Bray contributed to her eventual departure, but she survived in what was a man's world and made a decisive and highly beneficial contribution to BBC Drama.

Nesta Pain[42] was one of the most talented and creative producers at the BBC in the twentieth century. She began her career in 1942 working on the BBC's war effort and in particular the Overseas Service's propaganda programming 'Projection of Britain'. After the war she naturally moved to the newly independent Features Department under Lawrence Gilliam where she established a reputation for producing science features. Nesta Pain was a very active producer and writer, and during the 1950s she wrote books about history and science and, importantly, stage plays. In 1957 she completed BBC training as a television scriptwriter, and in the same year produced John Mortimer's Prix Italia winning radio drama, *The Dock Brief*.[43]

The play is a simple story of two men, one a man called Fowl who is accused of murdering his wife, which he freely admits to, and the other his severely incompetent and under-employed lawyer, Wilfred Morganhall. The lawyer is delighted to have been the case as a 'dock brief' meaning the defendant cannot pay and so the court will employ a lawyer for him. Despite his education and legal airs and graces, Morganhall is incompetent as a lawyer and a sad and lonely man. Fowl on the other hand, uneducated and working class, is a far more impressive and sympathetic character. The story concludes with the case being lost but eventually Fowl is released from prison because it was decided that the barrister who represented him, Morganhall, was no good. Clearly something about this unremarkable one-hour radio play resonated with audiences at the time and produced a great, popular success. Following its first broadcast the play was repeated in May and August 1957 before a BBC television version in September and two further broadcasts on the Home Service in 1957 and 1962. There was also a film of the play starring Peter Sellers and Richard Attenborough. The radio drama received a very positive review by J. C. Trewin who commended Mortimer's writing, 'in irony, pathos and comedy, ... subtly understated'.[44] He also praised the performances of David Kossoff as Fowl and Michael Hordern as Morganhall. Perhaps the key to understanding the success of *The Dock Brief* is its gentle critique of the class system. Running throughout the play is the argument that educated lawyers are in no way superior to uneducated working-class murderers who may in fact be their betters.

In the late 1950s and early 1960s, Nesta Pain managed to combine producing features, often about science or crime, with occasional but important contributions to radio drama. Following the success of *The Dock Brief*, she produced John Mortimer's *I Spy*[45] along with some crime-related drama for the Home Service. *Parkinson's Law*[46] was a musical satire written and produced by Pain, and in 1960 she adapted and produced T. H. White's *The Goshawk*. Evidence of the confidence the BBC had in Nesta Pain's ability to adapt novels and produce them as radio dramas is seen in the intriguing decision to use her to adapt and produce Alan Sillitoe's important social realist novel *The Loneliness of the Long Distance Runner*.[47]

Ray Bradbury's short story *There Will Come Soft Rains* was published in 1950 then appeared again as part of his influential collection of stories, *The Martian Chronicles*. In 1962, Nesta Pain adapted and produced the story with music composed by Antony Hopkins and further production by the Radiophonic Workshop.[48] The drama (or dramatized short story to be strictly accurate) begins with some haunting organ music, then the sound of a clock and woman's voice, 'tick tock, tick tock'. Music and radiophonic sounds continue for the thirty minutes of the programme, like a modern 'music bed' added to occasionally by female and male voices singing. There is a male narrator who tells the story in an adaptation which is very close to Bradbury's original although the tense has been changed from past to present. We are told that we are in a house served by robots who make coffee, pour milk and open the garage door. One of the robots speaks in an American accent, 'Today is August fourth in the year two thousand twenty six.' But there are no people in the house, only the robots who service it. We then learn that the side of the house bears a record of what happened to the occupants; one wall is black and on it are the silhouettes of the family who once lived in the house, the suggestion being that a huge explosion had blackened the house and captured the last moments of its occupants. Meanwhile the day passes in the empty house; lunch is cooked, uneaten it is disposed of; bridge tables appear and sandwiches and tea served to non-existent bridge players. In the evening a robot voice speaks, 'Mrs McLellan, which poem would you like this evening?' The voice is forced to make the choice and reads Sara Teasdale's 'There Will Come Soft Rains' which appropriately is a poem about the world after a war which had killed all of humanity. Then the house catches fire and is destroyed. This is arguably Nesta Pain's most interesting and successful radio drama, and given her intense interest in science, it was unsurprising that she succeeded so well with a science fiction story. The theme of Bradbury's story is of course nuclear destruction, and the timing of the broadcast could hardly have been more appropriate. Just four weeks later in October 1962 American and the Soviet Union were engaged in the nuclear stand-off of the Cuban missile crisis, arguably the closest the world has ever come to nuclear war.

Another woman who found space in the diminishing Drama department in the early 1960s was Caryl Churchill who went on to become one of Britain's most celebrated playwrights. *The Ants*[49] is a twenty-five-minute play produced by Michael Bakewell and benefitting from sound by the Radiophonic Workshop. In the play, Tim, a young boy, talks to the ants he sees by the seaside. With him is his grandfather and mother, who is evidently separated from Tim's father. The father arrives, 'we've dropped a big bomb' and the mother reads from a paper that a bomb has killed 10,000 people. Tim carries on playing with the ants and names one Bill. Tim's father uses the ants as a metaphor, 'You'll think you want to live with some girl and have lots of children and friends and jobs and live in a happy ant hill. But you don't.'[50] Tim's parents tell him they are separating, and his mother wants him to live with her; she cries. In the end Tim's father pours petrol on the ants, and the play ends with the sound of a roaring fire, a squeaking ant sound and then the sound of the sea. With its explicit cold war themes, *The Ants* impressed the critic Martin Shuttleworth. He praised Caryl Churchill's first radio drama and hoped that it would be broadcast many more times. Calling it a work of 'beauty and distinction' he added that some people had objected to the production of the play and in particular, 'the BBC seagulls, the electronic ant noises, the predictable BBC type middle-class mum, dad, granddad, and small boy'.[51] But he was not bothered by these production issues although they are an interesting comment on the occasional predictability of even the best radio drama at the time.

Being the last year covered by this book, 1963 was Val Gielgud's thirty-fifth and final year as a head of Radio Drama. On this occasion he was allowed a 'valedictory production' of his choice, and he chose Ibsen's *Brand*. Brand is a lonely priest, an Old Testament figure unable to compromise. Gielgud wrote that he had 'a personal sympathy for that harsh, uncompromising, indomitable figure' and wished that 'if only I could have found the courage and the certainty to face my problems like that'.[52] Brand had stood in defiance of the white onrush of an avalanche which killed him. It is tempting to draw similarities between Gielgud and Brand, between the isolated and often inflexible head of drama and the stubborn but certain priest. Perhaps for Gielgud the oncoming avalanche represented the arrival of television which almost swept radio drama to oblivion.

Notes

1 Hugh Greene, *The Third Floor Front* (London: The Bodley Head, 1969), 125.
2 Ibid.
3 It was replaced in October 1960 by the news at 10.00 pm.
4 Leonard Miall, *Inside the BBC* (London: Weidenfeld and Nicolson, 1994), 123–33.
5 Stoller, *Classical Music Radio in the United Kingdom, 1945-1995*, 98.
6 Ibid., 105.
7 *Waiting for Godot*, 27 April 1960. BBC Third Programme.
8 *Betsie*, 3 August 1960. BBC Third Programme.
9 *Rhinoceros*, 20 August 1959 repeated 29 March 1960. BBC Third Programme.
10 *Victims of Duty*, 21 August 1960. BBC Third Programme.
11 *East of the Sun and West of the Moon*, 25 July 1959 repeated 21 February 1960. BBC Third Programme.

12 *Peer Gynt*, 17 January 1960 (the broadcast ran for three hours twenty minutes including a short interval); *A Doll's House*, 3 May 1960; *The Pillars of Society*, 30 May 1960; *The Wild Duck*, 30 September 1960; *An Enemy of the People*, 12 October 1960; *The Lady from the Sea*, 7 November 1960. All BBC Third Programme. In addition there were two further Ibsen plays in the early 1960s, *Rosmersholm*, 17 January 1962; *Brand* 29 April 1963 (Val Gielgud's choice and his valedictory production).
13 *The Tempest*, 28 February 1960; *Antony and Cleopatra*, 3 March 1960; *King Lear*, 22 June 1960; *A Midsummer Night's Dream*, 17 August 1960 and *Hamlet*, 23 October 1960. All BBC Third Programme.
14 *The White Devil*, 16 February 1960. BBC Third Programme.
15 *The Changeling*, 6 April 1960. BBC Third Programme.
16 *Death of a Salesman*, 12 January 1960. BBC Third Programme.
17 *Free Fall*, 27 January 1960. BBC Third Programme.
18 *Miss Pulkinhorn*, 20 April 1960. BBC Third Programme.
19 *On the Run*, 13 February 1960. BBC Third Programme.
20 *La Nausée*, 7 December 1960. BBC Third Programme.
21 *A Resounding Twinkle*, 20 July 1960. BBC Third Programme.
22 *The Cocktail Party*, 9 October 1961. BBC Home Service.
23 *The Caretaker*, 20 March 1962. BBC Third Programme.
24 *The Dock Brief*, 16 May 1957. BBC Third Programme, repeated on 19 March 1962. BBC Home Service.
25 *A Resounding Tinkle*, 20 July 1960. BBC Third Programme, repeated on 19 March 1962. BBC Home Service.
26 *The Beggar's Opera*, 6 August 1961. BBC Home Service.
27 *Twelfth Night*, 6 January 1964. BBC Home Service.
28 *The Shoemaker's Holiday*, 1 January 1959. BBC Third Programme.
29 Rob Turnock, *Television and Consumer Culture* (London: I.B. Tauris, 2007), 75.
30 Ibid., 88.
31 *Quatermass*, 6 parts from 18 July 1953. BBC Television.
32 *Nineteen Eighty-Four*, 12 December 1954. BBC Television.
33 John Ellis, 'Is it possible to construct a canon of television programmes?' in *Reviewing Television History*, ed. Helen Wheatley (London: I.B. Tauris, 2007), 15–27.
34 *A Night Out*, 24 April 1960. ITV.
35 *The Lord of the Rings*, from 12 April 1981, 26 parts. BBC Radio Four.
36 *The Square*, 9 February 1958. BBC Third Programme. *Moderato Cantibile*, 9 December 1958. BBC Third Programme.
37 *En Fiacre*, 10 December 1959. BBC Third Programme.
38 *Ubu Roi*, 23 February 1960. BBC Third Programme.
39 *The Old Tune*, 11 September 1960. BBC Third Programme.
40 *The Dwarfs*, 2 December 1960. BBC Third Programme.
41 *La Nausée*, 7 December 1960. BBC Third Programme.
42 For a full account of her career at the BBC, see Kate Terkanian and Hugh Chignell, 'Nesta Pain, the entangled producer'.
43 *The Dock Brief*, 16 May 1957. BBC Third Programme.
44 J. C. Trewin, 'The critic on the hearth', *The Listener*, 21 May 1957.
45 *I Spy*, 19 November 1957. BBC Third Programme.
46 *Parkinson's Law*, 25 December 1958. BBC Third Programme.

47 *The Loneliness of the Long Distance Runner*, 26 April 1961. BBC Third Programme. Music composed by Antony Hopkins.
48 *There Will Come Soft Rains*, 12 September 1962. BBC Third Programme.
49 *The Ants*, 27 November 1962. BBC Third Programme.
50 Ibid.
51 Martin Shuttleworth, 'The critic on the hearth', *The Listener*, 6 December 1962.
52 Gielgud, *Years in a Mirror*, 186.

CONCLUSION

There can be little doubt that in the post-war period a number of remarkable radio dramas were broadcast by the BBC Drama and Features departments. Some of the most interesting and ambitious of these can be grouped under three headings: 'epic', 'absurdist' and 'realist'. Those may be problematic and loose categories, but they have informed the structure of this book and are at least a useful starting point for future discussions. The epic dramas of the immediate post-war period are epitomized by the grand ambition of Louis MacNeice's *The Dark Tower* and Douglas Cleverdon's production of David Jones's epic poem *In Parenthesis*. These large-scale productions benefitted from music composed by Benjamin Britten (*The Dark Tower*) and Elizabeth Poston (*In Parenthesis*) and from performances by some of the most distinguished actors of the day. It is tempting to see the overarching ambition and generous institutional support for these productions as making a statement about the BBC and its commitment to radio drama at the time. In more recent years the same ambition can be seen in the twenty-six-part adaptation of Tolkien's *Lord of the Rings*[1] which also featured a star cast and specially composed music. The first episode was accompanied by souvenir posters based on the special cover of the *Radio Times*. Some episodes were even produced by Michael Bakewell, harking back to the 'golden age' of radio drama. Similarly epic was the more recent *Neverwhere*[2] adapted from the novel by Neil Gaiman and produced by Dirk Maggs. The cinematic aesthetic of Maggs's production combined with the celebrity of the cast reinforces the sense of this as an epic radio drama of scale and ambition.

The absurdist trend in post-war radio drama was of course influenced by the dominance of writers whom Martin Esslin was to categorize as writers of the 'theatre of the absurd'. In fact he only included Beckett, Pinter and Ionesco of those who contributed significantly to radio drama, but there is no doubt that Giles Cooper drew from the creative well of absurdism without being a card-carrying absurdist. The absurdist approach to radio drama, no matter how uncomfortable we might be with that label, created extraordinary and bizarre worlds which seemed to work particularly well on radio, as I have argued here. Being some of the most important and memorable (and still existing) absurdist radio dramas of the 1950s, Beckett's *All That Fall* and Cooper's *The Disagreeable Oyster* and *Under the Loofah Tree* are all explorations of the inner world of their characters. Maddy Rooney's journey to the station to pick up her husband and then return home is, as Everett Frost argues, a journey of the imagination, an exploration of her inner world.[3] Similarly, Edward Thwaite's dreams and fantasies as he lies in his bath in Cooper's *Under the Loofah Tree* are a nightmarish but convincing study of human psychology, the anxieties and neuroses of the powerless male. It follows, as I have argued, that these psychological and fantastic dramas are radiogenic; they are best suited to radio and any attempt to stage them must necessarily fail.[4]

The realist approach to radio drama, heard in the work of writers like Rhys Adrian and, to an extent, Harold Pinter, reflected the success of social realist drama in the theatre and on television. Rhys Adrian's *Too Old for Donkeys* is both realist in the sense that it reflects a deeper truth about Britain and in particular working-class experience and attitudes, but it is also a naturalist drama with close attention paid to capturing everyday speech and idiom. Arguably, this approach to radio drama would hold sway in the radio drama world after the departure of Val Gielgud, a less challenging form of storytelling, drawing on the success of the radio soaps to provide a secondary accompaniment to domestic life.

It is tempting to suggest, as I have done, that the era of epic, absurdist and early realist drama, especially as broadcast on the cultural Third Programme, was the 'golden age' of radio drama. Others have used that term to describe post-war Britain. For Eric Hobsbawm, the increased affluence and opportunities of the 1950s heralded a golden age.[5] The television historian Rob Turnock is not the only commentator to suggest that the 1960s was the golden age of television drama in which improvements in technology of production and consumption and the launch of series like Armchair Theatre established television drama as an important part of British cultural life.[6] The American radio historian and theorist Neil Verma frequently refers to pre-television era radio drama as the golden age of the genre,[7] and Michael Billington also called the late 1950s 'a radio drama's golden age' in his book on Harold Pinter.[8] Applying the term 'golden age' to post-war British radio drama would imply that the dramas made after the early 1960s were inferior which is not my intension.

In the 1950s and early 1960s the Third Programme and, to a lesser extent, the Home Service broadcast a large number of original plays for radio written by some of the leading playwrights of the time. In addition there were many highly successful adaptations of novels and contemporary stage plays; Louis MacNeice's adaptation of Virginia Woolf's *The Waves* and Giles Cooper's adaptation of William Golding's *Lord of the Flies* are just two examples of adaptations in which the sonification of the novel seems to add a further dimension and so enriched the original. Michael Bakewell's triumphant adaptation of Ionesco's *Rhinoceros* also demonstrates radio's ability to add more to the original; our inability only to hear and not to see residents of the French town turn into rhinoceroses heightens the drama and is somehow more convincing and more terrifying. In addition to contemporary dramas were the regular broadcasts of stage classics; Shakespeare, Strindberg, Somerset Maugham, but especially Ibsen, deemed by Val Gielgud to be the playwrights most suited to radio adaptation. Inspired by the belief that radio was the 'national theatre of the air' (before the opening of the National Theatre in 1963[9]) BBC radio drama was not seen as an adjunct to more interesting things happening on the stage or in television but as a central part of British dramatic life. No one expressed that certainty better than the BBC radio script editor Barbara Bray whose belief in the importance of the genre is forcefully expressed in her revealing BBC oral history interview. Her weekly visits to the London theatre to see new plays and actors and, where necessary, recruit them for radio drama helped establish BBC radio drama as the lifeblood of the theatre, supporting writers and performers at often crucial moments in their careers. The presence of Bray, McWhinnie, Bakewell, Gielgud and others in the audiences for London stage plays must have been a great fillip to writers and actors and a reminder of the central role of the BBC in the arts. McWhinnie's sponsorship of Giles Cooper, Nesta Pain's encouragement of John Mortimer and, most importantly, McWhinnie and Bray's nurturing of both Samuel Beckett and Harold Pinter resulted in some of the greatest achievements of radio drama's 'golden age'.

A particularly striking quality of some of the extant radio dramas of the period is their concern with a central male character often struggling with his identity and the victim of other peoples' actions and the circumstances in which he finds himself. This was true of some of the earlier epic dramas; in *The Dark Tower*, Roland is uncertain about the quest which has killed his brothers, but his mother drives him on to self-destruction; he is a man, as he states, without free will. In *The Ascent of F6*, we encounter different masculinities: the hero (Michael Ransom), the coward, the obsessive, all of whom are victims of society's need for simplistic stories to maintain the status quo. In MacNeice's last radio drama, the autobiographical *Persons from Porlock*, Hank, the artist, is caught between his creative impulse and the need to make money and is the victim of drink and the demands of women. That last element of the assault on masculinity is clearly present in some of the most important post-war radio dramas and especially in the work of Giles Cooper and Harold Pinter. Cooper's *The Disagreeable Oyster* is a terrifying tale of the downtrodden Mervyn Bundy, harassed by his demanding wife, stripped by the posse of women and forced to remain naked until he escapes back to his domestic prison. Pinter's *A Night Out* is another deeply disturbing examination of a man oppressed by women: his controlling mother, the 'girls' at the party and the prostitute. Like Bundy, Albert finds no escape in this deeply pessimistic account of a powerless and impotent man. There was little room in post-war radio drama for a woman's view of the world, and it hardly needs to be stated that these dramas were pre-feminist and misogynistic. However, they were dramas that explored the existential crisis of masculinity, admittedly from the point of view of men and heavily imbued by anxieties about and ignorance of women. For all their faults these were dramas that spoke to core issues of gender and identity and provide us with some important insights into the inner (largely male) worlds of the 1950s.

If it is indeed the case that this was a golden age for radio drama then it seems right to ask what lessons can be learnt for the art and craft of sound drama. Much has been made about the 'decline' of radio and its inevitable demise as the non-visual medium. This can certainly be traced back to the late 1940s and the re-emergence of the BBC's television service, to Val Gielgud's temporary transfer to work in television in 1949, to the *New Statesman*'s failure to review radio in the 1950s and has been repeated endlessly since. The great potential of radio drama, as revealed by many of the examples discussed in this book, suggests that radio dramas are not a rather inadequate alternative to film and television, but have the power to tell stories that cannot be told in any other way. The ambitious and often demanding, difficult and disturbing dramas on the Third Programme point to the potential of sound drama, but for that potential to be realized it would seem to be necessary for new approaches to production and listening to emerge.

One of the most interesting and unexpected truths discovered by writing this book is that most, if not all, of the great 1950s' radio drama producers were not only very young but also very nearly complete amateurs when they were let loose on drama production. How much experience did Donald McWhinnie have of drama production when he was asked to produce the extremely important and high-profile *Ascent of F6* in 1951? Slightly over one year. What experience did Barbara Bray or Michael Bakewell have when in their early twenties they were given some of the most important jobs in radio drama editing and production? Almost none at all. Similarly John Tydeman, although he had directed a number of student plays at Cambridge, was professionally speaking totally inexperienced when given the job of BBC radio drama producer. To put it rather more bluntly, they may have presided over the 'golden age' of radio drama, but they were amateurs. What they lacked in professional training or experience was compensated for by their intelligence and enthusiasm. It surely follows that the relative amateurism of podcast drama should not be seen as a sign of weakness. Lacking drama experience should not deter those wanting to try and tell stories in sound. Radio or audio drama amateurs are just following in the footsteps of some of the best of all radio drama producers.

Another possible lesson for contemporary radio playwrights emerges from the work of Jacob Stulberg[10] who reminds us that radio dramatists have not lacked advice and guidance from some of the most prominent producers and authors, including Val Gielgud and Lance Sieveking. Today, potential writers are faced by a plethora of advice including online guides and the support of the BBC 'Writers Room' which aims to 'discover, develop and champion new and experienced writing talent across the whole of the UK'. Not to mention script writing and creative writing degrees and academic texts with analysis of radio drama. Is there a danger that this advice produces a combination of conformity and caution in modern radio writing? Stulberg reminds us that Pinter's *A Slight*

Ache is an explicit rejection of the exhortation to write in a clear and coherent style by being mysteriously unclear and incoherent; we do not even know if the central character exists. It is tempting to wonder if radio dramatists are being mentored away from the recklessly brave experimentation of Cooper, Ionesco and Pinter towards writing well-structured, coherent but fundamentally dull radio dramas.

Another lesson from this account of post-war radio drama is that there needed to be an audience motivated to listen to often quite challenging sound stories. Despite the very small size of the Third Programme audience, there were enough listeners to make the venture worthwhile. Some of those were cultural enthusiasts wanting to hear the latest play by Anouilh, Betti or Cooper and so keep abreast of dramatic developments on the stage as well as listen to work written specifically for radio. At the same time, drama series like *The National Theatre of the Air* and *World Theatre* were unashamedly didactic and reflected a thoroughgoing Reithianism in the Drama department, a commitment to educational broadcasting by presenting the listener with the theatrical canon. The abundance of Chekhov, Shakespeare, Strindberg and Ibsen was based on the belief that the BBC should provide listeners, and especially those without access to the theatre, a regular offering of stage classics. The success of this didactic programming would have been greatly assisted by the fact that the adult population had grown up listening to radio and so developed the ability to listen in a relatively concentrated way for hours at a time. So, for example, the 1949 production of Ibsen's *Brand*[11] produced by Val Gielgud lasted two hours fifteen minutes with no interval and the 1963 version,[12] also produced by Gielgud, was a slightly more manageable one of two hours but with no interval. There are many examples of listening experiences which would surely not be attempted today; the 1955 production of *The Waves*, Virginia Woolf's stream of conscious novel based on the utterances of four characters without the benefit of plot or any additional sound or music lasted two hours fifteen minutes, although there was a ten-minute interval. The resilient and committed listenership or 'listening public' to use the term used by Kate Lacey[13] was no doubt supported by the programming of some dramas in series at fixed times of the week. *The National Theatre of the Air* was scheduled for Sunday evenings at 8.30 pm and *World Theatre* was always on a Monday evening usually after 8.00 pm. The radio drama enthusiast could plan in advance to listen. The weekly reviews of radio drama in *The Listener* as well as in the national and local press would also have supported and encouraged listening to radio drama in a culture which valued and supported sound drama.

Clearly we no longer have either the listening competences or the commitment to sound drama which existed in the 1950s and early 1960s. We are not members of a 'listening public', prepared and able to listen to hours of uninterrupted radio drama. But it does not follow that the radio dramas discussed in this book, the products of the 'golden age', are inaccessible and beyond our reach or indeed that there is no place for the production of ambitious and challenging sound plays. A possible solution to the challenge not only for contemporary producers but also for those who want to listen and appreciate radio dramas from the past may be public listening. We tend to think of listening to radio as an individual act, more so than watching television; the excitement of visits to the cinema or watching football on large screens in the pub appears far removed from the more solitary and intimate world of radio. However, in recent years and since the beginning of the century there has been a steady growth of public-listening events. In Paris, ARTE Radio holds regular listening events sometimes attended by several hundred people, and there are similar public-listening activities in Chicago and Copenhagen. In London, 'In the Dark' organizes regular 'gatherings' to listen to different types of audio including documentary or drama and work mainly designed for podcasting or for radio broadcast. Sometimes at In the Dark events the producer or writer is present to join a discussion about the work. In the Dark has also collaborated with the British Library to create public-listening events at which complete radio features and dramas, often from the post-war period, have been played and discussed. The founder of In the Dark, Nina Garthwaite describes the communal listening events as a bit like belonging to a film club[14] while adding that the audio listening experience should not be reduced to 'cinema without pictures' or a 'theatre of the mind' because of the suggestion that we can only understand collective listening with reference to visual media. She describes the listening experience as having a 'mind wandering' quality in which the following of a clear narrative is often replaced by 'poetic resonances, meditative moments, associative meaning'.[15] Sean Street makes a similar point about radio's poetic quality and suggests an important link between radio and poetry.[16]

Somewhere in the public-listening phenomenon is at least one approach to help us reconnect to great but largely neglected radio dramas and find new possibilities for creating and experiencing their modern equivalents. I know from personal experience that listening to historic radio dramas in a solitary booth at the British Library can be strangely confusing and unsatisfactory. Sharing the same drama with a group of people is perhaps not 'collective listening' as listening is always a personal and individual experience, but as Garthwaite correctly states, it is 'gathered listening' and offers the chance to share an often strange experience with others and then learn from each other in post-listening discussion.

During the post-war period, from 1945 to 1963, radio maintained a place at the heart of British cultural life. Although radio drama would be overtaken by the growing success of television drama, the surviving examples from that 'golden age' include plays which are remarkable and deserve to be listened to and so provide inspiration for writers and producers today. Most of the successful post-war radio dramas were ambitious in their effort to address issues of identity and psychology, to examine in different ways the inner worlds of their characters. Sound drama can achieve the same heights of artistic expression as its visual equivalents, and especially when exploring inner worlds, but we have lost touch with a whole era of creative radio production; who today working in the field knows of the work of Giles Cooper or Rhys Adrian? Reclaiming radio drama's past has become more possible with the increased digitization of old audio and the use of searchable databases like the BBC Genome. Sharing our experience of historic radio in gathered listening events will facilitate our understanding and appreciation of historic radio and could inspire today's radio drama writers and producers.

Notes

1 *The Lord of the Rings*, 8 March 1981 (26 parts). BBC Home Service.
2 *Neverwhere*, 16 March 2014. BBC Radio 4.
3 Frost, 'Fundamental Sounds'.
4 Jacob Stulberg, however, makes a case for staging *A Slight Ache* in 'How (not) to write radio plays'.
5 Eric Hobsbawm, *The Age of Extremes, the Short Twentieth Century, 1914–1992*. (London: Abacus, 1995).
6 Turnock, *Television and Consumer Culture*, 37.
7 Verma, *Theatre of the Mind*.
8 Billington, *The Life and Work of Harold Pinter*, 95.
9 Originally based at the Old Vic theatre.
10 Stulberg, 'How (not) to write broadcast plays'.
11 *Brand*, 11 December 1949. BBC Third Programme.
12 *Brand*, 29 April 1963. BBC Home Service.
13 Kate Lacey, *Listening Publics: The Politics and Experience of Listening in the Media Age* (Cambridge: Polity, 2013).
14 Nina Garthwaite, email to dissertation student, 1 June 2016.
15 Ibid.
16 Sean Street, *The Poetry of Radio: The Colour of Sound* (London: Routledge, 2012).

LIST OF PROGRAMMES

Radio dramas cited

The dates shown are for the first transmission and all sourced from BBC Genome (genome.ch.bbc.co.uk). Most but not all of the works cited in the book are listed here.

Year	Date	Title	Network	Writer	Producer
1946	21 January	The Dark Tower	Home Service (Home)	Louis MacNeice	Louis MacNeice
	1 October (in 4 parts)	Man and Superman	Third Programme (Third)	George Bernard Shaw	Peter Watts
	4 October	Huis Clos	Third	Jean-Paul Sartre	Mary Hope Allen
	21 October (in 7 parts)	The Canterbury Tales	Third	Chaucer adapted by Nevil Coghill	Stephen Potter
	29 October	Agamemnon	Third	Aeschylus translated and adapted by Louis MacNeice	Val Gielgud
	19 November	In Parenthesis	Third	David Jones	Douglas Cleverdon
	3 December	Enemy of Cant	Third	Aristophanes translated and adapted by Louis MacNeice	Louis MacNeice
1947	14 January	Animal Farm	Third	George Orwell	Rayner Heppenstall
	26 January	Moby Dick	Third	Herman Melville adapted by Henry Reed	Stephen Potter
	20 February	Scenes from the Frogs	Third	Aristophanes	Raymond Raikes
	11 March	The Death of the Gunnar	Third	Louis MacNeice	Louis MacNeice
	12 March	The Burning of Njal	Third	Louis MacNeice	Louis MacNeice
	25 May	Pytheas: A Dramatic Speculation	Third	Henry Reed	Henry Reed
1948	3 and 4 March	The Rescue	Third	Edward Sackville-West	Val Gielgud
	31 March	A Single Taper	Home Service	R. C. Scriven	Rex Tucker
	19 September (in 13 parts)	Great Expectations	Home	Charles Dickens	Raymond Raikes
	19 December	The Christmas Child	Home	D. G. Bridson	D. G. Bridson
	22 December	Trimalchio's Feast	Third	Petronius adapted by Louis MacNeice	Louis MacNeice
1949	14 March	Silence in Heaven	Home	Lance Sieveking	Cleland Finn
	5 May	Broken Battlements	Home	Frederick Lidstone	Donald McWhinnie
	9 May	The Unblest	Third	Henry Reed	Rayner Heppenstall
	1 August	The Fool's Saga	Third	Rayner Heppenstall	Rayner Heppenstall
	1 November (in 4 parts)	Faust	Third	Goethe	E. A. Harding
	11 December	Brand	Third	Henrik Ibsen	Val Gielgud

List of Programmes

Year	Date	Title	Station	Author/Adapter	Producer
1950	7 March	*The Monument*	Third	Henry Reed	Rayner Heppenstall
	29 March	*Thieves Rush In*	Home	Giles Cooper	Donald McWhinnie
	2 April (in 8 parts)	*The Country House*	Home	John Galsworthy	Donald McWhinnie
	3 July	*Never Get Out*	Home	Giles Cooper	Donald McWhinnie
	22 August (first broadcast 5 December 1938)	*The Ascent of F6*	Third	W. H. Auden and Christopher Isherwood	
1951	3 June (in 6 parts)	*The Dynasts*	Third	Thomas Hardy adapted by Henry Reed	Not known
	13 September	*The Rescue*	Third	Edwards Sackville-West	Raymond Raikes
1952	6 January to 30 March (in 12 parts)	*Oliver Twist*	Home	Charles Dickens adapted by Giles Cooper	Charles Lefeaux
	3 March	*Swann in Love*	Third	Pamela Hansford Johnson adapted by Rayner Heppenstall	Rayner Heppenstall
	16 March	*The Streets of Pompeii*	Third	Henry Reed	Douglas Cleverdon
	18 March	*The Waves*	Third	Virginia Woolf adapted by Louis MacNeice	Louis MacNeice
	2 June	*The Return of the Prodigal*	Third	André Gide adapted by Rayner Heppenstall	Rayner Heppenstall
	26 October	*The Great Desire I Had*	Third	Henry Reed	Douglas Cleverdon
1953	12 April	*The Dance of Death*	Third	August Strindberg	Adapted and produced by Donald McWhinnie
	10 August (5 parts)	*Artists in Crime*	Light	Ngaio Marsh adapted by Giles Cooper	Martyn C. Webster
	7 September	*A Very Great Man Indeed*	Third	Henry Reed	Douglas Cleverdon
	20 September	*Men and Wives*	Third	Ivy Compton Burnett	Christopher Sykes
1954	24 January	*Under Milk Wood*	Third	Dylan Thomas	Douglas Cleverdon
	27 April	*Prisoners Progress*	Third	Louis MacNeice	Louis MacNeice

(Continued)

List of Programmes

Year	Date	Title	Network	Writer	Producer
	24 May	The Private Life of Hilda Tablet	Third	Henry Reed	Douglas Cleverdon
	24 August (in 4 parts)	The Nine Tailors	Light	Dorothy L. Sayers adapted by Giles Cooper	Norman Wright
	17 October	The Queen and the Rebels	Third	Ugo Betti adapted by Henry Reed	Donald McWhinnie
	14 November	Emily Butter	Third	Henry Reed	Douglas Cleverdon
1955	16 January	The Death of Wallenstein	Third	Schiller	Donald McWhinnie and Michael Bakewell
	18 March	The Waves	Third	Virginia Woolf	Adapted and produced by Louis MacNeice
	22 May	The Golden Butterfly	Home	Walter Besant	Val Gielgud
	28 August	The Lord of the Flies	Third	William Golding adapted by Giles Cooper	Archie Campbell
	26 October	The Great Desire I Had	Third	Henry Reed	Douglas Cleverdon
1956	5 February	Also Among the Prophets	Third	Louis MacNeice	Louis MacNeice
	29 February	Through a Hedge Backwards	Third	Henry Reed	Douglas Cleverdon
	6 May	La Photo du Colonel	Third	Eugene Ionesco	Michael Bakewell
	18 June	Mathry Beacon	Third	Giles Cooper	Donald McWhinnie
	8 October	Carpe Diem	Third	Louis MacNeice	Louis MacNeice
	19 November	The Man on the Gate	Third	Rhys Adrian	Archie Campbell
1957	13 January	All That Fall	Third	Samuel Beckett	Donald McWhinnie
	14 January	The Horse's Mouth	Home	Joyce Carey	Donald McWhinnie
	29 April	The Picture	Third	Eugene Ionesco	Michael Bakewell
	16 May	The Dock Brief	Third	John Mortimer	Nesta Pain
	15 August	The Disagreeable Oyster	Third	Giles Cooper	Donald McWhinnie

List of Programmes 171

Date	Title	Channel	Author	Producer
17 August	Private Dreams and Public Nightmares	Third	Frederick Bradnum	Donald McWhinnie
27 September	The Passionate Thinker	Third	Rhys Adrian	Donald McWhinnie
28 September	Hedda Gabler	Home	Ibsen	Donald McWhinnie
13 October	Morel	Third	Rayner Heppenstall	Rayner Heppenstall
19 November	I Spy	Third	John Mortimer	Nesta Pain
25 December	Parkinson's Law	Third	Nesta Pain	Nesta Pain
1958 24 January	Without the Grail	Third	Giles Cooper	Donald McWhinnie
9 February	The Square	Third	Marguerite Dumas	Barbara Bray
10 March	The Drunken Sailor	Home	Robert Bolt	Donald McWhinnie
11 March	The Primal Scene – As It Were	Third	Henry Reed	Douglas Cleverdon
2 August	The Deep Blue Sea	Home	Terence Rattigan	Val Gielgud
3 August	Under the Loofah Tree	Third	Giles Cooper	Donald McWhinnie
23 November	Unman, Wittering and Zigo	Third	Giles Cooper	Donald McWhinnie
9 December	Modernato Cantibile	Third	Marguerite Dumas	Barbara Bray
1959 20 April	Caretaker	Home	Giles Cooper	H. B. Fortiun
6 May	Not a Drum Was Heard	Third	Henry Reed	Douglas Cleverdon
4 June	Before the Monday	Third	Giles Cooper	Michael Bakewell
24 June	Embers	Third	Samuel Beckett	Donald McWhinnie
25 July	East of the Sun and West of the Moon	Third	Louis MacNeice	Louis MacNeice
29 July	A Slight Ache	Third	Harold Pinter	Donald McWhinnie
20 August	Rhinoceros	Third	Ionesco	Michael Bakewell
27 October	Musique Discrete	Third	Henry Reed	Douglas Cleverdon
10 December	En Fiacre	Third	Arthur Adomov	Barbara Bray
1960 12 January	Death of a Salesman	Third	Arthur Miller	Peter Watts
17 January	Peer Gynt	Third	Ibsen	Donald McWhinnie
27 January	Free Fall	Third	William Golding	Donald McWhinnie
13 February	On the Run	Home	Bill Naughton	Martyn Webster

(*Continued*)

List of Programmes

Year	Date	Title	Network	Writer	Producer
	23 February	Ubu Roi	Third	Alfred Jarry	Barbara Bray
	1 March	A Night Out	Third	Harold Pinter	Donald McWhinnie
	27 April	Waiting for Godot	Third	Samuel Beckett	Donald McWhinnie
	3 May	A Doll's House	Third	Ibsen	Frederick Bradnum
	30 May	The Pillars of Society	Third	Ibsen	Not known
	3 July	A Resounding Tinkle	Third	N. F. Simpson	Charles Lefeaux
	3 August	Betsie	Third	Rhys Adrian	Michael Bakewell
	21 August	Victims of Duty	Third	Eugene Ionesco	Martin Esslin
	11 September	The Old Tune	Third	Robert Pinget	Barbara Bray
	30 September	The Wild Duck	Third	Ibsen	Frederick Bradnum
	4 October	Pig in the Middle	Third	Giles Cooper	H. B. Fortuin
	12 October	An Enemy of the People	Third	Ibsen	R. D. Smith
	7 November	The Lady from the Sea	Home	Ibsen	R. D. Smith
	2 December	The Dwarfs	Third	Harold Pinter	Barbara Bray
	7 December	La Nausee	Third	Jean-Paul Sartre	Barbara Bray
1961	10 March	The Administrator	Third	Louis MacNeice	Louis MacNeice
	26 April	The Loneliness of the Long Distance Runner	Third	Alan Sillitoe	Nesta Pain
	11 May	The Collection	Third	Harold Pinter	Cedric Messina
	15 July	The Return of General Forefinger	Third	Giles Cooper	Michael Bakewell
	19 July	The Bridge	Third	Rhys Adrian	Michael Bakewell
	21 August	Victims of Duty	Third	Ionesco	Martin Esslin
	22 October	The Cocktail Party	Home	T. S. Eliot	Not known
	9 November	Living Time	Third	Arthur Adomov	Michael Bakewell
	14 November	One Eye Wild	Third	Louis MacNeice	Louis MacNeice
	29 December	The Lark	Third	Jean Anouilh	Val Gielgud

1962	17 January	*Rosmersholm*	Third	Ibsen	Charles Lefeaux
	20 March	*The Caretaker*	Third	Harold Pinter	Michael Bakewell
	8 May	*The American Dream*	Third	Edward Albee	John Gibbon
	22 May	*Endgame*	Third	Samuel Beckett	Michael Bakewell
	12 June	*The Collection*	Third	Harold Pinter	Cedric Messina
	12 September	*There Will Come Soft Rains*	Third	Ray Bradbury	Nesta Pain
	27 November	*The Ants*	Third	Caryl Churchill	Michael Bakewell
1963	14 January	*Too Old for Donkeys*	Third	Rhys Adrian	Michael Bakewell
	29 April	*Brand*	Third	Ibsen	Val Gielgud
	19 May	*Room to Let*	Third	Rhys Adrian	Michael Bakewell
	4 June	*The Maids*	Third	Jean Genet	John Tydeman
	30 August	*Persons from Porlock*	Third	Louis MacNeice	Louis MacNeice
	13 September	*All the Way Home*	Third	Giles Cooper	Charles Lefeaux
	16 October	*A Nice Clean Sheet of Paper*	Third	Rhys Adrian	Michael Bakewell

BIBLIOGRAPHY

Post-war radio drama

Avery, Todd. *Radio Modernism: Literature, Ethics, and the BBC, 1922-1938*. Aldershot: Ashgate, 2006.

Bignell, Jonathan. '"Random dottiness": Samuel Beckett and Harold Pinter in 1958', in *Beckett Influencing / Influencing Beckett*, ed. N. Johnson, A. Rokoczy and M. Tanaka. Budapest and Paris: Károli Gáspár University Press/L'Harmattan, forthcoming.

Billington, Michael. *The Life and Work of Harold Pinter*. London: Faber and Faber, 1996.

Billington, Michael. *State of the Nation: British Theatre since 1945*. London: Faber and Faber, 2007.

Billington, Michael. *The 101 Greatest Plays: From Antiquity to the Present*. London: Faber/Guardian, 2015.

Bloom, Emily C. *The Wireless Past: Anglo-Irish Writers and the BBC, 1931-1968*. Oxford: Oxford University Press, 2016.

Briggs, Asa. *The History of Broadcasting in the United Kingdom*, 5 vols. Oxford: Oxford University Press, 1995.

Bull, Michael and Back, Les, eds. *The Auditory Culture Reader*. Oxford: Berg, 2003.

Calder, John. *The Philosophy of Samuel Beckett*. London: Calder Publications, 2001.

Chignell, Hugh. *Public Issue Radio: Talks, News and Current Affairs in the Twentieth Century*. Basingstoke: Palgrave Macmillan, 2011.

Chignell, Hugh. 'Out of the dark, Samuel Beckett and radio', *Peripeti* 22, 2015: 10–22.

Chignell, Hugh. 'Sam Hanna Bell and the ideology of place', in *Regional Aesthetics*, ed. Ieuan Franklin, Hugh Chignell and Kristin Skoog. Basingstoke: Palgrave Macmillan, 2015, 185–95.

Chignell, Hugh. 'British radio drama and the avant-garde in the 1950s', *Historical Journal of Film, Radio and Television* 37, issue 4, 2017: 649–64.

Cochrane, Claire. *Twentieth Century British Theatre, Industry, Art and Empire*. Cambridge: Cambridge University Press, 2011.

Cohen, Debra Rae, Michael Coyle and Jane Lewty. *Broadcasting Modernism*. Gainesville: Florida University Press, 2009.

Coulton, Barbara. *Louis MacNeice in the BBC*. London: Faber and Faber, 1980.

Craig, George et al., eds. *The Letters of Samuel Beckett, 1957-1965*. Cambridge: Cambridge University Press, 2014.

Crisell, Andrew. *An Introductory History of British Broadcasting* (2nd edn). London: Routledge, 2002.

Cronin, Anthony. *Samuel Beckett, the Last Modernist*. New York: Da Capro Press, 1999.

Cronqvist, Marie and Hilgert, Christoph. 'Entangled Media Histories: The Value of Transnational and Transmedial Approaches in Media Historiography', *Media History* 23, no. 1, February 2017: 130–41.

Crook, Tim. *Radio Drama, Theory and Practice*. London: Routledge, 1999.
Douglas, Susan. *Listening In; Radio and the American Imagination*. Minneapolis: University of Minnesota Press, 1999.
Drakakis, John. 'The essence that's not seen: Radio adaptations of stage plays', in *Radio Drama*, ed. John Drakakis. Cambridge: Cambridge University Press, 1981, 111–34.
Ellis, John. 'Is it possible to construct a canon of television programmes?' in *Reviewing Television History*, ed. Helen Wheatley. London: I.B. Tauris, 2007, 15–27.
Ellis-Woods, Portia. 'BBC Northern Ireland Drama and features Programming 1924-1956: Development, identity, and cultural history', PhD diss., Queen's University Belfast, 2018.
Esslin, Martin. *Pinter the Playwright*. London: Methuen, 1970.
Esslin, Martin. *The Theatre of the Absurd*. London: Penguin, 1962/1980.
Frost, Everett, C. 'Fundamental sounds: Recording Samuel Beckett's radio plays', *Theatre Journal* 43, no. 3, October 1991: 361–76.
Gielgud, Val. *British Radio Drama, 1922 – 1956, A Survey*. London: George Harrap, 1957.
Gielgud, Val. *Years in a Mirror*. London: The Bodley Head, 1965.
Gray, Frances, 'Giles Cooper: The medium as moralist', in *British Radio Drama*, ed. John Drakakis. Cambridge: Cambridge University Press, 1981, 139–58.
Gray, Frances. 'The nature of radio drama', in *Radio Drama*, ed. Peter Lewis. London: Longman, 1981, 48–78.
Greene, Hugh. *The Third Floor Front*. London: The Bodley Head, 1969.
Guralnick, Elissa S. *Sight Unseen*. Athens: Ohio University Press, 1996.
Hendy, David. *Life on Air, A History of Radio Four*. Oxford: Oxford University Press, 2007.
Hendy, David. 'Biography and the emotions as a missing "narrative" in media history; a case study of Lance Sieveking and the early BBC', *Media History* 18, no. 3/4, 2012: 361–78.
Hendy, David. *Public Service Broadcasting*. Basingstoke: Palgrave Macmillan, 2013.
Hennessy, Peter. *Never Again, Britain 1945-1951*. London: Vintage, 1993.
Heppenstall, Rayner. *Portrait of the Artist as a Professional Man*. London: Peter Owen, 1949.
Hewison, Robert. *In Anger, Culture in the Cold War 1945-1960*. London: Methuen, 1988.
Hilmes, Michele. *Radio Voices, American Broadcasting, 1922-1952*. Minneapolis: University of Minnesota Press, 1997.
Hilmes, Michele. *Network Nations, A Transnational History of British and American Broadcasting*. New York and London: Routledge, 2012.
Hobsbawm, Eric. *The Age of Extremes, The Short Twentieth Century, 1914-1992*. London: Abacus, 1995.
Holme, Christopher. 'The radio drama of Louis MacNeice', in *British Radio Drama*, ed. John Drakakis. Cambridge: Cambridge University Press, 1981, 37–72.
van Hulle, Dirk. 'The BBC and Beckett's non-radiogenic plays in the 1950s', in *Samuel Beckett and BBC Radio*, ed. David Addyman, Matthew Feldman and Erik Tonning. New York: Palgrave Macmillan, 2017, 43–58.
Huwiler, Elke. 'Storytelling by sound: A theoretical frame for radio drama and for radio drama analysis', *The Radio Journal – International Studies in Broadcast and Audio Media* 3, no. 1 (2005): 45–59.

James, Mary. 'British radio drama: A critical analysis of its development as a distinctive aesthetic form', PhD diss., University of Hertfordshire, 1994.

Jarlbrink, Johan. 'News work behind and beyond the desk', *Media History* 21, no. 3, 2015: 280–93.

Jarlbrink, Johan. *Informations- och avfallshantering i papperstidningens tidevarv* [trans: Information and waste management in the age of the newspaper]. Lund: Mediehistoriskt arkiv, 2018.

Kynaston, David. *Austerity Britain, 1945-51*. London: Bloomsbury, 2007.

Lacey, Kate. *Listening Publics: The Politics and Experience of Listening in the Media Age.* Cambridge: Polity, 2013.

Lacey, Stephen. *British Realist Theatre: The New Wave in Its Context, 1956-1965.* London: Routledge, 1995.

Lax, Stephen. *Media and Communication Technologies*. Basingstoke: Palgrave Macmillan, 2009.

Lessing, Doris. *Walking in the Shade: Volume Two of My Autobiography, 1949-1962.* London: Flamingo, 1998.

Lewis, Peter. 'The radio road to Llareggub', in *British Radio Drama*, ed. John Drakakis. Cambridge: Cambridge University Press, 1981, 72–111.

Maschler, Tom, ed. *Declaration*. London: MacGibbon and Kee, 1957.

Maud, Ralph, ed. *Dylan Thomas, The Broadcasts*. London: J. M. Dent, 1991.

McWhinnie, Donald. *The Art of Radio*. London: Faber and Faber, 1959.

Miall, Leonard. *Inside the BBC*. London: Weidenfeld and Nicolson, 1994.

Morgan, Kenneth O. *The People's Peace; British History 1945-1990*. Oxford: Oxford University Press, 1990.

Murphy, Kate. *Behind the Wireless, A History of Early Women at the BBC*. Basingstoke: Palgrave Macmillan, 2016.

Niebur, Louis. *Special Sound: The Creation and Legacy of the BBC Radiophonic Workshop*. Oxford: Oxford University Press, 2010.

Pattie, David. *Modern British Playwriting in the 1950s*. London: Methuen Drama, 2012.

Priestley, J. B. *Postscripts*. London: William Heinemann, 1940.

Rodger, Ian. *Radio Drama*. London: Macmillan, 1982.

Sandbrook, Dominic. *Never Had It So Good; A History of Britain from Suez to the Beatles*. London: Abacus, 2006.

Savage, Roger, 'The radio plays of Henry Reed', in *British Radio Drama*, ed. John Drakakis. Cambridge: Cambridge University Press, 1981, 158–91.

Shellard, Dominic. *British Theatre since the War*. New Haven and London: Yale University Press, 1999.

Shellard, Dominic, ed. *The Golden Generation: New Light On Post-war British Theatre*. London: British Library, 2008.

Shellard, Dominic, ed. *Twentieth Century British Theatre: Industry, Art and Empire*. Cambridge: Cambridge University Press, 2008.

Stallworthy, John. *Louis MacNeice*. London: Faber and Faber, 1995.

Stoller, Tony. *Classical Music Radio in the United Kingdom, 1945-1995*. Basingstoke: Palgrave Macmillan, 2018.

Street, Sean. *Crossing the Ether; British Public Service Radio and Commercial Competition 1922-1945*. Eastleigh: John Libbey, 2006.

Stulberg, Jacob, 'How (not) to write broadcast plays: Pinter and the BBC', *Modern Drama* 58, no. 4 (2015): 502–23.

Svømmekjær, Heidi. 'Radio in proportion: *The Hansen Family* and strategies of relevance in the Danish Broadcasting Corporation 1925-50', PhD diss., Roskilde University, 2014.

Taylor, John Russell. *Anger and After: A Guide to the New British Drama*. Harmondsworth: Penguin, 1963.

Terkanian, Kate and Chignell, Hugh. 'Nesta Pain, the entangled producer', *Media History*, 2019 (forthcoming).

Thomas, Jeanette. 'A history of the BBC Features Department, 1924-1964', D.Phil diss., University of Oxford, 1993.

Tonning, Erik. 'Mediating modernism: The Third Programme, Samuel Beckett and mass communication', in *Samuel Beckett and BBC Radio*, ed. David Addyman, Matthew Feldman and Erik Tonning. New York: Palgrave Macmillan, 2017, 59–81.

Turnock, Rob. *Television and Consumer Culture*. London: I. B. Tauris, 2007.

Tynan, Kenneth. *Kenneth Tynan: Theatre Writings* (selected and edited by Dominic Shellard). London: Nick Hern Books, 2007.

Verma, Neil. *Theatre of the Mind, Imagination, Aesthetics and American Radio Drama*. Chicago: The University of Chicago Press, 2012.

Wade, David. 'Popular radio drama', in *Radio Drama*, ed. Peter Lewis. London: Longmann, 1981, 91–111.

Weiss, Katherine. *Plays of Samuel Beckett*. Huntingdon: Methuen Drama, 2012.

Whitehead, Kate. *The Third Programme, A Literary History*. Oxford: Clarendon Press, 1989.

Whittington, Ian. 'Radio studies and twentieth-century literature: Ethics, aesthetics, and remediation', *Literature Compass* 11, no. 9, 2014: 634–48.

Worton, Michael. '*Waiting for Godot* and *Endgame*: theatre as text', in *The Cambridge Companion to Beckett*, ed. John Pilling. Cambridge: Cambridge University Press, 1994, 67–87.

Wrigley, Amanda. 'A wartime radio *Odyssey*: Edward Sackville-West and Benjamin Britten's *The Rescue* (1943)', *The Radio Journal – International Studies in Broadcast and Audio Media* 8, no. 2, 2010: 141–59.

Wrigley, Amanda. *Greece on Air: Engagements with Ancient Greece on BBC Radio, 1920s – 1960s*. Oxford: Oxford University Press, 2014.

Wrigley, Amanda and Harrison, S. J., eds. *Louis MacNeice: The Classical Radio Plays*. Oxford: Oxford University Press.

Zilliacus, Clas. *Beckett and Broadcasting: A Study of the Works of Samuel Beckett for and in Radio and Television*. Abo: Abo Akademi, 1976.

Published scripts

Auden, W. H. and Isherwood, Christopher. *The Ascent of F6*. London: Faber and Faber, 1937.

Beckett, Samuel. *All That Fall*. London: Faber and Faber, 1957.

Beckett, Samuel. *Endgame*. London: Faber, 1964.

Cooper, Giles. *Giles Cooper: Six Plays for Radio*. London: BBC Publications, 1966.

Ionesco, Eugene. *Rhinoceros and Other Plays*. New York: Grove Press, 1960.

Jones, David. *In Parenthesis*. London: Faber and Faber, 1937/2014.

MacNeice, Louis. *The Dark Tower*. London, Faber and Faber, 1947.
MacNeice, Louis. *Persons from Porlock and Other Plays for Radio*. London: BBC, 1969.
New *Radio Drama*. London: BBC Publications, 1966.
Pinter, Harold. *A Slight Ache and Other Plays*. London: Methuen, 1961.
Thomas, Dylan. *Under Milk Wood*. London: Dent, 1975.

Commercially available recordings

Giles Cooper, four radio dramas. The Centre for Media History, Bournemouth University, 2016. CD boxed set.
'Samuel Beckett, works for radio. The original broadcasts'. BBC/ The British Library, National Sound Archive, 1996. CD boxed set.

INDEX

absurdism   16, 20, 65–82, 92, 129,
Administrator, The   118–19
Adomov, Arthur   31, 65, 129, 150, 152
Adrian, Rhys   3, 6, 9, 31, 74, 128, 141–5, 147, 150–1, 160, 165
aesthetics   3, 5–8
Agamemnon   111
Albee, Edward   82
Alexander Nevsky   24, 111
All That Fall   29–30, 62, 70–4, 76, 79, 80, 94, 134, 159
All the Way Home   103–4, 105
Also Among the Prophets   116
AM   58, 59
American Dream, The   82
Amis, Kingsley   18, 19
angry young man   16, 18
Animal Farm   109
Anouilh, Jean   14, 28, 30, 31, 67, 127, 150, 163
Ants, The   154–5
Archers The   1, 28
Armchair Theatre   128, 135
Artists in Crime   88
Arts Council   14–15
Arts Theatre Club   30
Ascent of F6, The   2, 33, 38, 47–9, 53, 161, 162
Auden, W. H.   29, 38, 47, 49, 110, 120–1
Autumn Journal   110
Avery, Todd   8

Bakewell, Michael   4, 5, 15, 25, 26, 29, 30–3, 35, 60, 62, 78–82, 102, 132, 139, 142–3, 150, 151, 152, 154, 159, 160, 161, 162
Baldwin, Barry   114
Barnes, George   17, 25
Barnett, Correlli   12

BBC Genome   4, 165
BBC Written Archives   3, 26
Beaumont, Hugh   13
Beckett, John   75
Beckett, Samuel   1, 2, 3, 4, 5, 7, 15, 17, 20, 26, 29, 30, 31, 33, 62, 65–79, 82, 87, 93, 102, 104, 129
Before the Monday   100–1, 103
Beggar's Opera, The   150
Betsie   89, 141, 143–3, 150
Billington, Michael   16, 73, 105, 129, 131–2, 134, 137, 139, 140, 160
Birthday Party, The   30, 129–31
Blin, Roger   67, 74
Bloom, Emily   73
Bloomsbury   17, 18, 25, 31
bomb, atomic   13, 38
Bower, Dallas   111
Bradbury, Ray   154
Brand   45, 155, 163
Bray, Barbara   4, 26, 28, 29, 30, 31, 33, 35, 69, 70, 74, 75, 76, 82, 89, 96, 104, 131–2, 138, 151, 152–3, 161, 162
Brecht, Bertolt   16, 68
Bridge, The   143
Bridson, D. G.   25, 26, 110, 132
Briggs, Asa   4, 111
British Drama 1600–1642   150
British Library   3, 5, 9, 164
Britten, Benjamin   15, 29, 38, 39, 40, 44, 47, 49, 110, 159
Broken Battlements   29
Brook, Peter   14
Burgess, Guy   13
Burning of Njal, The   112
Burton, Richard   42, 50, 53

Cambridge Arts Theatre   31, 130
Canterbury Tales, The   25
Caretaker, The   30, 31, 139, 150

Carpe Diem 112
Cary, Tristram 117
Chairs, The 15, 65
Changeling, The 150
Chekhov, Anton 27, 32, 33, 37, 38, 45, 52, 79, 127, 151, 163
Christopher Columbus 24, 111
Churchill, Caryl 31, 154–5
Churchill, Winston 11
Cleverdon, Douglas 25, 27, 34, 41, 43, 49–50, 51, 111, 116, 122, 159
Cocktail Party, The 122, 150
Cohen, Debra Rae 8
Cold War 12, 13, 15, 20, 26, 131
Collection, The 139–40
Cooper, Giles
    arrives at BBC 88–9
    early life 87–8
    radio dramas 7, 29, 31, 62, 65, 74, 82, 89–106, 112, 118, 119, 129, 130
    research 4, 5
    television (*Maigret*) 101–2, 103
    women 19, 91–4, 97, 99, 100, 103–4, 105
Coronation Street 17, 128
Coulton, Barbara 116, 119
Count of Monte Cristo, The 104
Country House, The 29
Critic on the Hearth, The 4, 44, 52
Critics, The 121
Cronin, Anthony 66, 70
Cronqvist, Marie 8, 9

Dales, The 32
Daring Dexters, The 32
Dark Tower, The 2, 6, 38–41, 53, 109, 111, 119, 121, 159, 161
Death of Gunnar, The 112, 121
Death of Vivien, The 128
Death of Wallenstein, The 31
Deep Blue Sea, The 14, 28, 105
Delaney, Shelagh 16, 17, 127
Denham, Maurice 80, 132
Devlin, J. G. 66, 70
Dick Barton 28, 32, 112
Dillon, Francis 'Jack' 25, 125

Disagreeable Oyster, The 62, 91–4, 96, 97, 100, 104, 105, 135, 138, 141, 159, 161
Dock Brief, The 150, 153
Donat, Robert 111
Douglas, Susan 57, 58
Drakakis, John 57
Drama Department 2, 5, 23–33, 37–8, 41, 45, 67–70, 74, 79, 88, 90, 95, 109, 149, 150, 151, 153
Driberg, Tom 20
Dumas, Marguerite 152
Dwarfs, The 30, 129, 132, 138–9, 152
Dynasts, The 25, 122

East of the Sun and West of the Moon 116–18, 150
Eden, Anthony 12
Electra 149
Eliot, T. S. 17, 18, 38, 41, 122, 130, 150
Embers 75–6
empire 19, 20, 96, 102–3, 105
Endgame, (Fin de Partie) 31, 65, 66, 74, 77–9
Enemy of Cant 111
En Fiacre 82, 152
English Stage Company 15
Entertainer, The 18
Epitaph for a Spy 88
Esslin, Martin 2, 15, 27, 29, 31, 32, 65, 66, 68, 76, 80, 82, 129, 131, 135, 150, 151, 159
Evening Standard 130
Eyre, Richard 16

Fall of the City, The 110
Farquhar, George 104
Features Department 2, 23, 25, 26, 37, 38, 41, 50, 109, 123, 153
Festival of Britain 15
Fifties, the (1950s) 11–19
First Reading 18
Fleming, Ian 19
FM (VHF) 5, 58, 60, 62
Fool's Saga 109
Forster, E. M. 17
Forsyth, James 3

Fortuin, H. B.   101
Free Fall   150
frequencies, *see* FM; VHF
From an Abandoned Work   74
From the Fifties   150, 151
Frontline Family   1, 27–8
Frost, Everett   73, 160

Gaiman, Neil   159
Galsworthy, John   28, 29
Genet, Jean   32, 82, 129
Gibson, John   122
Gide, André   31, 109
Gielgud, John   17, 28, 37
Gielgud, Val   2, 4, 23, 24, 26–9, 31, 33, 37, 38, 44–5, 46, 47, 52, 54, 59, 60, 62, 65, 68–70, 72, 74, 77, 91, 104, 109, 132, 149, 150, 151, 152, 153, 155, 160, 161, 162, 163
Gilliam, Lawrence   24, 26, 37, 38, 114, 123, 153
'golden age'   1, 7, 18–20, 29, 31, 33, 131, 159–62, 164
Golding, William   88, 100, 150, 160
Goon Show, The   62, 102
Gordon, Archie   88
Goshawk, The   154
Gray, Frances   6, 90, 91, 93, 102–3
Great Desire I Had, The   122–3
Great Expectations   33
Green, John   60
Greene, Hugh Carleton   149
Grisewood, Harman   114
Guinness, Alec   14
Guralnick, Elissa   134

Haley, William   24–5
Hall, Peter   15, 68
Hamlet of Stepney Green, The   127
Hancock, Tony   17
Hansen Family, The   1, 9
Hansford Johnson, Pamela   109
Harding, E. A., 'Archie'   29, 110
Hare, David   16
He Had a Date   24
Hendy, David   4, 45
Heppenstall, Rayner   25, 67, 109, 122

Hewison, Robert   18
Hilgert, Christoph   8
Hobsbawm, Eric   160
Hobson, Harold   13, 14, 68, 131
Hoggart, Richard   128
Holme, Christopher   116
Home Service   2, 8, 24, 27, 29, 32, 33, 37, 38, 45, 51, 58, 87, 88, 89, 95, 104, 121, 138, 142, 149, 150, 151, 153, 154, 160
Hope-Wallace, Philip   44, 45, 46, 52, 62
Hopkins, Antony   122, 154
Hordern, Michael   7, 153
Horns of the Dilemma, The   80
Huis Clos   14, 25
Hungary, invasion of   12

Ibsen, Henrik   27, 32, 33, 37, 38, 44–5, 52, 54, 79, 104, 127, 132, 150, 151, 155, 161, 163
inner world   7, 8, 30, 40, 41, 73, 91, 93, 97, 98, 104, 138, 160, 162, 164
In Parenthesis   2, 41–4, 53, 159
In the Dark   5, 164
Ionseco, Eugene   80–2
Isherwood, Christopher   29, 38, 47, 49, 110
I Spy   153

Jacob, Ian   58
Jacobi, Derek   32
James, Mary   11
Jarry, Alfred   152
Jones, David   41–4, 159
Joyce, James   41, 66, 80

Kaleidoscope, The   45
Kind of Loving, A   128
King Bull, E. J.   78
'kitchen sink drama'   16–17, 127
Kops, Bernard   127
Korean War   12
Krapp's Last Tape   73, 74
Kynaston, David   12

Lacey, Kate   163
Lark, The   28

Larkin, Philip   18
Laws, Frederick   118, 137, 142
Leavis, F. R.   18
Lefaux, Charles   88, 103
Lehman, John   18
Les Miserables   103
Lessing, Doris   11, 18
Lesson, The   15, 65, 68
Let's Go Yellow   119
Lewis, Peter   51
Lidstone, Frederick   29
Light Programme   2, 8, 24, 37, 58, 87
Listener, The   3, 4, 20, 44, 52, 59, 61, 62, 76, 79, 81, 89, 140, 143, 144
listening   6, 8, 9, 52, 57–9, 61, 62, 135, 162, 163
listening events   5, 9, 164, 165
Littlewood, Joan   16
live radio   45, 59, 60, 62, 73, 111, 151
London   11, 13–17, 25, 28, 110, 111, 114, 127–9, 131, 135–6, 161
Loneliness of the Long Distance Runner, The   154
Look Back in Anger   15, 16–17, 19, 127, 128
Lord Chamberlain   21, 68, 77
Lord of the Flies   88–9, 100, 160
Lord of the Rings   152, 159
Lucky Jim   18, 18
Lyric Theatre   30, 130–1

MacColl, Ewan   16
MacGowran, Jack   75
McKellen, Ian   32
Maclean, Donald   13
MacLeish, Archibald   110
MacNeice, Louis   2, 6, 20, 23–4, 25, 26, 29, 38, 40, 104, 109–21, 123, 150, 159, 160, 161
McWhinnie, Donald   3, 7, 26, 27, 28, 29–30, 31, 32, 33, 40, 41, 47, 49, 61, 62, 70, 71, 73, 74, 75, 76, 77, 78, 80, 89, 90, 91, 92, 94, 95–8, 100, 102, 104, 122, 123, 131, 132, 135, 141, 142, 151, 152, 161, 162
Madame Bovary   103
Magee, Patrick   7, 74, 75, 76
Maggs, Dirk   159

Maids, The   32
Maigret   101, 102, 103, 152, *see also* Cooper, Giles
Malone Dies   66, 67, 74
Man and Superman   25
Man Born to be King, The   23, 27
Man on the Gate   141
Marriott, R. D. A.,   132
Marsh, Ngaio   88
materiality   6, 9, 57
Mathry Beacon   89–91, 92, 97, 104, 105
Merchant, Vivien   132, 135, 139, 143
Messina, Cedric   139, 150
middle-brow   24, 46, 149, 150
Miller, Arthur   14, 150
Mitchell, Denis   25, 26
Moby Dick   121
Molloy   74
Monument, The   122
Morel   109
Morris, John   25, 68, 70, 77, 91, 96, 132, 141–2
Mortimer, John   150, 153, 161
Movement, The   18
Mrs. Dale's Diary   1, 28

National Service   12, 31, 128
National Theatre of the Air   33, 150, 153, 161, 163
naturalism   55, 80, 91, 98, 102, 105, 116, 143–4, 160
Naughton, Bill   150
Nausée, La   150, 152
Never Get Out   87–8
Neverwhere   159
Newby, P. H., ('Howard')   77, 119
New Soundings   18
New Statesman   18, 19–20, 121, 162
Night Out, A   30, 132, 135–8, 152, 161
Nine Tailors, The   88
Nuclear weapons, *see* bomb, atomic
Nude with Violin   17

O'Farrell, Mary   70, 73, 80, 102
Ogilvie, F. W.   110
Old Tune, The   152
Olivier, Lawrence   18, 24, 43, 111
One Eye Wild   114–16, 118, 119, 121

On the Run 150
Orton, Joe 144
Orwell, George 109
Osborne, John 15, 16, 18–19, 33, 105, 127

Pain, Nesta 4, 7, 25, 153–4, 161
Paris 13, 66, 67, 68, 70, 71, 152, 164
Parkinson's Law 154
Passionate Thinker, The 3, 141–2
Persons From Porlock 119–21
Photo du Colonel, La 80
Pickles, Wilfred 113
Pig in the Middle 101–2
Pinget, Robert 152
Ping Pong, Le 65
Pinter, Harold 1, 2, 13, 17, 20, 29, 30, 31, 33, 65, 68, 74, 80, 82, 101, 104, 105, 106, 129–30
    and radio 131–45, 150, 151, 152, 159, 160, 161, 162, 163
Poet and his Critic, The 121
Poston, Elizabeth 41, 53, 159
Pound, Ezra 18, 41
Power, Chris 43
Priestley, J. B. 11
Prisoner's Progress 116
Prix Italia 25, 34, 51, 90, 116, 122, 141, 153
public listening 5, 9, 164
Punishment without Vengeance 128
Pytheas: a dramatic speculation 122

Queen and the Rebels, The 122

Radio Drama Repertory Company 23
radiogenic 17, 46, 50, 54, 74, 79, 81, 82, 90, 101, 104, 121, 134, 142, 160
Radiophonic Workshop 30, 61–2, 74, 81, 90, 96, 97, 104, 118, 154
radio studies 3, 6–8
Radio Times 4, 29, 59, 61, 109, 132, 159
Raikes, Raymond 26, 32–3, 44, 69, 122, 123, 150, 151
Rattigan, Terence 14, 28, 105–6, 129, 150

Rawsthorne, Alan 113
realism 16, 20, 39, 40, 41, 73, 92, 100, 104, 127–45
Reed, Henry 25, 119, 121–3
Reeves, Cecilia 67, 70
Reith, John 24, 60
Rescue, The 33, 44, 53
Resounding Tinkle, A 150
Return of General Forefinger, the 102–3, 105
Return of the Prodigal, The 109
Rhinoceros 5, 15, 31, 65, 80–2, 150, 160
Richardson, Ralph 28, 45, 122
Robinson Family, The 32
Rodger, Ian 23, 57, 76, 81, 115–16, 134, 143
Rodgers, W. R. 25, 34, 38, 125
Room, The 129
Room at the Top, A 128
Rosencrantz and Guildenstern are Dead 110
Royal Court Theatre 15, 16, 17, 77, 127
Ruffian on the Stair, The 145
Rylands, George, 'Dadie' 31, 130

Sackville-West, Edward 33, 44
Sartre, Jean-Paul 14, 25, 30, 37, 150, 152
Saturday Night and Sunday Morning 128
Saturday Night Theatre 24, 37, 150
Sayers, Dorothy, L. 23, 27
Scenes from the Frogs 32
Script Unit 26, 28, 30, 70
Scriven, R. C. 128
Seagull, The 52
Second World War 1, 2, 5, 41, 60, 65, 66, 89, 102, 121, 144
    Dunkirk 11
Shakespeare, William 16, 27, 32, 33, 37, 74, 123, 127, 150, 151, 153, 161, 163
Shaw, George Bernard 25, 32, 38, 52
Shellard, Dominic 15, 17
Shoemaker's Holiday, The 150
Shuttleworth, Martin 79, 140, 144, 155
Sieveking, Lance 26, 45–6, 135, 162
Silence in Heaven 45, 46

Sigal, Clancy 20
Sillitoe, Alan 128, 154
Simenon, Georges, *see Maigret*
Single Taper, A 128
Slight Ache, A 30, 131–5, 136, 139, 140, 144, 152, 162–3
Somerset Maugham 16, 23, 27, 33, 150, 161
sound effects 3, 30, 45, 46, 50, 61, 62, 70, 72, 73–6, 81, 92, 96, 98, 103, 104, 116–17, 119, 132
Stoller, Tony 34, 149
Stoppard, Tom 82, 110
Strindberg, August 37, 45, 127, 151, 161, 163
Stulberg, Jacob 135, 162
Suez crisis 12, 17, 19
Sunday Times 13
Svømmekjær, Heidi 1
Swann in Love 109

tape recorder 6, 25, 26, 57, 59–61
Taste of Honey, A 16, 17, 128
technology
  reception 57–60, 62 (*see also* transistor radio; valve radio)
  transmission (*see* AM, FM)
television 1, 2, 4, 12, 17, 30, 47, 52, 58, 58, 61, 62, 74, 77, 88, 90–1, 100, 101, 103, 111, 128, 135, 138, 139, 140, 141, 143, 160, 161, 162, 164
  threat of 20, 29, 31, 53, 149, 151, 152, 155
Tennent, H. M., 13, 14, 105
Tennessee Williams 14
theatre 13–17, 29, 66, 70, 93, 105, 127, 129–31, 161, 163, *see also* Arts Theatre Club; Cambridge Arts Theatre; English Stage Company; Harold Hobson; Kenneth Tynan; Theatre Workshop
Theatre of the mind 1, 7
Theatre Workshop 16
There Will come Soft Rains 154
Thieves Rush In 87
Third Programme 1, 5, 7, 8, 17, 24, 25, 28, 29, 32, 37, 38, 41, 44, 45, 47, 50, 58, 61, 62, 67, 70, 73, 74, 75, 77, 78, 79, 88, 89, 96, 100, 102, 104, 111, 113, 114, 119, 121, 123, 127, 128, 132, 140, 141, 142, 144, 149, 150, 153, 160, 162, 163, *see also* George Barnes; John Morris; P. H. Newby
Thomas, Dylan 25, 37, 42, 43, 49–51, 53, 72, 113, 121, 122
Times 68, 90, 101, 102, 118, 131, 132, 139, 143, 144
Tonning, Erik 73, 74
transistor radio 6, 58, 60, 62
Trewin, J. C. 44, 89, 123, 153
Trimalchio's Feast 112, 113–14
Turnock, Rob 160
Tydeman, John 4, 26, 29, 30, 31–2, 33, 82, 130, 131, 145, 151, 162
Tynan, Kenneth 13, 14, 15, 17, 68, 138

Ubu Roi 152
Unblest, The 122
Under Milk Wood 25, 34, 37, 49–51, 52, 53
Under the Loofah Tree 29, 62, 96–8, 100, 104, 105, 118, 138, 159, 160
Unman, Wittering and Zigo 87, 89, 98–100, 105
Unnamable, The 66, 74

valve radio 5, 6, 57–9
VanCour, Shaun 7
Verma, Neal 1, 7, 9, 160
verse drama 29, 38, 41, 45, 47, 48, 50, 53, 110, 111, 122
Very Great Man Indeed, A 122–3
VHF, *see* FM
Victims of Duty 80, 150

Wade, David 2, 120
Wain, John 18
Waiting for Godot 15, 65, 66–9, 72, 73, 74, 77, 79, 143, 150
Walker, Roy 72, 95
Walton, William 24, 110, 111
War Reports 23
Waves, The 112, 116, 160, 163

Wednesday Play, The 128
Weiss, Katherine 75, 76
Wellington, Lindsey 24, 59, 60, 69
Wesker, Arnold 127
White Devil, The 150
Whitehead, Kate 37, 50, 89, 90, 96
Whittington, Ian 7
Williams, Raymond 128
Wilson, Colin 18

Without the Grail 3, 94–5, 105
Wood, Helena 69
Woolf, Virginia 22, 31, 112, 116, 160, 163
World Theatre 37, 151, 163
Worton, Michael 79
Wrigley, Amanda 113

Zilliacus, Clas 73, 76, 83

www.ingramcontent.com/pod-product-compliance
Lightning Source LLC
Chambersburg PA
CBHW052045300426
44117CB00012B/1985